Witch Beliefs and Witch Trials in the Middle Ages

Witch Beliefs and Witch Trials in the Middle Ages

Documents and Readings

P.G. Maxwell-Stuart

continuum

Continuum International Publishing Group
The Tower Building 80 Maiden Lane
11 York Road Suite 704
London SE1 7NX New York, NY 10038

www.continuumbooks.com

First published 2011

British Library Cataloguing-in-Publication Data
A catalogue record for this book is available from the British Library.

ISBN: HB: 978-1-4411-4965-7
PB: 978-1-4411-0980-4

Typeset by Fakenham Prepress Solutions, Fakenham, Norfolk NR21 8NN
Printed and bound in India

CONTENTS

Part II
Literature on Magic and Witches, c.1270–c.1505

PART III
TRIALS OF WITCHES AND OTHER WORKERS OF MAGIC

PART IV
TRIALS OF WITCHES AND OTHER WORKERS OF MAGIC

ILLUSTRATIONS

INTRODUCTION

When a Mediaeval peasant and a Mediaeval scholar looked up into the sky by day or night, what they saw was evidence of a *universum*, a whole complete in all its parts, a single thing tending always in one direction, its Creator, who, as Genesis explains, made the sky and the earth, the darkness and the light, the waters below and above the sky and the lights which shine in the sky and illumine the earth. Beyond this first sky, however, as both the Old and New Testaments bore witness, there were other skies, other heavens. 'Therefore, the heavens and the earth were completed' (Genesis 2.1); 'the heavens expound the glory of God, and the sky brings news of the works of His hands' (*Psalm* 19.1); 'Our Father, who are in the heavens' (Matthew 6.9); 'I knew a man in Christ ... who had been snatched up to the third heaven' (2 Corinthians 12.2). We can see what our two Mediaeval individuals were looking at in illustrations such as the one to be found in Hartmann Schedel's *Historia aetatum mundi et civitatum descriptio*, published in Nuremberg in 1493 (see illustration of the Mediaeval universe). Here, the earth is at the centre of a large number of enclosing spheres, with those of water, then air, then fire expanding round the onlookers, and beyond these, the spheres of the known planets – the moon, Mercury, Venus, the sun, Mars, Jupiter and Saturn. Beyond Saturn is the sphere of the 'firmament' which contains the fixed stars, those luminaries which, unlike the planets, do not move individually but all together, each keeping an immutable station; and beyond that again a 'crystalline heaven' and the *primum mobile*, the sphere first set in motion by God's hand. Outwith these, and beyond the range of human sight, was the dwelling place of God, where ranks of created spirits were ranged around God's throne in a strict hierarchy: seraphim, cherubim, thrones, dominations, principalities, powers, virtues, archangels and, in the humblest place, angels. Somewhere within this *universum*, too, in localities or positions or states of spiritual being never definitely fixed in 'maps'of the *universum*, were Purgatory and Hell,[1] again not visible to the human eye, except in vision, until death supervened and opened the eyes of the soul.

Now, this was not a *universum* which had come into being by chance, existed merely because it existed and had no purpose or meaning beyond the fact of its own existence. It had been created by an act of rational will and existed to

---

1.   The Nuremberg *Chronicle* notes, 'the mouth of Hell appeared in dreadful fashion in the middle of a huge fissure in the ground' (folio 70r), and this indeed is how artists often depicted it.

provide a series of suitable planes of being for an immense variety of *creaturae*, individual creations, whose purpose was to worship God in the ineffable and perpetual joy of His presence and, in the case of humanity, to advance to that state of salvation which would result in such enjoyment. In this *universum*, therefore, everything which exists has been created – it is a *creatura*, not an emergence *ex nihilo* – and thus each type of *creatura* is linked with every other type in an immense connectedness which begins and ends with God. Hence, nothing happens by chance. *Fors*, and its personification as Fortuna, does not operate blindly, of itself, but under the ultimate direction of God whose will and purposes give meaning to even the slightest motion, sight or sound.

The inhabitants of the Mediaeval world thus lived in a meaningful, purposeful *universum* of which they were an integral part and whose spheres, visible and invisible alike, impinged upon one another, interpenetrating and interacting in rhythms dictated by divine intention.[2] Angels, demons and souls of the dead, for example, might leave the realm of spirit and enter the realm of matter to be seen by, converse with or physically abuse living human beings. 'Devils many times appear to men', wrote Robert Burton in the seventeenth century and as truly of the Middle Ages as his own times, 'and affright them out of their wits, sometimes walking at noonday, sometimes at night, counterfeiting dead men's ghosts'.[3] Such visitations were not surprising – not, at least, in our sense of causing astonishment because such things are assumed to be impossible. If they were surprising, it was merely because they were unexpected. Their possibility could be taken for granted – not that that necessarily lessened the fear naturally attendant on coming face to face with these intruders from other planes of being. All this can be seen in an incident which took place during the life of Rabanus Maurus. Adelhard, the steward of Rabanus's monastery, was given strict instructions to distribute to the poor the allowances of food which had been allotted during life to some of his brethren who had recently died. Adelhard, however, was seduced by greed and kept these offerings for himself. The consequences were dire.

> Divine justice did not endure his rash insolence without revenge. For one day, when he had been very much preoccupied with worldly affairs, it became rather late and the rest of the brethren were already asleep. Adelhard was making his way alone to the dormitory through the chapter house carrying a small oil lamp, as usual, when he saw a large number of monks seated there in rows, wearing their usual black. Seized by an immense fear, he did not know what to do; for it was too late at night for him to believe that a chapter had been assembled. When he looked more closely, he realized that each was the ghost of one of the recently deceased brethren whose allowances he had held back. Terrified out of his wits, he began to try to withdraw. But his blood drained away

2.   It can also be said that Mediaeval *mappae mundi* in the West mirrored this concept of an integrated universal whole and could be read 'as depictions in time and space of the world as subject to divine will' and as 'pictorial representations of universalism in geographical, legal-political, and religious dimensions', H. Kleinschmidt, 2008, *Ruling the Waves* (Utrecht: Hies and De Graaf BV) pp. 15.

3.   *Anatomy of Melancholy*, Part 1, section 2, member 1, subsection 2.

and panic made his legs and feet grow stiff, as with freezing cold, so that he could not move from the spot. In an instant, the dreadful ghosts of the dead, seeing him struck down by great fear, rose up with sudden violence and, with hidden power, stripped him of his clothes and beat the wretched man with sticks – not just on his naked back, as is the custom in monastic punishments, but over his whole body – in such a way that he could really feel it. While they struck him, they uttered [the following words] in an awful semblance of a voice: 'Wretched man, take the punishment you deserve for your greed. You will receive worse in three days' time, and then you will be numbered with us among the dead'. At about midnight, when the brethren got up to sing Matins and Lauds, they found the wretched man who had been beaten, lying in the chapter house more dead than alive. They took him to the infirmary and, after a while, when the brothers' efforts had restored him to himself, he told them what awful things he had suffered and that, according to the spirits who had appeared to him, he was going to die in three days' time. Lest they imagine he had dreamed it, or that it was merely a sick fantasy of his mind, he said, 'Look at the blows. Observe the livid marks. No one could get the signs of a violent assault and remain asleep' (Trithemius, *Beati Rabani Mauri Vita*, book 2).

Notice that this encounter between the living and the dead has been permitted by God for a purpose; Adelhard is terrified, not because ghosts cannot happen, but because they can and he is faced by that reality; and the ghosts, though spirits, are able to make themselves heard and felt, the bruises they leave being proof that they are no fantasy or dream.

Within what appeared to be the physical world, however, there existed beings neither spirit nor human, but of an order seemingly partaking of both, living in a species of time different from that of humans and able to manipulate the interconnectedness or 'sympathy' of things to produce effects not possible to humans by ordinary means. These creatures had a great variety of names – fairies, trolls, goblins, elves and so forth – and European folklore teems with stories about human encounters with them. People honoured them and sought their help or blessing. During the trial of St Jeanne d'Arc, for example, questioning her elicited the following information about her childhood:

24 February 1431. She was asked about a certain tree which grew near her village. She answered that quite near the village of Domrémy there was a tree called 'The Ladies' Tree'. Some people called it 'The Fairies' Tree'. Not far away there is a spring of water. She has heard it said that people who are ill with fever drink from this spring, and come to seek its water to restore their health. She has seen this herself, but she does not know whether they are cured thereby or not. She says she has heard that when the sick can get up, they go to the tree in order to walk round it. It is a big tree, called a 'beech', from which comes many a [blossom] ... . She said that sometime she used to walk round it with other young girls; and close by that tree she used to make garlands of flowers for the statue of the Blessed Virgin of Domrémy. On many occasions, she has heard from the very old – not those of her own family – that the fairy ladies used to visit it frequently ... . She said she has never seen the fairies at the tree, as far as she knows. Has she seen them elsewhere? She does not know whether she has or not. She said she has seen young girls putting garlands on the branches of the tree, and she herself has sometimes put

them there, in company with the other girls. Sometimes they would take the garlands away with them, sometimes they would leave them there.

Procès de condemnation de Jeanne d'Arc

Fairies and similar spirits had a helpful side to their character – 'a bigger kind there is of them', wrote Burton, 'called with us hobgoblins and Robin Goodfellows, that would, in those superstitious times, grind corn for a mess of milk, cut wood or do any manner of drudgery work'[4] – but they could also be menacing or malicious. Human babies were sometimes taken by fairies who left a caricature of their own, a changeling, in its place; men might take their fancy and be invited into the fairy realm whence, years later, they emerged, thinking they had been absent for only a day – a good example of the human's entering a different dimension, as we might say; and fairies also hunted in packs, letting fly arrows at unwary human beings and careering through the countryside in a company which might include the dead and other spirits. Uninhabited or sparsely inhabited places were actually not as empty as they seemed, for it was quite likely they were alive with spirit life whose uncertain moods had to be negotiated with care; and deep underground in mines, there existed yet another variant, equally disconcerting and potentially unpleasant.

Among the number of subterranean entities or (as theologians prefer) 'substances', one can include evil spirits who busy themselves in mines. There are two kinds. They are aggressive, frightening to look at and, for the most part, dangerous and hostile to miners. Such was the Anneburgius who, with his breath, killed more than 12 workmen in a cave. He is called 'the rosy crown' because he used to emit breath from his open mouth. He is said to look like a horse with a long neck and savage eyes. Belonging to this type, too, was Sneburgius, clad in a black cowl. In a Georgian mine, in a big cave which was once very rich in silver, he lifted a workman from the ground and put him in a higher place, bruising his body in the process ... . Then there are the gentle ones which some of the Germans (like the Greeks) call 'Cobali' because they imitate human beings. These smile, as if longing for pleasure, and seem to do many things when actually they do nothing. Some people call them 'little men of the mountain'. This usually refers to their height. They are actually dwarfs, 27 inches long. They look like old men and wear miners' clothes, i.e. an outer tunic and an animal skin round their loins. These do not usually cause miners trouble. They wander about in wells and burrows and although they do not do anything, they give the appearance of occupying themselves with every kind of work such as digging veins, or pouring into jars what they have dug out, or turning the hoist. Although they sometimes assail miners with gravel, they very rarely hurt them; and they never hurt them unless they themselves have first been hurt with laughter or insults. So they are as completely different from evil spirits as are those who rarely appear to humans but who finish the housework every day and look after the farm animals (George Agricola, *De animantibus subterraneis*).

4.   *Anatomy of Melancholy, loc. cit.* supra. By 'those superstitious times', of course he means Catholic England.

Humanity, then, lived cheek by jowl with non-human entities whose states of realms or habitations stretched from the presence of God Himself to the infernal regions where Satan exercised sway over demonic hierarchies no less complex than those of Heaven, each rank of which seemed to contain numberless spirits, and people, surrounded by a constant flux of interactive, intrusive, intelligent entities, were caught, as it were, in the middle of strong currents which could sweep them in one direction or in another or pull them both ways at once. Such a precarious existence, which mirrored that of a physical life always subject to disease, famine, sudden death, alarming falls from fortune and, above all, the wills and caprices of powerful individuals, might have been unbearable were it not for three things. First, we should not suppose that people lived in a constant state of immediate awareness of these circumambient spirits. As always, the attendant circumstances of each daily task informed the character of the moment. But, in contrast with modern Western experience, any change in those circumstances might trigger awareness of the spirits and hence affect emotional reaction and consequent behaviour. Secondly, because the interconnectedness of the *universum* stemmed from God, the Church, which had been entrusted by Him with authority reaching beyond this physical world – 'I shall give you the keys of the kingdom of Heaven, and whatever you bind on earth will be bound in Heaven, and whatever you loose on earth will be loosed in Heaven' (Matthew 16.19) – and which was thus the repository of ultimate power, under God, over the *creaturae* of the *universum*, was able to protect, help and heal human beings and release them, if need be, from the consequences of interaction between them and the spirit worlds. Thirdly, because everything was connected with everything else, everything existed in a state of sympathy or antipathy with everything else, and there were those who understood or claimed to understand how these reactions worked or could be made to work separately and conjointly. Hence, spirits could be invoked, made to appear and constrained to answer questions or do a human's bidding – even, in some circumstances, imprisoned in a ring or bottle, to be used more or less as a servant – and because even the simplest of objects were likely to reflect or possess within themselves hidden powers not otherwise available to human beings: marks in sand or earth could foretell the future, precious and semi-precious stones could make spirits visible, sticks or brooms carry people through the air and a verse or two of St John's Gospel written on paper and worn about the person ward off all kinds of evil from disease to demons. Magic, from its simplest to its most complex forms, provided a beleaguered humanity with powerful means to exercise some kind of control over the forces and entities of and in the *universum*, and the knowledge that such possibilities existed mitigated what might otherwise have been an all too troubling consciousness that human powers are very limited, especially when asked to exist beside and cope with those of non-human beings whose puissance is God-given and superior.

The Church on the one hand, however, and magical practitioners on the other offered everyone ways to cope with these problems. Religion and magic provided reassurance that humans need not be overwhelmed by obtrusive spirits, nor feel themselves hapless in the face of powers greater than they. Religion and magic also gave people access to authority. In the case of the Church this was an authority which gave its consent to, and therefore rendered licit, the use of prayers, blessings and sacramentals such as holy water, which would act as channels of communication between humans and God, the ultimate authority, or as instruments of His responses to people's pleading and expectation. In the case of magic, the authority was illicit, either because people used words, gestures or things to which they attributed what was, in fact, a non-existent power;[5] or they applied to an authority other than divine or divinely sanctioned, in which case they were at least tacitly substituting that authority for the authority of God. The former was 'superstition', the latter 'idolatry and apostasy' the assumption being that a lesser power which was willing to allow itself to be elevated in such a fashion could not be good, since good 'powers' must always be conscious of their subordinate relationship with God; and if good 'powers', such as angels or saints, would not let themselves be used thus – unless, of course, God made them a special case and permitted it – then those lesser 'powers' must be evil, and evil 'powers', being governed by pride, would not hesitate to let themselves be addressed and used as having authority.

It is easy to see, therefore, why the Church attacked any whom she considered to be idolaters and apostates and was deeply suspicious of those she called 'superstitious'. Their willingness to apply to authorities other than God amounted to *lèse majesté* and needed to be dealt with as such. Only the Church's mission to save souls – to do so with mercy if she could, with rigour if she could not and with final rejection of those who proved obdurate if they gave her no other choice – meant that she exercised any patience at all with people who ignorantly, recklessly or intentionally put their souls in jeopardy by venturing themselves into alliance or traffic with spirits of any kind. Hence, one of the principal concerns of a succession of Popes (as we see from Part I), was to suppress superstition on the one hand and demon worship on the other.

But while it may be said that a simple, uncomplicated act of magic by a peasant who undertook it for a practical end – to increase a cow's flow of milk, for example, or make someone fall in love – can readily be accepted by us as a genuine action actually performed by an individual, can we bring ourselves with equal readiness to accept that some people actually did worship a demon or demons, as was alleged of them by their contemporaries? Here we come to one of the most difficult points of difference between ourselves and earlier times. The temptation is for us to dismiss that type of allegation as fantasy or lies or

5.   For example, during the 1130s David of Ganjak noted in his *Penitential* that magical curers 'make passes with the hand over their young children and say, "Let there be no pain in their bodies". And they rub the spittle of their mouths on them with their hand, and say, "The evil eye is upon him, he has become sick. May he not attract the evil eye". And wicked old crones yawn and stretch round the sick child; and they cast sparks into water and give it to the children and other sick persons to drink, in order [to see] whether they have been the victim of the evil eye or not. Also they melt lead and cast it into water in a vessel and place it upon people's chests, saying that it is a cure for palpitations and toothache. In remote places, they cut roots of plants and stuff them in pear trees and other bushes around the room, and say it is a cure for fever'.

malicious gossip, and indeed one would be unwise to thrust any of these on one side altogether, since the nature of many of our records and the context in which such a thing is said suggest that particular instances of demonolatry may well owe much to fantasy, lies or gossip. Nevertheless, 'particular instances' do not amount to 'all', and we must surely be prepared to allow that the Church's concern with demon worship was based on sufficient fact to make that concern legitimate.

'Insulting to God', observed the French Dominican, Étienne de Bourbon in the thirteenth century, 'are superstitions which pay divine honours to evil spirits or to any other created being – as idolatry does, and as wretched female diviners and sorcerers [*sortilegae*] do when they heal by worshipping elder trees or making offerings to them, despising churches or the relics of the saints' (*Anecdotes historiques*). 'Why do you supplicate the sun with blessings and incantations to protect you, fool', asked Nicholas of Cusa in 1431, 'and the new moon to do likewise, by fasting on the day she first makes her appearance? The Lord is your spouse. He created them, and you are an idolater!' (*Ibant Magi* 20). Pope John XXII summarized similar activities carried out under his very nose by both priests and laymen at the Papal Court in 1318 (see below, Part I, no. 3).

The involvement of priests in acts of ritual magic – and one can see and appreciate the difference between these complex ceremonies and the simple words and gestures which, on the whole, constituted non-learned magic, even if the basis on which both learned and non-learned acted was the same, that is, an appeal to an authority other than God – was clearly disturbing to the Pope, as it had been to his predecessors and would continue to be to his successors. Priests, who had access to power legitimately authorized, had no business, to say the least, in perverting that access in the service of ends for which it was not given. Thus, during the trial of Gilles de Rais in 1440, it was alleged he had been assisted in his invocation of demons by a cleric, Francesco Prelati. 'On one occasion, [Gilles] brought to Francesco's room a jar containing the hands, the heart, the eyes and the blood of a child and gave them to him. Then Francesco made an invocation to offer them to the demon if the demon came in answer to the invocation' (Deposition of Francesco Prelati). But even if he were a layman, the magician was likely to dress and act as a priest – 'you should wear a priest's garment, if possible', recommended Pietro d'Abano in his *Heptameron*, a detailed account of how to perform a complex magical ritual – and when he spoke, he was likely to speak with the assumed authority of a priest-exorcist:

I mark you with the sign of the cross, o air. I adjure you, o Devil and your angels. I adjure you not to bring a hailstorm or any distress into this district, and not to have anything to say in the presence of God on the grounds that no one has spoken against you. May God speak against you, and the Son of God who is the beginning of all created things. May holy Mary speak against you. I adjure you, Merment, along with your companions, you who have been given charge of the storm. I adjure you in the name of Him who made heaven and earth in the beginning. I adjure you, Merment, by the right hand of Him who formed Adam, the first human being, in His own image. I adjure you, Merment, by Jesus Christ, the only Son of God. I conjure you, demon and Satan, I conjure you that you have no power in this place or in this village either to do harm or to cause damage, to send a storm or throw down very violent rain.

Eleventh-century spell

Should priests be allowed to continue to practise magic, or wink at others who did so, by co-operating in their blasphemies – the altar cloths of churches frequently concealed an extraordinary array of objects waiting to be 'consecrated' by having Mass celebrated over them – lay people might well come to believe that the authority and therefore the power of Satan and his demons was as legitimate and effective as that of God Himself, a muddling of comprehension which in any case was already often evident in individuals who developed highly peculiar theological notions out of their misunderstanding the Christian doctrine they heard expounded during sermons, or from their own meditations upon the pictures in glass and paint and stone which they saw round them in church. To give only one example, Domenico Scandella, a miller from the mountainous region of Friuli in the north of Italy, had an odd notion of creation:

> I have said that, in my opinion, all was chaos ... and out of that bulk a mass formed – just as cheese is made out of milk – and worms appeared in it, and these were the angels. The most holy majesty decreed that these should be God and the angels, and among that number of angels there was also God, He too having been created out of that mass at the same time.
>
> C. Ginzburg, 1980, *The Cheese and the Worms*, English trans. (London: Routledge and Kegan Paul), 53

Christianizing Europe had been a long, drawn-out process and Christianizing its thousands of isolated communities a challenge which was clearly not complete even by the time the Protestant and Catholic reformations began to make their several impacts, and their separate confessional authorities were making serious efforts to bring doctrinal uniformity to bear upon the quirks, bizarreries or plain ignorance of their widespread laities. Even before these sixteenth-century endeavours, however, the Church had been involved in recurrent battles with those whose particular interpretations of Scripture or doctrine led both themselves and those who accepted their views away from that orthodoxy the Church felt herself charged to preserve and defend. Heresy, in other words, had fertile ground in which to plant its seeds.

Now, heresy by its very nature challenges the Church's claim to have been constituted by God the only legitimate source of true and valid teaching on matters of faith and morals, and although the problems presented to the Church by heresy on the one hand and magic on the other were in many ways separate and distinct, they had in common their dissension from the Church anent legitimacy of authority. For the Church, this dissent was a serious matter. If she was to fulfil her role as pastor of souls and guide them to salvation, she could not stand by and let people stray into or deliberately embrace behaviour which would result in their soul's damnation. Again, reading Hansen's selection of Papal letters and decrees illustrates the range of problems relating to magic alone with which the Popes were faced: heretical groups, odd rituals, Jewish intransigence, invocation of demons and outright demon worship, the misuse of the altar and the Mass by priests and clerics and a growing unease that humanity was battling against one conspiracy after another, each fuelled one way or another by Satan himself. Correction of ignorance, therefore, and punishment of wilful defiance were the Church's duty, and in order to correct or punish with greater effectiveness than had been managed hitherto by bishops' tribunals, the Popes, starting with Gregory IX (1227–1241), began to appoint special investigators ('inquisitors') whose task was to detect and then deal with heretics in whatever way seemed appropriate to the individual case which came before them.

Changes in the legal systems of several European countries at about this time were also significant. Instead of having accusations brought and presented by one individual against another and defended in a court where the judge acted as an arbitrator between the two parties concerned, the Roman inquisitorial system became more common. Here, the *iudex* – an individual appointed to hear and collect evidence and decide a case at law – whether ecclesiastical or secular – now evaluated accusations brought before him, accusations which might stem from direct statements made by one person accusing another, or from rumour or anonymous information picked up by legal officials, and it was the *iudex* who heard and controlled the whole process from beginning to end. The system was meant to be thorough and impartial, with built-in safeguards to ensure that both the accused and witnesses had fair hearings. Written records were kept and rules governing the ways in which evidence was collected – by torture, for example – were strict and weighted, if anything, in favour of the accused. Practice, as always, might turn out differently, of course, but the theory was intended to enable *iudices* to uncover the truth to the benefit of the individual accused as well as society at large, and, interestingly enough, as time went on, secular courts tended to be more severe in their dealing with magical operators than their ecclesiastical counterparts. But it was not only legal systems which underwent widespread changes at this period. So too did official perceptions of magic and of witchcraft in particular. The Church had always been suspicious of magic and divination, but from at least the fourteenth century onwards magic and divination of all kinds began to be seen as irretrievably tainted with heresy. This opened a kind of floodgate of learned speculation on the nature of magic and its actual operation in certain communities, particularly, as it turned out, those belonging to or bordering upon the Duchy of Savoy. For much of the fifteenth century, Savoy itself was subject to unsettling influences. Duke Amadeus VIII attracted hostile attention from the Papacy for his apparent laxity in attending to manifestations of magic and heresy in his domains, manifestations which actually seem to have stemmed from reality rather than fantasy or anti-Savoyard propaganda, although one has to bear in mind that Amadeus did split the Church in 1439 when a group of dissident cardinals elected him 'Pope' Felix V – in fact, an antipope. His ducal successor, Louis, was weak, more interested in music, especially that for the flute, than the complex political situation of his duchy in which France played an increasingly major role, an influence continued and augmented during the reign of his successor, Amadeus IX, a deeply religious epileptic whose French wife effectively controlled Savoy and governed it in his stead.

Schism in the Church and weak government throughout the areas in which magic appeared to be burgeoning, combined with the geography of those areas – mountainous regions difficult of access whose scattered, somewhat isolated communities presented major problems for anyone who wanted or tried to preach and maintain orthodox doctrine – meant that it was possible for popular disinterest in the exact balance to be achieved between Church teaching traditional belief anent the physical and spirit worlds to allow magic of all kinds to flourish. What began to make a notable difference, however, was the Church's growing conviction that magic's dependence on spirits as a legitimate source of power and authority had morphed into open demon worship, and that the tacit mutuality hitherto existing between human and spirit had turned into something deeply sinister, an actual pact – unspoken or overt – according to which the practitioner, in return for the spirit's help, would abandon God altogether and substitute Satan for Him. Such an interpretation was not new. The Council of Paris in 829, for example, had hinted at it:

> [Practitioners of magic] say that by their acts of harmful magic they can upset the air and send hailstorms, predict the future, take away fruit and milk and give them to others: and are said to accomplish innumerable things by such methods. When it may be discovered that they are people of this sort, whether men or women, they are to be chastised severely by the vigorous instruction of the Prince, *since they are not afraid to serve the Devil by means of a crime which is both abominable and reckless.*
>
> section 16, my italics

But by the fifteenth century, theologians were openly talking about it and warning their flocks against it:

It is not lawful for anyone of his own authority to add to or subtract from those things established by the Church for the worship of God', said Nicholas of Cusa in a sermon delivered on 6 January 1431. 'Likewise, it is a superstition when worship is paid to to another cult rather than to God. It is, in fact, idolatry. Therefore it is idolatry to make a pact with evil spirits, to sacrifice to them and to accept advice from them. (section 20)

One potent force driving theologians towards this notion of an abandonment of God was a long-standing schism in the Church itself, made vivid by the Papacy's exile from Rome and the election of counter-Popes of whom 'Felix V', Duke Amadeus had been the latest. Add to this the prevalence of various heresies – Waldensians, Utraquists, Bohemian Brethren – which were seen as virulently opposed to the Church and a resurgence of the fear that humankind was living in the Last Days when Antichrist would be born and flourish and tear society apart, and the soil was ripe for conspiracy theories to catch ears and hearts and intensify that fear. The Jews, it was said, would co-operate with Antichrist in destroying the Church – illustrations often depict them and renegade Christians as his followers and worshippers – and block-book *vitae* show him surrounded by demons from his very conception onwards.[6] There was also a growing emphasis on the role played by women in these conspiracies. Certain elements in the narratives of the Sabbat – flight upon a stick or broom, subservience to male authority, sealing the pact with sexual intercourse, infanticide – make particular sense when related of women rather than men. The carnality of women, which was described by both theologians and physicians, laid them open to easy seduction by Satan or one of his demons who targeted that weakness, and one can appreciate therefrom aspects of the psychology underlying the Sabbat story which, whatever its variants over time and geographical origin, emphasized three features which were likely to make the idea of a Sabbat attractive: (i) plenty of food and drink, as opposed to a real world of borderline hunger or starvation, and while this may have been as alluring to men as to women, nourishing the family was seen as a particular female role; (ii) uninhibited sex, as opposed to a real world of ecclesiastical strictures and constant pregnancies; and (iii) encouragement to exercise power over others who had not the means to retaliate. Living in tight-knit communities meant that power emanated from one's hierarchical position, and that one was under constant scrutiny from one's neighbours and kinsfolk. Women, subject to various types of authority from lord of the manor to husband, were thus – in theory, at any rate, whatever the reality of particular cases – liable to be on the receiving end of the exercise of power rather than exercise it themselves. Being given the ability to break free from those constraints and dominate instead of being dominated must therefore have seemed, to those reading contemporary female psychology in an effort to explain why women were so prominent in Satan's plans for the overthrow of humanity, an almost irresistible gift and one which a woman would grasp without hesitation. Hence the rapid, often near-immediate concurrence with Satan's temptation to apostasy, which is evident in so many accounts of a witch's seduction. Likewise, the lessons learned in a 'school' of the Sabbat are seen as opening channels for the outpouring of women's innate malice, again an interesting comment on how those who recorded narratives of the Sabbat interpreted women's characters: seething cauldrons of lust and resentment liable to boil over and scald those nearest to them unless securely lidded and controlled. Thus Last Days, Antichrist, Jews, women's instability and demons feed into what became a common stream, convincing the Church and secular society that, whatever lenience may have been shown towards magic in the past – and there had indeed been lenience: older law codes tended to prescribe periods of penance or fines rather than death for simple breaches of the relevant legislation – now was not the time for unwarranted patience or mercy. Diabolism appeared to be rampant and increasing. In a battle between Good and Evil, it behoved Christians to fight on the side of the Good, supporting the Church and supported by her. Shilly-shallying could not be countenanced.

---

6.   See further Emmerson, *Antichrist in the Middle Ages*, pp. 126–9. Notice that 'synagogue' becomes one of the terms used to describe an assembly of witches.

In the light of these conspiracy theories, we should note the increasing interest shown by scholars in particular, but also by all kinds of literate individuals, ecclesiastical and lay, in the theory of this growing diabolism. From the 1330s onwards, as Hansen illustrates with an anonymous 'A Gleaming of Demon Worship, or, A Little Work dealing with Demons and especially those people who invoke them', manuscripts and then printed works appeared in gathering numbers, dealing with the various phenomena of these conspiracies and debating how far they were real or misleading illusions slipped into people's minds by Satan's craftiness. A key question anent illusion or reality involved witches' flight to the Sabbat: did this happen physically, and if so, how did one explain the continuing corporeal presence of the witch in her bed or kitchen? Did Satan substitute an appearance of the witch real enough to fool her husband while her actual body was absent at the assembly? Or was her absence entirely illusion, and if so, was it a genuine illusion caused by Satan, or merely self-delusion by the witch who genuinely believed that she flew and attended a Sabbat and there did what was said to be done, before coming to and finding herself at home? Or did she merely lie, in which case why would she want to do so on such a subject, with all its attendant dangers to soul and body? Authors, then, were divided. What they all agreed on, however, was the reality of Satan and his demons, the possible efficacy of magic of all kinds, helpful or malicious, and the reality of intercourse between the worlds of matter and of spirit. Thus far, at least, the learned and the unlearned were at one.

Now, one of the more difficult steps that we and our contemporaries are obliged to take is the realization that magic, witchcraft, divination and the rest of the occult sciences were at basis both rational and logical. Given the *universum* of which our forebears were a part, there was nothing in the least irrational in the notion that the various aspects of creation both might and actually did interact; and given the possibility and likelihood of interaction, along with the belief that the *universum* was directed and purposeful, it was logical to presume that everything existed for an end and that everything which happened did so for a reason. The end might not be perceivable by human intellect, the reason might turn out to be unfathomable, but step by step rationality, allied to traditional wisdom on the one hand and divine revelation on the other, might be able to discover the sense underlying the whole. Whatever else magic or witchcraft might be, therefore, they were not bizarre or anomalous. Rather, they were particular manifestations of the workings of the *universum* and, as such, clues to the innermost thoughts of God Himself.

Joseph Hansen (1862–1943) belongs to what has been termed the 'rationalist' school of thought in the historiography of witchcraft. His principal post was that of Director of the city archive of Köln, and this and his contacts with other scholars in Germany and abroad enabled him to assemble the collection of source material partly translated here, *Quellen und Untersuchungen zur Geschichte des Hexenwahns und der Hexenverfolgung im Mittelalter* ('Sources, and Investigations into the History of Belief in Witches and the Witch Hunt in the Middle Ages'), and to write a study of witch prosecutions between 1258 and 1526, *Zauberwahn, Inquisition und Hexenprozess im Mittelalter und die Entstehung der grossen Hexenverfolgung* ('Magical Delusion, Inquisition and

Witch Trials in the Middle Ages and the Origin of the Great Witch Persecution'),
published in 1901. Eighteenth- and nineteenth-century approaches to witchcraft
among writers had become increasingly dismissive as post-industrial Europe
struggled to come to intellectual and emotional terms with the rapid changes
technology and the physical sciences began to have on everyday life and the
consequent alterations in people's reactions to and interpretations of the working
and intention of the cosmos and humanity's place and purpose within it. Gone
(or at least going) was the sense of a *universum*, as something more mechanistic,
colder and impersonal took its place. 'Science' now appeared to offer challenges
to religion in particular, which suggested modes of being or existence outwith
that of physical matter, and set its face, especially in France, against the Catholic
Church whose importance during the Middle Ages was now deemed to have
held back 'progress' and 'advance' in favour of the thraldom of 'superstition'
and 'irrationality'. As Roy Porter puts it, 'Christian transcendentalism no longer
seemed to provide the blueprint for an orderly, smooth-running commercial
society. Witches ceased to be prosecuted and began to be patronized'.[7]

Rearguard actions were fought, of course, but not by Hansen. His researches
had convinced him that witchcraft as an idea had had a long gestation, perhaps
lasting for three hundred years, until its various strands had merged to form
a single coherent, if composite notion by the end of the fifteenth century. The
American scholar, George Lincoln Burr (1861–1942), with whom Hansen
was in contact, came to the conclusion that this concept of witchcraft owed
its origins and development to a theology many of whose ideas were driven
by fear of heresy, and that the witchcraft theory was imposed upon society by
religious authorities, especially inquisitors, motivated by a desire to maintain
their spiritual, intellectual and imperial dominance. Hansen agreed completely,
and his choice of sources is clearly driven by that view of the Church and her
place in Mediaeval history. The virulence of English anti-Catholicism and French
anti-clericalism, so evident during the eighteenth and nineteenth centuries, had
left their mark on historians' perceptions of the earlier period.[8] Hansen was
also convinced that the appearance of Heinrich Institoris's treatise, *Malleus
Maleficarum*, in 1486 had been an important factor in stimulating widespread
prosecution of witches, a view he had inherited from Soldan, and he devotes the
whole of the third section of his source collection to documents dealing with the
origins of the *Malleus* and the lives of its authors.[9] The importance he attributes
to this book made an impact on subsequent scholarship which tended, first to
accept Hansen's view that by the end of the fifteenth century there was a more
or less unified theory of witchcraft among contemporary scholars, and secondly

7.   Porter, 'Witchcraft and magic in enlightenment, romantic, and liberal thought', p. 236.
8.   This is evident, for example, in the work of Wilhelm Gottlieb Soldan (1803–1869)
whose history of the witch trials applauds the end of those trials as a sign that the oppressive
and overweening authority of the Catholic Church was also on its last legs.
9.   Like all his contemporaries and, indeed, many modern scholars, Hansen believed the
Malleus was written by both Institoris and Sprenger. Opinion now is beginning to suggest that
Institoris alone was the author.

that the *Malleus* did indeed play a major role in driving forward the urge to prosecute witches in large numbers. Today, scholarship largely disagrees with both these propositions. Nevertheless, Hansen's collection still has a great deal to offer modern readers. The diversity of his selected material and its range across Latin and several European vernaculars presents us with details and voices which generally go unheard or are scarcely noticed in modern collections and enable us to catch those undercurrents of fear and growing conviction that something was loose in the world and preparing to to create a havoc destructive of souls. That such a fear and conviction did not result in widespread prosecution and execution of magical practitioners until a hundred years after the appearance of the *Malleus* is one of the more fascinating contradictions with which historians of the subject have to come to terms.

Quellen und Untersuchingen is divided into eight parts. The first contains 47 extracts from or notices of Papal decrees between 1258 and 1526. Where these are not mere notices, I have translated them. Part 2 has 76 extracts from or notices of learned treatises and other remarks or reminiscences or observations from literate sources dealing with magic, divination, witchcraft and demonology; Part 3, as I said earlier, deals with the authorship and background of the *Malleus*; Part 4 is a fairly short notice on Vauderie during the fifteenth century; Part 5 is devoted to Johannes Nider and contains extracts from his writings; Part 6 is divided into two sections, the first of which deals with trials before inquisitorial courts and the second with those before secular courts. Part 7 is a study of the German word for witch and Part 8 a few additional extracts and notices. My translations are based on material from Parts 1, 2 and 6.

Latin terminology

My title, *Witch Beliefs and Witch Trials in the Middle Ages*, is half that of Hansen's book but, as is clear from its contents, Hansen's use of the words 'witch' and 'witchcraft' may mislead the unwary English reader about the nature of his material, because his sources deal with a very wide range of magical activity and its practitioners should not really be lumped together under these catch-all English words, which tend to be used to translate a variety of Latin terms. Note, for example, the procurator fiscal of Köln who, on 4 April 1489, issued a formal warning that 'several persons of both sexes within the city and diocese of Köln ... are not afraid to put their trust in necromancers [*nigromanticis*], chanters of spells [*incantatoribus*], diviners [*divinatoribus*], fortune tellers [*sortilegis*], and women who predict the future [*phitonissis*]'. These terms are not synonymous and none refers to 'witch', unless it be argued that *sortilegus/a* can be so translated. Its position within a clear list of seers into the future, however, suggests not in this context. At the risk of producing somewhat cumbersome phraseology, therefore, but for the sake of greater accuracy, I have tried to avoid the words 'witch' and 'witchcraft' except in certain circumstances explained below and have employed words or phrases which reflect the actual meaning of the Latin.

Maleficium
This is a crime or an offence or a wrongdoing in general. Its technical usage refers to 'an act of harmful magic'. A man who perpetrates such an act is a *maleficus* and a woman a *malefica*. These I have translated as 'worker of harmful magic', indicating the gender by the addition of 'male' or 'female,' as the case may be.

Veneficium
This is either an act of poisoning or the poisonous substance itself. Those who used plants to concoct drinks of one kind or another ran the risk of miscalculating the strength of the dosage – unless murder was their actual objective – and so serious illness or death might follow from ingestion of such a drink. *Veneficium* may therefore also be translated as 'an act of poisonous magic'. A male practitioner was a *veneficus* and a female, a *venefica*. I have translated accordingly.

Strix
Originally an owl or bird of ill omen, this was used even in Classical times to refer to a kind of vampire, and later became one of the standard terms for someone we call 'witch'. The implication of *strix* in this latter sense is twofold: (i) a woman who is able to change her shape and fly; and (ii) a woman who seeks to kill children. Depending on the context in which the word or its variants appear, I have translated it with reference to one or other of its implications, or simply as 'witch'. The variants are *striga*, *strega*, *stria* and *strigo* which usually refers to a male.

Lamia
This was originally a figure in Greek folklore, a female monster who devoured children. Once again, I have translated it according to its immediate context, either as 'monster' or 'witch'. Every so often, the word appears as *lania* which means 'butcher'.

Sortilegium
This was a method of predicting the future by casting lots. A *sortilegus* (male) or *sortilega* (female) was therefore a fortune teller, and this is clearly the intended meaning in certain contexts, since we know that the authorities regarded all forms of divination with suspicion or hostility. Sometimes, however, the context is either not clear or seems to indicate that magic rather than fortune telling is the activity being described. Under those circumstances, I have adopted the translations 'sorcery', 'male/female sorcerer', which are etymologically connected with *sortilegium* through *sors* = 'lot, share, portion'.

Punctuation convention

I have used square brackets [ ] either to supply the word or words of the original language or to indicate my own words to construct an intelligible English sentence or to give the context of the passage. I have used parentheses ( ) to show an aside or modification made by the original author. Dots ... indicate that Hansen himself has omitted part of his text.

Part I

Papal Decisions, Decrees and Letters
1258–1524

1. Should inquisitors investigate and punish fortune tellers? 1258

Hansen I, no. 1 (p. 1)

[Alexander IV's intervention in a debate between Franciscans and Dominicans over whether divinatores *and* sortilegi *should or should not be regarded as tainted with heresy.]*

13 December

When anyone is denounced to inquisitors for practising divination and fortune telling,[1] is it the business of the inquisitors to find out about such things and punish them? Our brief reply [is that] since the business of the Faith, which carries with it the highest privileges, should not be hindered by other concerns, inquisitors themselves, because of the duty entrusted to them, should in no way concern themselves with these things unless they manifestly smack of heresy, but should leave these people to be punished appropriately by their own legal authorities.

2. A demon-worshipping bishop, 1303

Hansen I, no. 2 (p. 2)

[Boniface VIII comments on a case brought to his attention. The Pope later referred the bishop to the Archbishop of Canterbury, who cleared him of the charge.]

8 June

Not long ago it was brought to Our attention that Our venerable brother Walter, Bishop of Coventry and Lichfield, was in England and that elsewhere he had been publicly slandered of having done homage to the Devil,[2] had kissed him on the backside and had spoken to him many times.

3. Magicians, fortune tellers and demon worshippers at the Papal Court, 1318

Hansen I, no. 3 (pp. 2–4)

[John XXII (Papal reign, 1316–1334), was embroiled in magical conspiracies of one kind or another for most of his Papacy. More than one of these plots was directed against him personally. In 1317, for example, the Bishop of Cahors tried to kill him by use of magic, and in 1320 the ruler of Milan and his son were accused of trying to do the same thing. Annual experience of hearing about or having to deal with magic and demon worship, then, caused him in 1320 to order inquisitors in Toulouse and Carcassonne to act against those against whom such practices were alleged, and in 1326 to issue a Bull, Super illius specula, *in which*

---

1.   Or 'acts of sorcery'.
2.   *Diabolo,* which could also simply mean 'a devil'.

he threatened workers of magic and worshippers of demons with immediate excommunication if they did not repent and give up their illicit and idolatrous behaviour. The allegation of magic, and demon worship in the Papal Court itself, described below, is therefore one in a succession of such incidents which served to convince the Pope that a serious evil was beginning to make itself visible in the world and needed to be dealt with firmly.

Necromancy (nigromantia) should refer to raising a dead person in such a way that he or she, or a spirit using the corpse as a medium, can answer questions. During the Middle Ages especially, this was a form of magic particularly associated with the clergy. Geomancy (geomantia) involves making marks on an earthen or sandy surface, and using those marks as indicators of some future event. Mirrors could be used in the same way as modern crystal balls, as media in which images of past, present or future could be seen. Imprisoning demons in mirrors, rings or small stoppered bottles was a common magical practice. Questioning demons about the past or present was a useful way to find out what had happened or was happening in a distant place. In a period without access to instant communication such as we are used to enjoying, news might take days or weeks or even months to reach one place from another, so the demons' intelligence represented speedy communication on a scale otherwise unobtainable.]

27 February

To Our venerable brother Bartholomew, Bishop of Fréjus, Our beloved son Pierre le Tessier, Doctor of Canon Law, Prior of the Monastery of St Antony in the diocese of Rodez, and Pierre de Pratis, Professor of Civil Law and Provost of the church at Clermont.

The Roman Pontiff, who is obliged by his office to direct his efforts principally to the salvation of souls, must be able to devote immediate attention to the correction of sons who deviate from the Faith, while at the same time making it clear that nothing can have the power [to bring people] to salvation if it is not grounded in the root of faith. But a credible allegation, and a report of what was being said by common gossip earlier, has recently reached Our ears that Jean de Limoges, Jacques known as 'the Brabantine', Jean d'Amato, a physician, and the clerics Rudolf Penchaclau, Walter Loflamene, Gulielmo Marini, Conrad 'the German', the late Thomas known as 'the German' and Innocent, the barber of Our venerable [blank line], Archbishop of Leiden, and several others residing at Our Court, unwilling to show calm good sense in accordance with the Apostle's teaching, but striving in a drunken state of extravagant vanity to throw their good sense aside in base adventurings, have entangled and continue to entangle themselves in endeavours [to practise] necromancy, geomancy and other magical practices. They have in their possession manuscripts and books[3] [dealing with] this kind of practice; and since they are the practices of demons and have come

---

3.   *Scripta et libros.* Since books, too, were handwritten at this period, the *scripta* are likely to refer to single sheets of paper or small notebooks containing, perforce, a limited amount of material.

into existence out of a noxious association between humans and evil angels, they should certainly be avoided by absolutely every Christian and condemned from the bottom of one's heart with every kind of imprecation.

On many occasions they have used mirrors and images consecrated according to their detestable ritual. They have placed themselves in circles and frequently invoked malignant spirits so that, by their means, they may work against people's salvation, either by killing them through the destructive force of an incantation or by cutting short their life by directing the destructive force of a debilitating weakness against them. Every so often they have enclosed demons in mirrors, circles or rings so that they may question them, not only about the past but also about the future, with the aim of being able, through that consultation, to predict that same future (which is for God alone to know in advance). They have involved themselves in [various types] of divination and fortune telling, sometimes making use of 'dianas/dianuses' by mistake.[4] But no matter how many attempts[5] they have made, and no matter when they have made them for these and other purposes, demons have been invoked. Nor do they have any scruples about claiming they are able to shorten or prolong people's lives, destroy them completely or cure them of any illness, not just by giving them something to eat or drink, but merely by uttering a single word; and they steadfastly maintain they have made use of such things. Moreover, they have abandoned their Creator and, thinking them worthy of it, have put their trust in the aid of this kind of demon. They have taken it upon themselves to act as their servants, offer them divine honours and worship them as idolaters do, with a display of veneration and deference.

The foresaid clerics and barber and any one of them, as well as a number of others residing at Court, are said to have pursued these and other detestable superstitions, not once but several times, to the danger not only of their own souls but to those of very many others, too. Therefore, because common sense regards the reprehensible followers of this kind of superstition as enemies of social well-being and opponents of the human race, We are neither willing nor able to close Our eyes and let this pestilence pass by, especially as [these superstitious acts] give the impression that heretical wickedness has brought about their fall. We recommend, by zeal for the Faith whose business ought to be pursued

4.   This may be a reference to the canon *Episcopi* which talked about some women who mistakenly claimed they used to go riding at night with the pagan goddess Diana. A gloss on the word *dianus*, however, explains that it referred to a peasant name for a demon. Hansen suggests that Pope John means 'succubus', a female demon who has sex with human men. While it is true that 'involved themselves' (*se immiscuerunt*) may also be a euphemism for having sexual intercourse, the context does not suggest any such thing, and it is more likely that the *dianis* here – the Latin does not allow one to know the gender involved at this point – are merely thought of as 'demons' in a general sense. The Pope may be using a peasant word because the source of his information came via Italian or French vernacular, or because Latin had absorbed *dianus/diana* to a greater extent than our dictionaries suggest.

5.   *Experimenta.* It is possible that this word also means 'instruments of magic', in which case it would refer to the mirrors, circles or rings used to enclose demons who could then be questioned about the past and future.

everywhere in such a way as to gain approval, that inquisition be instituted against the clerics, barber and others foresaid regarding each and every point We have mentioned. It makes no difference that the late foresaid Thomas has died, for it is the practice when dealing with crimes such as these to permit a charge to be brought against the reputation of a deceased person whose proven heresy ought to be duly punished after death.

In consequence, by the authority of these presents, We commit [this task] conjointly to you and to any one of your people (whose discretion We trust fully in the Lord), and We instruct you to make inquiries about each and every one of the foresaid things We have specified, and those things deriving from them and about any slanders you find which have been made publicly about the foresaid clerics, barber and anyone else at Court. [Do this] without wasting time, unofficially, without fuss and formal judicial proceedings, and without right of appeal, having God alone before your eyes. With due diligence, settle the truth and [deal with] the collection of evidence which that entails (on the assumption it has been done in accordance with the law), and come to a due conclusion. For (on condition that there is not a better way of doing this, but that whenever one of your people has started, or however many times he has done so, another has the ability to pick things up, or carry on and bring them to a conclusion), We grant, by the authority of these presents, full and unrestricted power conjointly to you and any one of your people to receive, summon and cite, in their individual capacity, witnesses to [the fact that] each and every one of the foresaid things was done. [You may also cite] other individuals appropriate for this purpose in whatever way and as often as you think expedient, and use Apostolic authority and ecclesiastical censure to round up those who object and those who offer assistance, and do and carry out other things which prove useful with regard to the foresaid, or touch upon them: [and this] notwithstanding what two sessions in a General Council have said, or any other decrees published by the Roman pontiffs, Our predecessors.

4. Instructions to root out demon worship and sacrilegious magic in Carcassonne, 1320

Hansen I, no. 4 (pp. 4–5)

[The Cardinal of Santa Sabina writes to the Inquisitor of Carcassonne.]

Our most holy father and lord, John, by God's providence, Pope [John] XXII, fervently wishing to drive away from the middle of God's house workers of harmful magic, who are infecting the Lord's flock, wishes and ordains that you undertake, with his authority, [to move] against those:

(i)   who sacrifice to demons, or worship them, or do homage to them by giving them a signed written document or anything else, or who make explicit pacts with them which [they consider] legally binding;

(ii)   who make or get someone else to make some image or anything else to bind a demon to them, or invoke demons to get them to perpetrate some act of harmful magic;

(iii) who, in an abuse of the sacrament of baptism, baptize or get someone else to baptize an image made from wax or anything else, or, in other circumstances, invoke demons in some fashion to make [such an image] or get someone else to make it, or knowingly repeat baptism, ordination or confirmation.

Likewise, when it comes to sorcerers and workers of harmful magic [*sortilegis et maleficis*] who abuse the sacrament of the Eucharist or the consecrated Host and the other sacraments of the Church and use either their outward form or the stuff of which they are made in their acts of sorcery or harmful magic, you can make inquiries and in other respects proceed against them, but only in accordance with the restrictions laid down in advance for you by canon law which has determined procedure in the case of heresy. Moreover, our foresaid lord himself, as a result of indisputable expert knowledge, enhances and extends to each and every one of the aforementioned cases the power lawfully given to inquisitors with respect to the investigation of heretics and the areas of their jurisdiction, until such time as he decides to revoke [this extension].

Accordingly, we convey all the foregoing to you via this our letter patent from our foresaid lord, the Pope, by a specific command given to us by his authoritative utterance.

[Throughout the 1320s and 1330s, John XXII was obliged to continue dealing with rumours and reports of magic and demon worship, warning the faithful in his decretal, Super illius specula *(1326/1327), that those who worshipped demons, entered into pacts with them, or enclosed them in rings, mirrors or small vessels, would be excommunicated and suffer all the punishments appropriate to heretics, with the exception of confiscation of goods; and on 4 November 1330 he wrote to the Inquisitor of Toulouse and the Archbishop of Toulouse and his suffragans that they were to complete all trials dealing with 'errors and abominations' in the areas under their jurisdiction and send him the relevant papers.]*

5. Parish clergy and monks threaten the life of Philippe de Valois with harmful magic, 1331

Hansen I, no. 7 (pp. 7–8)

[A letter from John XXII to the Bishop of Paris.]

12 April

A bishop's authority ought to pursue men who do evil[6] – enemies, so to speak, of the human race – with greater fervour the more dangerously they lay a trap for public safety and are not even afraid to strike at the royal dignity with secret

---

6. *Viros maleficos*, which could also mean 'men who work harmful magic'.

acts of harmful magic. Hence it is that We, dismayed by the complaint of Our beloved son in Christ, Philippe, illustrious King of France, and influenced by the petitions to Your Fraternity [directed] against Hercaud, Abbot of the Benedictine monastery of Versilhac in the diocese of Autun, and Jean Aubri, Dominican, and several other ecclesiastics, secular and regular,[7] by the wording of this present We grant you full and unrestricted power, by Our authority, to investigate those named by the said King, concerning the acts of harmful magic and transgressions which they are said to have carried out against the King himself and members of his Court, particularly by perpetrating the crime of high treason against the King. [You should carry out your inquiries] straightforwardly, unofficially, without fuss and without formal judicial proceedings. [You are to] proceed against them and each one of them according to canon law, as far as arresting them in connection with the foregoing and doing anything else against them which justice recommends anent the foresaid [offences]. [You may also] constrain them by means of ecclesiastical sanction, any privileges notwithstanding.

6. An English necromancer and his magical apparatus, 1336

Hansen I, no. 8 (p. 8)

[Benedict XII writes to the Bishop of Paris.]

13 April

William Altafex, a necromancer from England, has been arrested and is being held in your prison because of certain acts of harmful magic and [magical] images he is alleged to have employed. For certain specific reasons, We want him brought to the Apostolic See, [and] We instruct Your Fraternity not to delay sending this William to the said Seat under trustworthy guard as soon as possible. Likewise, you should have certain *lamina*[8] (with which he was said to operate while carrying out these acts of harmful magic and [using] his images), investigated, recovered and sent on to Us, as Our beloved son, Maître Guillaume Lombardi, canon of Mirepoix and official in Avignon, writes to you in greater detail in his account of the foregoing.

---

7.   Secular clergy were those 'living in the world', that is, not members of a monastic order. Regular clergy belonged to a monastic community.

8.   These will have been thin sheets or strips, usually of metal, with magical characters or images engraved or drawn or painted thereon. *Lamina* were a very common feature of magical practice at this period and later.

7. Payment to a notary for recording the trial of fortune tellers and other criminals, 1336

Hansen I, no. 10 (pp. 8–9)

7 August

Item: Since Our beloved Maître Foulques has been busy for several days and months, making a record of the trial and investigation of Brother Pierre Thomas, a penitentiary, Garin de Layto of Pisa (fortune tellers and necromancers),[9] Bertrand de Narbonne (counterfeiter and under sentence of banishment), Rostagne Botayhs (accused of fortune telling), Maître Jean, rector of the church at Méthon in the diocese of Langres, and certain women, Decelma and [*illegible*] (accused of fortune telling), Gerald de Ycuria, cleric (accused of forgery), Maître Fernand Egidius, and several other individuals, We pay Maître Foulques five gold florins for his living expenses, writing and effort.

8. Payment to the same notary for bringing a necromancer to and from court, 1336

Hansen I, no. 11 (p. 9)

17 August

Because Maître Foulques Peyrer, public notary of Cahors, had been sent to Montpellier by me, the Pope's treasurer, and Hugo Anger, at that time an official in Avignon, to arrest and bring to the Roman court Maître Fernand Egidius suspected and found guilty of necromancy, and [Maître Foulques] said it had taken him 16 days to go to the court, stay there, and come back with the said Fernand, [we pay him] £6 8s 8d for himself, his servant and the cost of horses.

9. Two magicians arrested in Béarn, 1336

Hansen I, no. 12 (pp. 9–10)

[Letter from Benedict XII to Gaston, comte de Foix]

21 December

From Your Nobility's report, We note that you, with a pure burning zeal for God and the Catholic faith, had two men arrested some time ago in your lands of Béarn: namely, Pierre de Coarraze, a priest, and the man known as 'Devi de Solies', who are said to be publicly vilified with and very strongly suspected of acts of sorcery [*sortilegiis*], the use of images [*factionibus*], acts of harmful magic, magical practices and other detestable crimes; and you are keeping them under guard in your prison, with the intention of restoring and committing them to

---

9.   The word *sortilegia* is used here and later in the passage. It could also mean 'acts of sorcery'.

the charge of the Church so that they can receive correction and punishment for those offences, as justice demands.

However, since We should like these men to be sent to the Apostolic See so that they can receive a better and more complete justice, We request Your Nobility and urge [you] expectantly in the Lord to make arrangements to send the said Pierre de Coarraze and 'Devi' under the trustworthy and secure [guard] of Our beloved sons, Raimond de Vonco, door keeper,[10] and Roger de Quimbal, sergeant at arms (whom We particularly nominate for this task), and others whom you may depute and assign to this task and see fit to make use of to ensure a more secure custody; [and] We shall hold you in such regard anent these matters that you will deserve to be honoured by Us and the [Apostolic] See with appropriate commendations as well as a monetary recompense for many years to come.

[This was followed by four more letters, also dated 21 December, to the Comte, the Comte's envoy to the Holy See and the Bishop of Tarbes, asking for further information about the two women's offences, and another dated 18 January 1337, addressed to Guillaume Lombardi, canon of Mirepoix. This tells us that Pierre was a priest in the diocese of Tarbes, that 'Devi' was a layman from Arles and that his name was actually Jean de Salins, and that their offences included invocation of demons, acts of harmful magic and the use of images and other magical practices. A letter dated 12 June 1337 authorizes payment to cover the expenses of keeping the two men in prison since 14 January.]

10. Benedict XII investigates a plot to kill John XXII by magic, 1337

Hansen I, no. 19 (pp. 11–12)

[A letter from Benedict XII to Arnaud of Verdala, deacon of the church of St Paul of Fenolhad in the diocese of Alet, and Pierre de Maupertuis, archdeacon of Lunas in the diocese of Béziers.]

13 June

Not long ago it was brought to Our attention that François Julien and Marcel des Murs, clerics of the diocese of Béziers, and several other clerics and lay folk, during the time of Our predecessor Pope John XXII of happy memory, on one occasion made an effort to commit a shocking crime – to kill an innocent person through their abominable activities. By means of false, treacherous letters and pieces of writing they themselves had written (or had had written), they falsely and deceitfully convinced [Our] foresaid predecessor, as well as certain members of his Court, that Our venerable brother Guillaume, Bishop of Béziers, had made (or had had made) a number of wax images which were baptized and [then] used to work acts of harmful magic against Our said predecessor and his life. So that such detestable deeds may not go unpunished (on the assumption that those who relate them were speaking the truth), and so that We can deal with the bishop's

---

10.   The lowest of the minor clerical orders: porter, lector, exorcist, cantor, acolyte.

loss of reputation, We wish to have the truth investigated and justice seen to be done. We are minded to commission you or one of your people by Our letter (the meaning of which cannot be misunderstood), to take pains, as Our letter lays out in detail, to investigate carefully, frankly, unofficially, without fuss and formal judicial proceedings, the truth about the forementioned [charges] and anything which may be relevant to them, including the foresaid François and Michel and the other clerics and lay folk who, We were told, have been arrested and are being held in the gaols of Béziers on account of [those charges], and including other people you may see fit [to examine]. So then, because, as We have noted from your communication, once you have read Our letter, you will institute the proceedings dealing with this business for the most part according to the procedure [laid down] therein, in order that the truth about the foregoing may start to shine more clearly, We, in Our desire to see [the business] completed and brought to a conclusion, commit it to your care by Apostolic letter so that, while you or one of your people, along with individuals you believe are useful in connection with this matter, are resourcefully and diligently investigating the truth by means of the courses of action, methods, procedures and rights of appeal of the kind [We have described] which you will decently be able to employ[11] in accordance with canonical sanctions, you may undertake to complete this investigation and, once it has been completed and brought to a conclusion, to send an accurate account of it to Us as soon as may be convenient.

[On 29 October 1337, Pope Benedict wrote to Pietro de Montespecchio, archdeacon of Lunas in the diocese of Béziers, and Guy, Professor of Canon and Civil Law, and precentor of the churches of Lodève, saying that he had looked at the judicial record in the case of François Julien and the others (no. 10) and was now passing it on to Pietro and Guy for their consideration. They were to call upon people whose judgement they could trust [sapientibus hominibus] to assist them in deciding who had been unjustly slandered and accused, and was therefore innocent, and who was guilty. The latter were to receive due punishment and penances.]

11. *Two women who have entered a devil's service, 1338*

Hansen I, no. 21 (pp. 13–14)

[A letter from Benedict XII to Guillaume Lombardi, Provost of the church of Barjols in the diocese of Fréjus.]

Not without horror and detestation have We noted that Catherine Andrieva of St Paul Lofrech and Simone Ginota of Baigneaux, women from the diocese of Le Vivier, who were arrested some time ago [and] on that account brought to the Apostolic See, were aroused by a devilish spirit and gave themselves to him, body

---

11. Adding *uti* to the text.

and soul, promising him annual tribute or labour in his wheat field[12] (paying it on a number of occasions), and doing in dreadful fashion other superstitious and damnable things in word and deed with that same devil. We, therefore, wishing to root out these and similar things from the domain of the faithful, and to have these women's great offences polished away by the file of justice, instruct Your Prudence in the case of these women, as in other cases, to take such pains as you deem appropriate to track down the truth of these things more fully, to investigate diligently the truth of the foregoing and anything stemming therefrom, and, if you find these women guilty, to punish them and correct them and impose penances on them as justice demands, but in a spirit of mercy, should their contrition merit it and you think it consistent with reason.

12. Image magic and buried treasure, 1339

Hansen I, no. 22 (pp. 14–15)

[A letter from Benedict XII to Durand, Abbot of the Cistercian monastery of Bolbonne in the diocese of Mirepoix.]

(3?) December

It has come to Our hearing that Guillaume de Mosset, otherwise known as 'the Bastard of Mosset', a cleric in the diocese of Rieux, Raimond Fenol, Arnald Gifre, Bernard Ainer and Bertrand de Causat, monks of your monastery, harking back to secular desires and worldly riches (which fight against the soul and ought to be regarded as pieces of dung), got together one day at the gate of the said monastery in order to be able to carry out alchemy in secret, and they bound themselves by a sacred oath not to reveal or make known to anyone the alchemical [experiments] they were going to make. Guillaume de Mosset told the monks that he knew of an enchanted hill near the village of Limoux, where an immense treasure had been hidden, and that a certain woman, similarly enchanted, had been appointed guardian of it, and that if the monks were going to carry out the said alchemy and remove the said treasure from the foresaid hill, they would need a wax image which would be baptized and afterwards would speak. This image Guillaume later procured and had a servant called Pierre bring it to the house of Pierre Giraud, a citizen of Pamiers. [He said] that later on this image was taken out of Pierre [Giraud's] house and secretly brought by Raimond Fenol to the foresaid monastery and put on top of the altar of the Chapel of St Katharine which is next to the monastery gate.[13] In spite of its having been made with a view to committing a sacrilege, it is said to have remained on top of [the altar] for several days without attracting attention. After this, Raimond brought

---

12.   *Servicium in blado.* This could refer to a money-payment, but *servitium* is perhaps more commonly associated with work of some kind. Is there a faint echo of the parable of the workers in the lord's vineyard, Matthew 20.1–16?

13.   Putting objects under the linen which covered the altar so that they could be 'consecrated' by having Mass said over them was a common procedure.

it back to Pierre's house and, in Pierre's presence, Guillaume asked Raimond if the image had been baptized. He replied it had not, because he had not been able to baptize it. So next Pierre Garaud handed over the image to you, and you – so We have heard – found in the basket in which it had been brought back nine pins with which the image was to be pricked. Raimond, it is said, confessed – and proof of this comes from a secular[14] – that he received and kept in his possession for several days a book in which the traditional rite of the sacrament of baptism had been written down.

Bernard is said to have confessed that he had got the book of holy baptism from the church in Montaillou and had sent it to Raimond who kept it for several days and then sent it back to the chaplain of the forementioned church. One of the church's clerics is also said to have mentioned that Bernard asked him to borrow the church's holy oil and give it to him. But the cleric refused to do so, saying that he was not authorized to give Bernard anything.

Therefore, since (provided the foregoing turns out to be true), these monks are known to have brought on themselves the stain of a serious charge by making the said image (or having it made), putting it on top of the altar and keeping it there for several days while Mass was being celebrated, with the intention of conferring the sacrament of baptism on the image in order to perform this kind of alchemy and acquire the hidden treasure, and [since these monks] should be punished severely on that account, We recommend to your discernment, and We strictly command by this Apostolic document, that you take pains to inform yourself privately about the things We have described and deal with them in such a way that the monks who have had the rash presumption to do these things cannot run away and, by doing so, evade the penance which is due to them. [We also instruct] you to seize books, manuscripts and other things belonging to them and to look after them carefully and, in addition, to report to Us by letter whatever you have found out about these matters and what you think should be done, by [employing] ecclesiastical censure with no right of appeal, to curb those who raise objections. If, however, the witnesses, whose names you will have [by then], dissociate themselves because of partiality, hatred or fear, you may compel them to provide the testimony to the truth by [employing] a similar censure with no opportunity of appeal.

---

14. *Per unum secularem*, that is, a cleric who was not a monk. It could also refer to a lay person, but it is perhaps more likely that another ecclesiastic may have had a chance to see the book and know what was in it.

13. Demon worshippers seek to obstruct the inquisitorial process, 1374

Hansen I, no. 23 (pp. 15–16)

[Letter from Gregory XI to Jacques de Morée, inquisitor in France.]

14 August

Although We, unworthy as We are, have been designated by divine Providence overseer of the Church Militant, We are made weak[15] by constant vigils and assailed by Our continually wondering how We may spend Our resources and effort as effectively as We possibly can, so that the sheep of the Lord's flock may be protected from a cunning enemy 'who seeks, like a roaring lion, whom he may devour',[16] and tries to rend the unity of the Church, wound her charity, poison the sweetness of her holy works with the bile of iniquity and in every way to ruin and throw into confusion the people of Christ: and [so that] they may be kept safe from the vices and ambushes and assaults of others who seek, in wretched fashion, [to tread in his] damnable footprints: and [so that] they may be imbued with good and virtuous habits (which are the gift of the Lord) and praiseworthily kept therein. Now, it is a fact that it came to Our hearing not long ago from a trustworthy source (and caused Us much disturbance of mind), that in the matters to which We have referred and which concern you as an inquisitor into heretical perversity, appointed by Apostolic authority, error of this kind has sprouted and continues to sprout because a very large number of people (even on occasion ecclesiastics), unmindful of their salvation, invoke demons to the peril of their souls, injury to the Christian faith and the scandal of many; and because when you wish to proceed against such individuals anent the foregoing, some of them (sometimes even those with education) oppose what you are doing, alleging that, according to canon law, this is not part of your duty.

We, therefore, as We are required to do by Our pastoral duty, wishing to take steps to deal with these people, by Apostolic authority grant to Your Circumspection by the wording of these presents full and unrestricted power to investigate fully, candidly, unofficially, without fuss or formal judicial proceeding, these particular invokers of demons: to correct and punish, according to the intentions and dictates of canon law, and without right of appeal, those you find guilty: also to restrain by means of ecclesiastical censure those who object, setting aside their right of appeal: [and this] notwithstanding Apostolic decrees from one, two or any other session to the contrary; [and this also applies] if anyone, either as part of a group or as an individual, [claims he] has an indult from the Apostolic See, [saying] that he cannot be interdicted, suspended or excommunicated or summoned to court outwith or beyond certain places, if [his] Apostolic letter does not make full and express mention, word for word, of an indult of this kind.

15.　Reading *languemus* for *angimur*.
16.　1 Peter 5.8: 'Be sober, be vigilant, for your adversary the Devil, as a roaring lion, walketh about, seeking whom he may devour'.

This present [letter] will cease to have any validity two years from the date of these presents.

[On 30 August 1409, Alexander V wrote to Pons Fougeyron, a Franciscan, commissioned as Inquisitor that same year, noting that he had heard there were, in the extensive province now under Fougeyron's jurisdiction, 'many Christians and Jews who are fortune tellers [sortilegi], invokers of demons, chanters of spells [carminatores], summoners of spirits [coniuratores], practitioners of superstition and interpreters of signs [augures], who employ wicked, forbidden practices'. These people, he said, should be prosecuted and punished even if it meant calling on the assistance of the secular arm. The word coniurator *has both a technical and a more general sense. Here it is being used in the former, but* coniurator *is also the ordinary word for 'conspirator', and this enables writers on magic and so on to hint that magic involves a conspiracy and oath taking between humans or between humans and evil spirits. On 3 February 1418, Martin V wrote to Fougeyron, urging him to similar action on the basis of his predecessor's letter; and on 24 February 1434, Eugenius IV confirmed Fougeyron's powers to deal with practitioners of magic and fortune tellers, quoting Pope Alexander's list as a comprehensive guide.]*

14. Eugenius IV addresses all inquisitors on the subject of demon worship and magical practice, 1437

Hansen I, no. 27 (pp. 17–18)

Not without grave bitterness of mind has it come to Our ears that the prince of darkness has, by means of his stratagems, cast such a spell on many people who have been redeemed by the blood of Christ, that he makes them accomplices in their own damnation and fall; that with criminal blindness they search out his detestable persuasions and illusions and those of his supporters, sacrifice to demons, worship them, await and receive responses from them, pay them homage; and moreover [that] they hand over to them a written document or something else as a sign, so that (i) they can lay on or take away from anyone they wish, by word alone or touch or sign, acts of harmful magic [*maleficia*] which they have bound themselves to the [demons] to perform (ii) they can cure the sick, and (iii) arouse extremes of weather. [We have also heard that] they make pacts in connection with other dreadful things, or that once they have had these ideas, they carry them out; [that] they conceive images or other things and have them made so that they can control demons with them, and carry out acts of harmful magic by invoking them; [that] they are not afraid to abuse baptism and the Eucharist and the other sacraments and the stuff of which they are made in their fortune telling and acts of harmful magic [*sortilegiis et maleficiis*];[17] [that] by means of this type of invocation, they baptize or get others to baptize images made from wax or something else. In addition to this, some of them, showing

17. *Sortilegiis* could also be translated as 'acts of sorcery'.

no reverence to the mystery of that most holy cross on which the Shepherd hung for us all, insult crucifixes and at other times the sign of the cross with reprehensible movements [of their body], and take it upon themselves with superstitious temerity to imitate the sacraments (which should not be imitated in any way).

[The Pope therefore empowers the inquisitors] to proceed without wasting time, straightforwardly, unofficially, without fuss or formal judicial proceedings, and, during the trials, observing the methods approved by canon law, which are to be embraced in cases of heresy with diocesan bishops and others. [They may] also examine those people, put them in prison and keep them there in accordance with what is demanded by the nature of their transgressions and strike them down with due punishments by means of ecclesiastical censure and any other appropriate remedies provided by law, calling upon the assistance of the secular arm, if need be.

15. Pope Eugenius rails against Amadeus, Duke of Savoy, as a protector of and a consorter with witches, 1440

Hansen I, no. 28 (pp. 18–19)

[Eugenius struggled with the Council of Basel over Papal authority. At one point he was 'deposed' by the Council which then elected Duke Amadeus as antipope Felix V. Amadeus presided over Savoy at a time when witchcraft was being re-formulated into a new kind of crime, that of conscious conspiracy with Satan to undermine and eventually overthrow Christianity, and Amadeus's law code, Statuta Sabaudiae (1430), laid emphasis on the crime of hostile magic. Thirteen years earlier, the Duke had had his Chancellor executed on a charge of attempted assassination by magic (see below III, no. 4)].

23 March

The leader and chief of these people [the Council] and architect of the whole damnable enterprise is that firstborn of Satan, Amadeus, Duke of Savoy, who has been thinking about this for a long time. A good many people maintain that he was led astray some years ago by the tricks, predictions and illusions of a number of most unfortunate men and silly women [*muliercularum*],[18] who have abandoned their Saviour and turned back to Satan, and are led astray by the fantasies of demons which are called *stregule* or *stregones* or Waldenses in the vernacular,[19] and which are said to be very numerous in his country. In order to get himself erected at some point as an unnatural Head in the Church of God,

---

18. *Muliercula* is a diminutive form of *mulier*, 'woman'. It is frequently used in this kind of context as a term of contempt.

19. *Stregones* and *stregule* are Italian terms derived from the Latin *strix* meaning 'night owl', often taken to be a bird of ill-omen, and associated with feeding upon young or small creatures. Hence, when it became one of the terms for 'witch', it implied shape-changing and attacks upon babies or infants, especially at night. *Stregula* is a diminutive form of *strego*. The Waldenses were an heretical sect originating in the twelfth century. They took their name from their founder, Waldo, a wealthy French merchant. The movement was difficult to suppress and

he put on the clothes of a hermit (or rather, of a most deceitful hypocrite), so that, under the fleece of a sheep and the appearance of a lamb, he might don the brutality of a most rapacious wolf. Then, conspiring with those attending [the Council of] Basel, by force, bribery, promises and threats, he brought a very large number of them under his dominion (or tyranny) so that they might desecrate themselves for the sake of Beelzebub, idol and prince of those demons, in opposition to Our Holiness, the undoubted and most genuine Vicar of Christ and successor of Peter in the Church of God.

16. Boniface IX writes to a priest who has been involved in magic and an unforeseen death, 1440

Hansen VIII (p. 672)

[Letter to Otto Synboden of Ameneburg, a priest in the diocese of Mainz.]

25 May

Recently you explained in Our presence that some time ago, while you were a chaplain in Meyrinchusen in the diocese of Paderborn, you performed an act of sorcery [*sortilegium*] in connection with the loss of large sums of money. You did so with a fine zeal and simple mindedness, as though you were ignorant of the law not to invoke a demon, but, by means of your own guile and with the instruction and advice of certain persons practised in sorcery, [you used] the divine words of the psalter, fervent prayers, pieces of bread and other things employed for this purpose, and invocations of male and female saints, to put right the theft of sums of money belonging to Our beloved son, Tilo Wulf, esquire, from the same diocese. Tilo, however, and Our beloved son, Bruno Francken, a lay man, his servant, received ample warning in advance that even if sorcery of this kind allowed one to guess the identity and guilt of a thief from reliable signs, such a person could not be harmed or hurt by any word, deed or sign from [Tilo and Bruno] or anyone else. But once you had carried out this act of sorcery in the manner described, Tilo and Bruno, in your absence, without doing you the favour of asking you and without your knowing anything at all about it, went to Conrad, a lay man from the said diocese, upon whom your act of sorcery had cast suspicion. You had told them beforehand that the human eye might be mistaken because of prompting from the Devil, and that there was no trust to be had in these acts of sorcery you were performing; and on another occasion you had taken as much care as ever you could to praise Conrad [to them]. However, stained by a spirit of malice, they gave him a fatal wound and then, it is alleged, Bruno strangled him.

[The Pope goes on to absolve Otto from the canonical penalties he had incurred as a result of the part he had played in these events.]

lasted, in scattered pockets, for a long time. Its members were accused of being practitioners of harmful magic and therefore apostates and followers of Satan.

17. Confirmation of an inquisitor's powers against a variety of offences, 1451

Hansen I, no. 30 (p. 19)

[Nicholas V writes to the Inquisitor General of France, Hugues Lenoir.]

1 August

[The Pope confirms and extends all the inquisitor's privileges to enable him] to proceed without wasting time, straightforwardly, unofficially, without fuss and formal judicial proceeding (but only as far as, and no more than, is required in looking for the truth), against each and every person of whatever rank, standing, degree, status, position or pre-eminence he or she may be, who has set aside fear of God and, to the loss of his or her soul, blasphemes God and the most glorious Virgin Mary and His saints: who, even if they do not obviously savour of heresy, commit sacrilege and foretell the future [*divinatores*], and who perpetrate that outrageous crime according to which 'God's anger comes upon the sons of disbelief'[20] – having sex carnally and damnably with brute animals[21] – and who are beasts of any other sect.[22]

18. Magicians in the north of Italy corrupt the faithful, 1457

Hansen I, no. 31 (pp. 19–20)

[Calixtus III to Bernardo da Bosco, Papal nuncio and commissioner, canon and sacrist of the church in Lerida and Papal chaplain in the cities and dioceses of Verona, Brescia and Bergamo.]

29 October

[The Pope is astonished that in the city and diocese of Brescia and Bergamo several ecclesiastics as well as lay people are disseminating false teachings about Christ and the Virgin Mary.] Indeed, a number of others who live there, too, from whose eyes the fear of God has departed in like manner, make use of invocations, chanted spells [*carminibus*], superstitious and conspiratorial evocations [*coniurationibus*] and magical and offensive practices; and by means of their deceptive tricks they do the best they can to teach, persuade, and induce those from among the Christian population whom they recognize as simple minded and gullible to turn away from their divine Creator and become soiled with their most deceptive practices ... .

[Bernardo therefore] may proceed with vigilance, by Our authority, against each and every person of either sex ... . Without wasting time, straightforwardly,

---

20.   Ephesians 5.6: 'Let no one lead you astray with empty words, for on account of these God's anger comes upon the sons of disbelief'.

21.   This is a reference to sodomy which very frequently means 'bestiality' not 'buggery of a human'.

22.   There are gaps in Hansen's text at this point, and I have emended *quarreristas*, 'stonecutters', to *querestas*, 'beasts', in the hope that it makes better sense in the context.

unofficially, without fuss and formal judicial proceeding, looking only for the truth of what has been done, [and pursuing the case] as far as definitive sentence and execution of the individual, both steps inclusive, with a view to the extirpation of the foresaid and any other errors, heresies and immoral behaviour in these same cities and dioceses, and also (if appropriate), in the city and diocese of Verona, the territory and town of Crema and the dioceses of Piacenza, Lodi and Cremona, once you have consulted and been fully informed about the foregoing by the ordinaries of those places and the inquisitor of heretical wickedness appointed to that region, should you consider [such consultation] profitable.

19. Heretics who practise fortune telling and magic and spread errors among the faithful, 1459

Hansen I, no. 32 (p. 20)

[Letter of Pius II to the Abbot of Sainte Marie in the diocese of Tréguier in Brittany and two canons of the church in Tréguier. The wording is very similar to that used by Eugenius IV over 20 years earlier.]

17 December

Not without disturbance of mind and great sorrow has it come to Our hearing that the prince of darkness has so engulfed a very large number of the inhabitants of the Duchy of Brittany, who have been redeemed by the blood of Christ, that he has made them accomplices in their own damnation and fall and has deceived them with his stratagems: that with criminal blindness they search out his detestable illusions and those of his supporters, strive to predict the times of people's deaths and other happenings and by the use of incantations cause other illnesses and debilitating sickness: [and that] they are not afraid to plant errors in the Christian faith, while carrying out wicked acts and persuading men and women that virginity, widowhood, and celibacy are necessary to eternal salvation ....

We long with the deepest feelings to drive away plague-bearing diseases of this kind which infect the Lord's flock when they come into contact with it, and, as far as lies in Us, to keep all peoples away from things which may cause them to fall, or which are forbidden, and We have been swayed by the entreaties of Our beloved and noble François, Duke of Brittany. [Therefore] We instruct you ... to investigate those who are actively engaged in magical practices and, with Apostolic authority, to proceed against those and others who disseminate fresh errors.

[On 17 June 1473, Sixtus IV asked the Vicar General in Bologna about certain Carmelites who were alleged to be saying 'that it is not heretical or contrary to the purity of the Faith to seek responses from demons. On account of this, it appears that many scandals have arisen, directed towards the purity of the Faith'; *and on 1 April 1478, he was obliged to forbid the making, blessing and sale of* 'stamped images of the most innocent Lamb, made from wax which are generally called Agnus Dei'. *These are reserved exclusively to the Pope,* 'to be bestowed

on those who devoutly ask for the remission of their sins, so that by touching [the Agnus Dei] and using it, the Christian faithful may be invited to the praise of God, be freed from fire and shipwreck, have tornadoes, lightning strikes, hailstorms, tempests and every malign turbulence driven away from them and be kept safe from the danger [attendant upon] childbirth if they are pregnant'.]

20. Grant of an indulgence to the Dominican house in Sélestat to help with its upkeep and contribute to the expenses of local inquisitors, 1483

Hansen I, no. 35 (pp. 21–4)

[Bull of Sixtus IV, probably written in answer to a request from Heinrich Institoris, an inquisitor in Upper Germany, who had been born in the town of Sélestat some 50 years or so earlier.]

31 October

To all Christ's faithful who will see this letter, greeting.

The mercy of God's clemency, contained in the treasury of the most holy Passion of our Lord and hidden in the sacraments of the Church, has arranged for it to be obtained for the salvation of the faithful in the form of the reward of eternal life. Although We who dispense it are endowed with insufficient merits, yet We believe We are worthily carrying out the ministry of dispensation when We convert the salutary commerce of that treasury into the work of the repair and upkeep of churches and other religious places of devotion, most especially those which are known to stand in need [of it], and also [use it] to aid a Christian state and those individuals who constantly labour for the salvation of souls on behalf of the Catholic faith against treacherous heretics.

So, then, We have heard, not without severe distress of mind, from a trustworthy source, that in several areas of Germany some heresies are sprouting under the ministration of the 'sower of weeds'.[23] [They involve] certain silly women who have been denying the Faith for some time past and continue to do so, particularly at the moment, having been led away from the Faith by that foster son of iniquity and perdition, Andrea, the former Archbishop of Krain,[24] whose aspiring vanity has corrupted his judgement; and by means of his deceitful illusions, [Satan] has also drawn many into his treacherous sect, who were once true Christians and genuine Catholics. In consequence, it is expedient to provide

---

23.   I.e. Satan. See Matthew 13.25: 'while the men were sleeping, his enemy came, sowed weeds in the middle of the wheat, and went away'.

24.   Andrea Zuccalmaglio, a Slav by birth, who joined the Dominican Order and in 1479 was sent to Rome as an envoy from the Holy Roman Emperor, Frederick III. Shocked by what he found there, Andrea spoke his mind too freely, angered the Pope and was briefly imprisoned until he was released, probably at the instance of the Emperor. Not long after, he went to Basel where he hoped to call a General Council to have the Pope deposed. By the Emperor's tolerance he was able to cause trouble between March and July 1482 in spite of his being excommunicated. But by December the Emperor had withdrawn his support and Andrea was arrested and thrown into prison where he endured until November 1484 when he committed suicide.

a suitable remedy so that errors of this kind may not grow stronger every day. For this, no small effort on the part of inquisitors of heretical wickedness is necessary to counter such things, and because these inquisitors cannot do their duty without great expense, since they are continually compelled to keep on the move all over the place, We wish and desire to provide both for their easement (so that they can support themselves), and for the needs of the church of the house of St Dominic in the town known as Sélestat in the Dominican diocese of Strasbourg. [Therefore], by Apostolic authority and the wording of this letter, We grant a plenary indulgence and remission of all their sins (i) to those of both sexes who have put their trust in the mercy of God and of St Peter and St Paul (by His authority Apostles); (ii) who in a spirit of devotion visit the foresaid church every year for three years between first and second Vespers on the fifth Sunday of Lent, when *Judica* is sung,[25] and the following day; (iii) and make offerings to help repair the fabric and buildings [and contribute to] the upkeep and maintenance of the said church; (iv) and, as far as their income allows and their confessors advise, give financial support to the inquisitors. [We do this] so that the Christian faithful may flock to that church more willingly out of devotion and more readily make offerings to help its repair, maintenance and upkeep, as well as the relief of the inquisitors, and thus perceive that by this action they have been restored the more fully by the gift of heavenly grace in that spot.

[The rest of the Bull deals with further privileges granted to the Dominican house and the inquisitors.]

21. Heinrich Institoris and Jakob Sprenger have their powers as inquisitors clarified in the face of objections from certain clergy and lay men, 1484

Hansen I, no. 36 (pp. 25–7)

[A Bull issued by Innocent VIII, which Institoris, author of the Malleus Maleficarum, *attached to his work in an apparent attempt to persuade readers that it had official Papal approval.]*

5 December

Bishop Innocent, slave of the slaves of God, for a perpetual reminder of this situation.[26] Desiring with the greatest eagerness, as careful attention to [Our]

25.　Psalms 42.1: *Judica me, Deus*, 'Judge me, o God'.

26.　*Servus* has an ambiguous status between 'slave' and 'servant', but the title is an ancient one, coming from a period when slaves were a common feature of society. There were still many slaves in Europe during the fifteenth century, and 'serfs' (*servi*) were in effect little better than slaves in their various societies. An awareness of the link between the Christian use of *Dominus* ('master of slaves') for God, and the term *servus* itself, is always acutely possible in a society which used Latin constantly as its mean of communication. Cf. Romans 6.16: 'Don't you know that when put yourselves at someone's disposal with regard to obedience, you are the slaves of the person you obey?' On balance, therefore, I have decided to use this slightly unorthodox version of the episcopal title, rather than the more traditional 'servant of the servants of God'.

pastoral duty requires, that the Catholic faith be increased and flourish every-where, most especially in Our times, and that all heretical wickedness be driven far from the domain of the faithful, We gladly proclaim and grant once again those things through which this devout desire of Ours may attain its end and, after every error has been weeded out with the help given by Our activity (as with the hoe of a far-seeing labourer), enthusiasm for and attentiveness to the Faith may be stamped more forcibly upon the hearts of the faithful.

Not without immense distress has it recently come to Our hearing that in several regions of Upper Germany, and also in the provinces, cities, lands, regions and dioceses of Mainz, Köln, Trier, Salzburg and Bremen, very many people of both sexes, unmindful of their own salvation and straying from the Catholic faith, have misbehaved with incubi and succubi, and are not afraid, by means of their own incantations, spells and invocations, other acts of superstitious abomination[27] and outrages, crimes and offences:

(i)   to cause and procure the death, suffocation and extermination of the offspring of women, the young of animals, the crops of the earth, the grapes of vines and fruits of trees, as well as men, women, beasts of burden, farm animals, livestock and other animals of various kinds, and also vineyards, orchards, meadows, pastures, corn, cereals and other pulses:

(ii)   to afflict and torture these men, women, beasts of burden, farm animals, livestock and animals with dreadful anguish and acute pain, both internal and external;

(iii)   to prevent these men from fathering children and women from conceiving, and making it impossible for husbands and wives and women and men to perform their conjugal acts;

(iv)   also to deny with sacrilegious mouth the very faith they embraced when they received the holy [sacrament] of baptism;

(v)   and to commit and perpetrate very many other abominable things, outrages and crimes while the enemy of the human race goads them on, to the peril of their souls, offence to the majesty of God and a deadly example and scandal to a very large number of people.

(vi)   [We have also heard] that although Our beloved sons Heinrich Institoris and Jakob Sprenger, [members] of the Order of Preaching Brethren and Professors of Theology, were appointed inquisitors of heretical wickedness by Apostolic letter (and still hold that office) – Institoris in the foresaid areas of Upper Germany in which the provinces, cities, lands, dioceses and other regions mentioned above are considered to be included, and Sprenger throughout specific areas along the course of the Rhine – yet several clerics and lay men in those regions, seeking 'to know more than is proper',[28] do not blush to maintain stubbornly that because the provinces, cities, dioceses, lands and other foresaid regions, and the individuals living

---

27.   Reading *superstitiosis* for *superstitiis*.
28.   Romans 12.3: 'For I say to all those among you, through the grace which has been given to me, don't [seek] to know more than is proper'.

there and the outrages [they commit], were not mentioned individually and specifically by name, those places are not included as part of those areas [under the inquisitors' jurisdiction], and therefore the foresaid inquisitors have no right to exercise their office of inquisitor in those provinces, cities, dioceses, lands and regions and should not be permitted to punish, imprison and chastise the people living there on account of the foresaid outrages and crimes. Because of this, in those provinces, cities, dioceses, lands and regions, those outrages and crimes remain unpunished, not without obvious loss of these people's souls and cost to their eternal salvation.

We, therefore, driven chiefly by zeal for the Faith, wish, as Our duty requires Us to do, to get rid of any obstacles whereby these inquisitors can be held back from doing their duty and to provide appropriate remedies so that the stain of heretical wickedness and other outrages of a similar kind may not pour out its poisons to the destruction of other innocent individuals, and so that it does not turn out that the provinces, cities, dioceses, lands and foresaid regions in these areas of Upper Germany lack the beneficial service of scrutiny which is their due.

By the wording of this present [letter] We decree, by Apostolic authority, that these inquisitors are permitted to exercise the duty of inquisition in those places, and to proceed to the chastisement, imprisonment and punishment of those individuals on account of the foresaid outrages and crimes in every regard and by all means, precisely as though the provinces, cities, dioceses, lands and regions, individuals and outrages, had been mentioned individually and specifically by name in the foresaid letter. As a further surety, We extend the said letter and appointment to provinces, cities, dioceses, lands and regions, and also to individuals and crimes of the sort mentioned above, and grant once again the foresaid inquisitors, by the same authority, full and unrestricted power to carry out the duty of inquisition in the foresaid provinces, cities, dioceses, lands and regions against any individuals, of whatever rank and pre-eminence they may be, and to chastise, imprison, punish and fine those individuals they find guilty in the forementioned [places], according to their faults.

This [they may do] themselves, as may one of them by inviting Our beloved son, Johann Glemper, a cleric of the diocese of Konstanz and Master in the Arts, their present notary (or any other public notary), [to act] with him, and by one or both of them deputizing him for the time being. They also have the power to explain and preach the word of God to the faithful populace freely and without restraint in every parish church of these provinces as many times as may be expedient, and as often as they think fit; and likewise they may also legally and without restriction do and carry out all other individual things necessary and appropriate in connection with the foregoing and these [particular] points.

Nevertheless, by written Apostolic [orders], We instruct Our venerable brother, the Bishop of Strasburg, that when, where or however many times he realizes it is expedient, and when, where or however many times he has been lawfully asked by these inquisitors, or by one of them, he make the foregoing public with due formality, either himself or via another person or persons; and that he do not allow them to be harassed or impeded by anyone [claiming] any authority contrary to the text of Our previous and present letters. By Our authority, he is to curb any trouble makers, obstructers, objectors and rebels, of whatever rank, status, social position, pre-eminence, nobility, superiority or condition they may be, or by whatever privilege of exemption they may be protected, by sentences of excommunication, suspension, interdict and other even more frightening censures and punishments he will think fit, with no right of appeal; and by Our authority, he is to ensure that he aggravates these sentences again and again as often as may be necessary in the legal proceedings he must employ in connection with these matters, calling upon the aid of the secular arm if necessary.

[The contents of this letter are not to be contradicted or restrained in any way by earlier Apostolic letters or grants of exemption or privilege. Anyone who attempts to do so will incur divine and Papal wrath.]

[On 18 June 1485, Pope Innocent VIII wrote to the Archbishop of Mainz, saying that he had issued a plenary indulgence, effective at the moment of death, to those who assisted Institoris and Sprenger in their work as inquisitors, namely, public officials and nobles who afforded them protection. In addition, Innocent instructed the Archbishop to appoint inquisitorial deputes to every diocese, since it was impossible for Institoris and Sprenger to visit every one.

On the same day he wrote to the Archduke of Austria, praising him for his zeal in protecting the Faith and acting against 'the sect of heretics and workers of harmful magic'. Innocent urged him to continue this work, 'especially in the suppression of workers of harmful magic of both sexes', and said that they should not be allowed to agree to undergo ordeal by red-hot iron, but that they should be punished according to canon law and Imperial statute.

A third letter from that day, addressed to the Abbot of Weingarten, praised him for supporting the inquisitors in the diocese of Konstanz and told him he had written to the Archduke of Austria, asking him to protect the abbot against any harassment.

A letter from Innocent VIII to the Bishop of Brescia and the local inquisitor, dated 30 September 1486, dealt with the intransigence of Brescian officials in carrying out punishments imposed by the bishop and the inquisitor in several cases of heresy. Neither magic nor fortune telling nor demon worship seems to be involved.

On the other hand, Alexander VI wrote to the Provost of Klosterneuberg and Heinrich Institoris on 31 January 1500 that in Bohemia and Moravia 'many people have been infected by the poisons of the most wicked Enemy' to blaspheme against the Faith and attach themselves to heretical doctrines. So the Provost and Institoris were going to be sent there to preach the Gospel and counter opposition with the usual armoury of ecclesiastical censures and sentences; and the Pope promised that they would be accorded the facilities needed to conduct their investigations (followed by trials) of local heretics and workers of harmful magic 'who run after illusions, follow Herodias (to use the words of St Augustine),[29] *and pursue magical practices', as well as 'the protectors and supporters of heretical workers of harmful magic and pursuers of magical practices'.]*

22. Incantations, acts of poisonous magic and superstitious practices are to be suppressed and punished, 1501

Hansen I, no. 42 (p. 31)

[A letter from Alexander VI to Brother Angelo of Verona, Inquisitor in Lombardy.]

Since We have heard that in the province of Lombardy various individuals of both sexes are devoting their energies to various incantations and devilish superstitions, and are giving rise to many dreadful crimes with their acts of poisonous magic [*veneficiis*] and superstitious magic [*vanis observationibus*], and are destroying people, draught animals and fields, introducing various errors and in consequence giving rise to great scandals, by virtue of the ministry of the pastoral duty which has been committed to Us from on high, We have decided to suppress crimes of this nature and to take measures to deal, as far as We can with God's [help], with the foregoing scandals and crimes. Therefore to you and your successors appointed to Lombardy (in whom We have complete confidence in the Lord with regard to these and other things), We commit and entrust the task of making diligent investigation of these individuals of both sexes and, using the means afforded by justice, of punishing and suppressing them – [a task] for you alone, although carried out in company with a respectable staff to be chosen by you. So that you may be able the better to carry out this commission, We grant you full and continuous power of every kind against them, Apostolic constitutions and decisions, indults and ordinary concessions made as circumstances require and any other such things to the contrary notwithstanding.

[In a letter addressed to Giorgio da Casale, Inquisitor of Cremona, dated somewhere between 1503 and 1513, Julius II noted that some people of both sexes were trampling on the cross, insulting, it, abusing the Church's sacraments, especially the Eucharist, reverencing the Devil as their lord, and harming people, animals and crops by means of incantations, spells [carminibus], acts of sorcery [sortilegiis] and other dreadful superstitious practices.]

29.   'Certain wicked women who … . believe they ride at night on certain beasts together with Diana (or Herodias), a goddess of the pagans'. This is not St Augustine, but Burchard's version of the canon *Episcopi* where 'Herodias' is added to the text.

23. *Lay interference in cases of magic, divination and demon worship, 1521*

Hansen I, no. 44 (pp. 32–4)

[Letter from Pope Leo X to the bishops of Venetia.]

15 February 1521

Anent the petition of Our beloved sons, the Duke and senators of Venice.

In the cities and dioceses of Brescia and Bergamo a most pernicious kind of people were utterly damned by the stain of heresy, which was causing them to renounce the sacrament of the baptism they had received, denying their Lord and giving their bodies and souls to Satan whose advice was leading them astray. In order to do something to please him, they were eagerly and indiscriminately slaughtering small children and were not afraid to carry out other acts of harmful magic and fortune telling. In the light of these facts, it started to become apparent that appropriate measures to extirpate their error would be called for. We suspect that a number of this sort have obstinately and willingly preferred to lose their life as heretics by means of an unspeakable punishment rather than acknowledge their error, and on account of this We are very much in two minds about what was being said anent the severity of your judges' proceedings against these people. We assigned Our venerable brother, the Bishop of Pula, to be attached to you, the Duke and Senate, as Apostolic Nuncio, with personal authority:

(i)   to examine and revisit the record of any one or more of the legal proceedings you have held, or have caused to be held, and whether you, as investigators, had the proceedings held properly, correctly and according to legal form;

(ii)   with your assistance to proceed against and investigate this class of damned people;

(iii)   to depute and pay suitable salaries to procurators and advocates, clerks and any other officials and court officers necessary and appropriate to carrying out the foresaid investigation;

(iv)   to deal with the foresaid [damned] people mercifully (whenever they are willing to return to the unity of the Church), to impose salutary penance on them and also to find them not guilty, in either an ecclesiastical or a secular court;

(v)   to condemn those who cannot be reformed and hand them over to the secular arm;

(vi)   and in accordance with what is contained above in this letter, to do, carry out and pursue anything else you could or should do by law or customary good practice.

Therefore, when the forementioned nuncio, by the legal force of this commission, deputed his venerable brother, the Bishop of Koper, who lives in that area, to study in detail the things We have mentioned and pursue them in company with you, and you and the depute went to the Val Camonica in the diocese of Brescia where people of this damned sort particularly flourish and sprout new growth, and discovered that a number of them had already been found guilty and sentenced and handed over to a secular court, it appears that the Venetian Senate instructed the Governor of Brescia not to persist with sentences of this kind and brought pressure to bear on you and the said depute not to proceed with their[30] execution, (on the assumption that the executions have indeed been stopped); and [ordered you] to remove and withdraw the payments and salaries necessary for carrying out this investigation, to transfer the proceedings against the foresaid guilty parties to Venice, or have them transferred there, and, what is worse, to force and compel the foresaid depute to appear before [the Venetian senate], (on the assumption that he has been forced and compelled to do so).

Now, because some people, on account of the foresaid letters in which the said nuncio was given his assignment, are undecided whether this means your authority has been diminished to the extent that you cannot proceed, (on the assumption that you had been able [to proceed] before these two letters [were written]), and because it is not seemly and is contrary to what is prescribed by law and the sacred canons and the liberty of the Church that lay people meddle with ecclesiastical persons and trials and carry out a sentence which We have not authorized, unless it were the case that they had already seen and examined the proceedings and sentences and had precedence and jurisdiction over clerics and ecclesiastical court proceedings. Since, however, no authority has been granted to lay people over clerics and proceedings of this kind, they have an obligation to comply and do their duty, not the authority to give orders; and because of this [situation], no small scandal arises among the Christian faithful.

Therefore, so that what has been proposed for the salvation of souls and the easier completion of the said proceedings may not be turned into loss and dismay: and especially because of the length of time the unfortunate souls continue to be weighed down to a greater extent by sins of this kind: and to remove all doubt concerning this, We decree and declare by the Apostolic contents of these presents that you can and should proceed, as the character of the crime demands, against workers of harmful magic, fortune tellers and apostates from the Faith, just as you had the power to proceed, lawfully and in accordance with custom and privilege, before these letters [of Ours] were issued. We engage and instruct you to admonish and exhort those Venetians, and their Duke and officials, not to meddle further in proceedings of this kind, but unhesitatingly to pursue the executions which have been and perhaps need to be enjoined upon them, now that they have been asked to do so, [and] without seeing or examining the trials conducted by the said ecclesiastical judges. If they fail or refuse to do this, you may compel them [to do so] by means of ecclesiastical sanctions and other appropriate legal means, without right of appeal.

[Two years later, on 20 July 1523, Adrian VI wrote to Modesto of Vincenza, Inquisitor in Cremona and other parts of Lombardy in answer to Modesto's

---

30.   *Illarum*, specifically feminine, although this is at odds with Leo's use of *homines* (not necessarily gender-specific, and masculine if it is) elsewhere in the letter as the collective noun for the offenders in question.

reminding him of the situation faced earlier by Giorgio da Casale and Pope Julius II's letter of authorization to him. A number of clerics and laymen had obstructed Giorgio in his efforts to suppress workers of magic and other forbidden practices, which was why Pope Julius issued his decree. Now Modesto had complained to Pope Adrian that these crimes were still being perpetrated day in, day out, not only in his jurisdiction of Cremona, but in all the other places and dioceses under the jurisdiction of inquisitors in Lombardy, and had asked for the provisions of Pope Julius's decree to be extended to himself. This request Pope Adrian now granted by this document.]

Part II

Literature on Magic and Witches
C. 1270–C. 1505

Preface: Canon Episcopi *c.900*

[Hansen begins his selection of literary texts with the tenth-century canon Episcopi, a direction to clergy anent certain popular beliefs which the Church was convinced needed to be combated vigorously before they got completely out of hand. Subsequent writers on magic and witchcraft very frequently referred to the canon and took it for granted either that its conclusions and provisions should be fully supported or that these were wrong and therefore should be corrected. Although the canon has been translated into English more than once, therefore, it seems advisable to include another version here as a preface to the later discussions.]

Bishops and their officials should endeavour, with all their strength, to erase completely from their parishes the pernicious practice of foretelling the future [*sortilegium*] and working harmful magic [*maleficium*], which was invented by the Devil; and if they find that any man or woman is a devotee of this criminal activity, they should throw them out of their parish in complete disgrace, because the Apostle says, 'After he has been given a first and second warning, steer clear of the person who is a heretic, because you know that someone of his kind has been subverted'.[1] Those who have abandoned their Creator and seek favours of the Devil have been subverted and are being held prisoner by the Devil. Therefore Holy Church must be cleansed from such a disease.

One must also not fail [to mention] that certain accursed women 'have been turned right back to Satan',[2] and led astray by the illusions and fantasies [produced] by demons. They believe and claim that, in company with Diana, a goddess of the heathens, a countless number of women ride during the hours of darkness on certain animals and, during the silence of the dead of night cross over many stretches of land and obey the commands [of Diana] as their mistress; and that, on particular nights, they are summoned to her service. If only these women had been the only ones to die in their treachery and had not dragged many other people with them into the violent and untimely death of faithlessness! For a countless number, deceived by this mistaken idea, believes that these things are true; and this belief of theirs draws them away from correct faith and makes them fall into the error of the heathens, which thinks that there is some kind of divinity or godhead apart from the one God.

This is why priests should preach to the people in the churches entrusted to them, with every possible urgency, so that they know these things are entirely false and that fantasies of this kind are inflicted on the minds of those without faith not by a divine, but by a malicious spirit. There is no doubt that Satan himself, who transforms himself into an angel of light, captures the mind of some silly little woman [*mulierculae*], subjugates her to him by using her lack of faith and

---

1.   Titus 3.10–11. The second verse continues, 'and he does wrong, because he has been sentenced by his own decision'.

2.   1 Timothy 5.15.

lack of belief, then transforms himself into the appearance and likeness of various individuals and dupes her mind, which he is holding prisoner, while she is asleep. He shows her happy things, sad things, people she knows, people she does not know, and leads [her mind] astray with every possible diversion; and while only her spirit suffers this, her faithless mind thinks these things are taking place, not in her mind but physically. Who is not taken out of himself in sleep and during nocturnal visions, and sees many things while he is asleep which he had never seen while he was awake? Who can be so stupid and so dim that he thinks all these things which are taking place only in his spirit are happening to him physically? The prophet Ezekiel saw his visions of the Lord spiritually, not physically, and the Apostle John saw and heard the mysteries of the apocalypse spiritually, not physically – as he himself says, 'At once I was in the spirit' [*Apocalypse* 4.2], and St Paul does not dare say he was snatched away physically.[3]

Therefore everyone must be told publicly that anyone who believes such things and things like them has lost his or her faith, and anyone who does not have the correct faith in God does not belong to Him, but to the one in whom he does believe, that is, the Devil. For it has been written about our Lord, 'Everything has been made by Him'.[4] Therefore whoever believes that anything can be done, or any created thing can be changed, except by the Creator Himself, who made everything and by whom everything has been made, or take on another appearance or likeness for better or worse, is undoubtedly a person without the Faith.

1. The form and method of questioning readers of signs and idolaters, anonymous, c.1270

Hansen II, no. 3 (pp. 43–4)

[From a Summary of the Duty of the Inquisition.]

Questions asked of idolaters and idolatrous people[5] about acts of idolatry and acts of harmful magic [*maleficiis*] should be asked in the same way.

If they[6] make something pertaining to the worship of demons, or if they have had [something] made or know who made it.

If they make trial of a mirror or sword or fingernail or sphere or ivory shaft to invoke the help of demons with any herbs or birds or other created things.

If they have tried anything [to achieve] anyone's hatred, anger or dissension, or to discover a thief or treasure, or to have honours, riches, or favours.

3.   See 2 Corinthians 12.2: 'I knew a man in Christ above fourteen years ago, whether in the body I cannot tell: or whether out of the body, I cannot tell: God knoweth; such a one caught up in the third heaven'.

4.   John 1.3.

5.   Reading *idolatricis* for *idolatriis*.

6.   I have changed the Latin singular to a plural in order to avoid having to say 'he or she' all the time.

If they have tried [to use] a circle or a child, or if they have made any sacrifice to get a response from demons.

If they have tried [to see anything] in water or fire or parts of the body, or [to do anything] with lead.

If they have made anything from the head of a person living or dead, or from their clothes or hair [to achieve] hatred or love.

If they have used the blood of a man or a woman to write anything on the Host or on anything else.

If they have sought the future in the intestines of animals or their shoulder blades or a person's hands.

If they have observed 'Egyptian' days[7] in the belief that these are unlucky for starting or stopping to do something, or [have done] anything such as this.

If they have done anything on 1 January to ensure good luck for the following year by exchanging New Year gifts with each other.

If they have taken note of months, times, hours of the day or years, or the course or stage of the moon or sun, in the belief that some days or hours or minutes or times are lucky or unlucky for doing, beginning or ceasing to do something such as a journey, marital sex or starting work on a building.

If they have investigated a number of letters, dots, drawings or [a number of] any signs, words or characters concerning someone's death or life or any future prosperity or adversity.[8]

If they have used dream writing or pages with signs and names [from the book] of Daniel written on them, or the lots which are called 'Apostles' lots', or if they have spoken charms while collecting herbs [intended to act] as preventatives[9]; or if they have worn small pieces of parchment with writing on them, or amulets, or placed them on people or animals in order to cure them of illness or for some other reason.

Likewise, if they have ill spoken [*fatavit*] a child or had someone else ill speak it; or if they have asked anyone to do this; or if they have furnished a table with rich foods and lamps for the fairies.

If they have taken note of portents from birds in flight or the song [of birds], or [have noted] sneezes or other similar things,[10] in the belief that they are the causes or signs of bad luck that day or month or year.

If they have taken note of things they have come across by chance, such as a bird sitting upon eggs, believing that because of this they [will] have fecundity or abundance; or they discover a cooking pot or a needle or a halfpenny; or if they run across a wolf or a snake and so forth, and believe that those things are the causes of good or bad luck.

---

7.   So called perhaps because it was believed they had been discovered by Egyptian astrologers. Popular belief in their significance goes back at least as far as an oblique reference in St Augustine's commentary on the Epistle to the Galatians, *Patrologia Latina* 35.2129.

8.   Dots probably refers to the divinatory art of geomancy, which involved making marks of some kind in sand or on a sheet of paper and interpreting the future from these.

9.   Reading *nomina* for *nomine*. On Apostles' lots, see further Cameron, *Enchanted Europe*, pp. 67–8. Reading *preventa* for *proventa*.

10.   Reading *similia* for *initialia*.

If they have taken note of the constellations, believing that the character, actions and fates of those being born can be known from the course of the stars.

If they have tried to jump across fires, or take [fire] from a number of hearths, or burn bones to a powder.

If they believed such things; if they had gone to the house of people who carry out such things, or if they had ever gone into the house to ask a question.

If they have tried [to use] any image, or (to be specific), if they have had an image or penny or halfpenny or amulet or anything else baptized.

If they have made any attempt [to use] the body of Christ or [holy] oil or baptismal water or any other sacred thing.

If they have tried [to use] characters written on skin, orchard fruit or any other fruit.

If they have tried [to use] drawings, marks, cuts, impressions or rings.

If they have tried to enchant snakes or other animals.

If they have used a fritter, a flat cake or any other foodstuff or a drink to make someone fall in love.

If they have used belts or pieces of silk[11] for divination.

If they have been reconciled [with the Church], by whom, when and in what way.

If they have been presented with money for these [magical purposes], if they have carried them out and if they have concealed any [of them].

If they have subsequently lapsed in any of the foregoing.

If they know that anyone has committed a sin by doing any of the foregoing.

2. Magically induced impotence and a mixture of remedies, Arnald of Villanova, attributed, c.1300

Hansen II, no. 4 (pp. 44–7)

[Arnald of Villanova (c.1240–1311) was of Catalan descent and was born in Valencia. He interested himself particularly in medicine and eschatology, but his theological views were regarded as unorthodox and he got into trouble not only with theologians in Paris, but also with two Popes, Boniface VIII and Benedict XI, who tolerated his medicine but not his theology. He wrote much on both medicine and alchemy, although the latter volumes under his name may be attributions rather than genuine works from his pen, as may 'Acts of Harmful Magic' (De maleficiis) from which the following extract is taken. The maleficium with which the extract deals may be one or any of three kinds: an act of harmful magic; 'harmful magic' as an abstract concept; and a physical instrument, such as something made from metal or a piece of paper with magical writing on it, which is used as a channelling device for the harmful magic to pass through and hit its target. NB: Hansen's version of the text differs in many places from that provided by Rider, Magic and Impotence, *pp. 218–23.]*

11.   *Cambalia.* Cf. Italian *cambellotto*, cloth originally made from camel-skin but, in the thirteenth century, referring to cloth made from silk.

There are certain men who cannot have sex with their wives because they have been prevented from doing so by acts [or instruments] of harmful magic, and I want my book to disclose a remedy for them because, unless I am mistaken, the remedy is one particularly blessed. So if it applies to you, you should put your hope in God and He will show you kindness. But because there are many different kinds of instruments of harmful magic, I should discuss them first.

Well now, certain instruments of harmful magic have their origin in living creatures; for example, a cock's testicles placed on top of a bed along with its blood stop those who lie in the bed from having sex; certain [consist of] characters written in bat's blood and certain [consist of things] originating in the ground: if, for example, you split a hazelnut or an acorn and put one half on one side of a path along which a husband and wife have to come and the other half on the other. There are others which are made from the seeds of beans which cannot be softened in hot water or roasted. The harmful magic is particularly bad if three or four of them are placed under a bed or on a path or on top of a door or on each side of it. There are also some which come from metallic substances and are made from iron, or lead and iron. But [there are also] those consisting of the needle used to sew dead men and women into their shrouds. Because these are devilish and practised especially by women, some people are cured with divine and others with human help. Therefore, if a husband or wife is disturbed by these instruments of harmful magic, it is undoubtedly more blessed to discuss them, because if these people get no help, they are split up and downcast, and the exercise of this harmful magic affects not only one's neighbours but also the Creator.[12]

If we want to eradicate harmful magic of the bed, we must see whether the instrument of harmful magic is still in its place and take it away. On the one hand, if the perpetrator of this magic takes it away during the day or puts it there during the night, or vice versa, the husband and wife should seek out another house in which they can go to bed. But if this magic is one which uses characters, [and] it is realized that the husband and wife do not love each other, one should look for [the instrument] above or below the door lintel and take whatever one finds to a priest. But if the instrument is not there, one should do as described later. If a hazelnut or acorn be the cause of the harmful magic, someone should take the magical substance[13] or the acorn which is causing the separation. A man [should take] his bit of it and immediately go from one side [of the path] to the other and place it there, and the woman should put the other piece of the nut from her side of the road [along with it]. Then husband and wife should take both parts of the nut, remove the shell and keep the whole nut bound fast together for six days. Once this has been done, they should eat it. If the magic has been done with beans, it can be cured with God's help rather than with human [remedies]. If the source of the magic lies in 'the needles of the dead', look for it in the mattress or the pillow, and if it not to be found there, [the couple] should have sex in another house and another bed.

12.   Reading *per hoc maleficium non solum exercetur in proximis sed etiam in Creatore*.

13.   *Venenum*, also 'poison'. People who worked magic with potent herbs were often called *veneficus* 'worker of poisonous magic' (male) or *venefica* (female).

Apotropaics against evil spirits and acts of harmful magic
The bile of a male black dog sprinkled upon a house combats an evil spirit so that harmful magic does not bring damage into it, [and] when the walls of a house have been sprinkled with dog's blood, that cleanses it of all harmful magic.[14]

If a husband and wife have the bile of any fish, but especially that of small shads [river herring] when they go to bed, and put it on live coals, thereby creating a fumigation, all forementioned harmful magic vanishes.

If, without the knowledge of a husband and wife, quicksilver[15] is taken and inserted into a cane or reed which is sealed with wax, they will not be troubled by harmful magic.

'If you put goat's bile in your house, all evil spirits will flee' (Gilbert).[16]

Likewise, 'if you carry a vulture's heart [with you], it makes all evil spirits and wild animals run away from a sinner, and makes a man pleasing to everyone, men and women, as well as rich and earnest' (Gilbert).[17]

Likewise, 'the jay either roasted or boiled and then eaten quickly restores health to the sick, releases and cures those who have been deceived by an incantation, cures them, and bestows serenity [of behaviour]' (Gilbert).

'To remove harmful magic, one responds with theriac, along with sap from St John's wort, and plasters to the kidneys' (Gilbert).[18]

Likewise, put quicksilver in a cane or hollow filbert, and place it under the pillow of those affected by harmful magic, or put it under the threshold of a door he or she uses to come into [the house], and the harmful magic will be dispersed.

Likewise, 'if coral is kept in the house, it disperses any harmful magic' (Dioscorides).[19]

Likewise, 'the blood of a black dog smeared on every wall of the house in which there is harmful magic removes it'.

---

14.   Cf. Pliny, 'The Magi say that the gall of a black male dog acts as an amulet against all noxious substances when the whole house is fumigated or purified with it. Likewise, when the walls are sprinkled with the dog's blood and his penis is buried under the threshold of the door', *Naturalis Historia* 30.82.

15.   Reading *argentum vivum*.

16.   Dioscorides records more than one plant under the name *tragon* or *tragion* ('goatish'). The latter, he says (*De materia medica* 4.50), stinks like a goat, so one may consider that this property rendered it suitable for driving away evil spirits. Cf. the fumigation of shad's bile supra. 'Gilbert' presumably refers to Gilbertus Anglicus (*c.*1180–*c.*1230), author of a *Compendium Medicinae* which appeared some time after *c.*1230.

17.   Pliny, 'The heart of a vulture's chick is worn as an amulet', *Naturalis Historia* 30.92.

18.   Theriac was a Classical medicament traditionally ascribed to Mithridates VI of Pontus who mixed together as many antidotes to venom and poison as he could, and so produced what he claimed was the ultimate remedy for poison of any kind. His recipe continued to be used until the eighteenth century.

19.   Dioscorides does not say this, so the information is more likely to have come from a writer such as Marbode of Rennes (1035–1123) whose *De Lapidibus* 20 notes that, among its other virtues, coral 'drives away demonic ghosts and dreadful creatures invoked by workers of magic [*thessala monstra*]'. Gaius Solinus (mid-fourth century), one of Marbode's principal sources for this passage, says that coral wards off storms and lightning, but does not mention magic or spirits, *Polyhistor* (Basel 1538), p. 22.

Likewise, if harmful magic has affected someone so that he is unable to love another person, he should put shit from the person he loves into his right shoe and tread on it. As soon as he smells the stink, the magic will cease. This has been shown to be true.

Likewise, wormwood (that is, chamomile) placed over or under the threshold of a house ensures that no harmful magic can harm that house.[20]

Likewise, if you cut the head off a hoopoe at the new moon, and swallow its still-beating heart, you will know everything which is happening, both people's thoughts and many heavenly matters.[21]

Likewise, if you keep St John's wort in the house, evil spirits are put to flight, and therefore many people call it 'Demons' Bane'.[22]

Likewise, when carried about the person, the stone known as 'the loadstone' completely calms discord between a man and a woman or wife.

Likewise, [let a person suffering from the effects of harmful magic] be fumigated with the powdered tooth of a dead man.

Likewise, let him or her drink a herb which has grown through a hole in the middle of a stone.

Likewise, a fresh squill hung in the doorway of a house removes harmful magic.[23]

Likewise, if you carry bryony root on your person, all acts of harmful magic will disappear.

Likewise, if a man carries the heart of a [male] crow, and his wife that of a female, they will always have satisfying sex.

Likewise, if someone carries a root of sea holly, neither he nor she will ever suffer the treacherous attack of any evil spirit.

Likewise, if [this] root is placed beneath the clothes of someone possessed by an evil spirit, the possessing spirit will confess who he is, what he is and whence he comes.[24] [Then] he will run away.

Likewise, if harmful magic is practised against a husband and wife who have not yet had sex, with the result that the husband is unable to have carnal knowledge of his wife, take a dish or a cup, draw a cross in the middle of it, and write these four 'names' on the four sides of the cross: 'avis, gravis, seps, sipa'.[25]

---

20.   Pliny, 'Those who carry wormwood about with them are not hurt by harmful drugs, or by any wild beast, or even by the sun', *Naturalis Historia* 25.130. Arthemisia (wormwood) and matricaria (chamomile) are members of the same family but belong to different genera. There are many different types of matricaria, so 'chamomile' is only one among several possible translations.

21.   *Celestia*. This could also imply knowledge of what was going on in the mind of God or in those of the angels, or simply a better understanding of the heavenly bodies – planets, stars, constellations – in their astrological or astronomical aspects.

22.   Reading *fugare demones* for *fuga demonis*.

23.   This may go back to Pliny the Elder who says, 'Squills hung in a doorway are said by Pythagoras to be able to exert influence over the entry of harmful poisons', *Naturalis Historia* 20.101.

24.   Desirable steps in the process of exorcism.

25.   Rhyming phrases – avis, gravis – were common in charms. Cf. 'rex, pax, nax' or 'max, max, pax, pater noster', Olsan, 'Latin charms of Mediaeval England', p. 126.

Round the inside of the cup write the entire Gospel of St John. Then, if you can, take holy water or wine or some other [kind of] water if you cannot get holy water, and put it in that cup. Wash away all the writing therein with your finger and let both husband and wife drink therefrom with devotion, and let them take it in the name of God. It has been shown to be true.

Likewise, write this name, Tetragrammaton,[26] on the four sides [of the cross] according to the pattern described above, provided you know how to write it. Say out loud what is signified by this name Tetragrammaton which you have written. It is most effective if it is done in Hebrew letters. Afterwards do the foregoing as well (that is, write the Gospel), and let a single male virgin child with a crown on his head write everything I have said.

Likewise, take a virgin child on a Friday, Saturday or Sunday in the hour before sunrise. Let him or her stand in front of a bramble bush, salute the Virgin Mary who has been represented by the bramble bush,[27] then say the Our Father three times and three times make the sign of the cross over the bush, saying, 'In the name of the Father and of the Son and of the Holy Spirit, Amen'. Then he or she must collect three fistfuls of its leaves and flowers (if there are any) and fruit, or simply the leaves if there is not anything else.[28] Withdraw, and when you are in the house, let the husband and wife shut themselves in a room. Let a brazier full of burning coals be placed in it. Let each of them in turn pray to God to grant [them] the fruits of marriage for His service. When they have done this, let them take the bramble leaves (and flowers, if there are any), and put them on the burning coals. [These] will fill the whole room with smoke, and the 'snake' [i.e. the demon] will flee. Then they should cross themselves and have sex in the name of God.

Likewise, another way of dealing with the same problem. To break every bit of the harmful magic, each of them should conscientiously confess his or her sins, and then both of them should hear Mass and communicate by dividing the Body of Christ in two, with a warning that they are to have sex not because of lust but for the fruit of marriage. I fully believe that if the harmful magic exists only in one person, and he or she conscientiously goes to confession and communion, every bit of harmful magic will be broken up and dispersed.

Likewise, if instances of harmful magic happen in fields or vineyards, one should do as I described earlier. Have the Gospel of St John written by a virgin child. Sprinkle the water in the four corners of the field, and in the middle of it make a [sign of the] cross and say, 'I exorcize you, unclean spirit, so that you leave this place which has been dedicated to God and go to the place of your eternal damnation'. Once you have said this, sprinkle water in the form of a cross in the four corners [of the field, saying], 'In the name of the Father and of the Son and of the Holy Spirit, Amen'.

---

26.   The four Hebrew letters Yod, He, Vau, He, which make up 'Yahweh' or 'Jehovah'.

27.   Reading *rubum* for *rubrum*. The Virgin was often associated with the burning bush of Exodus 3.2 (*rubus* in the Vulgate). See, for example, St Bonaventure, *Collationes de septem donis Spiritus Sancti* 6.2.8, which is part of a well-established tradition.

28.   Here the text suddenly deviates from a third person singular into a second.

3. Interrogating sorcerers, fortune tellers and invokers of demons and repudiating past practice of magic, Bernard Gui, c.1320

Hansen II, no. 5 (pp. 47–55)

[Bernard Gui (c.1261–1331) was a French Dominican and became an active inquisitor for Toulouse during the attempts to eradicate Albigensian and other heresies prevalent in Languedoc at this time. He wrote a good deal, but his best-known work is his Practica Inquisitoris Heretice Pravitatis *('The Inquisitor's Manual'). The extracts provided by Hansen (a) deal with divinatory and magical practices, and demon worship, and (b) provide formulae for a* sortilegus *to repudiate his magic and be reconciled with the Church, for the degradation of anyone in holy orders who has practised magic, and for sentencing anyone who has used the Host for magical purposes. I have translated only (a) and the first example from (b).]*

The sorcerer [*sortilegus*] or fortune teller [*divinator*] or invoker of demons who is to be examined should be asked which kinds of sorcery, fortune telling and invocations he knows, and how many and from which people he learned them.

Item: Let us get down to details. Pay attention to the character and status of the individuals, because they should not all be questioned in a uniform way or a single fashion. Men should be questioned one way, women another, and you will be able to formulate your questions from the following:

What do they know, or what did they know, or what have they done in connection with children or infants ill spoken or released from ill speaking?

Item: in connection with lost or damned souls?

Item: in connection with thieves who should be imprisoned?

Item: in connection with the harmony or discord of married people?

Item: in connection with the impregnation of those who are barren?

Item: in connection with those who give [people] hairs and finger- or toenails and certain things to eat?

Item: in connection with the condition of the souls of the dead?

Item: in connection with the prediction of future events?

Item: in connection with the female fairies [*fatis mulieribus*] who are popularly called 'good deeds'[29] and who, people say, go about at night?

Item: in connection with chanting or invoking by means of the words of spells, fruits, herbs, thongs and other things?

Item: Whom has he or she taught to chant or invoke by the use of spells, and from which people did he or she learn or hear this kind of enchantment or invocation?

Item: [What do they know, or what did they know, or what have they done] in connection with the sick by means of invocations or the words of spells?

---

29.   *Bonas res.* The phrase appears in Vincent de Beauvais's *Speculum morale* where he comments on the delusions of some women noted by the canon *Episcopi*, and adds that some of these women refer to non-human entities as '*bonae res*'.

Item: in connection with collecting herbs while kneeling down, facing east and saying the Lord's Prayer?

Item: in connection with a [sorcerer's] command to go on pilgrimage, hear Mass, offer candles and give to charity?

Item: in connection with discovering that thefts have been carried out, or with bringing to light things which have been hidden?

Item: You should ask especially about things which savour of any superstition or irreverence or insult with regard to the sacraments of the Church (and particularly the sacrament of Christ's Body), as well as with regard to divine worship and consecrated places.

Item: [You should ask] about retaining the Eucharist [instead of swallowing it], or the theft of chrism or holy oil from a church.

Item: [You should ask] about the baptism of wax images or other things, how they were baptized, the uses to which they were put and the intended outcomes.

Item: [You should ask] about making images from lead, how they were made and towards what ends.

Item: From which people did he or she learn or hear such things?

Item: How long is it since he or she began to use such things?

Item: Who has come to him [*ipsum*], especially during the last year, asking for consultations? How many people have come?

Item: Has he ever been forbidden to use such things before? By whom? Did he repudiate them and promise he would never do or use such things again?

Item: Did he later take back his repudiation and promise?

Item: Did he believe that what he learned from the others was true?

Item: What goods or gifts or favours did he have and receive for such things?

Formula for repudiating past practice of magic

I, N, of such and such a place and diocese, put on trial before you, N, inquisitor, from the bottom of my heart repudiate all error and heresy which raises itself against the Catholic faith of the Lord Jesus Christ, and I particularly and expressly repudiate all baptizing of images or any other object which has no ability to reason, and all re-baptizing of people who have been properly and legitimately baptized already.

Item: [I repudiate] any fortune telling [*sortilegium*] or practice of harmful magic [*maleficium*] done with or caused by a sacred object the holy Body of Christ or chrism or holy or blessed oil.

Item: [I repudiate] all divination or invocation of demons, especially when they are shown or expect to be shown worship or reverence, or are offered or expect to be offered homage, or any sacrifice, or immolation of any object offered to them as a sacrifice.

Item: I repudiate the practice and manner of making images from lead or wax or any other material in order to procure any kind of illicit outcome.

Item: I repudiate that practice which people call 'St George's'.[30]

Item: I repudiate completely every kind of fortune telling [*sortilegia*] which

---

30.   I have been unable to find out what this practice was.

had been judged condemnable, especially those kinds which are prescribed with a view to procuring any illicit or harmful outcomes.

Item: I promise and swear to pursue to the best of my ability, reveal and make known to inquisitors or prelates any person or persons wherever and whenever I may know that he, she or they are doing the foresaid things or any one of them.

Item: I swear and promise to observe and keep the Catholic faith [which the Roman Church teaches and practices].

[*Hansen II no. 6 is taken from Oldrado da Ponte, a jurist who flourished in the first half of the fourteenth century, serving at the Papal Court in Avignon from 1311. The extract offers opinions on the questions, 'May someone be condemned on strong suspicion of heresy? What king of a thing is heresy, and are fortune telling and love potions heretical?'*]

[*Hansen II no. 7 is taken from Zanchinus Ugolini's treatise on heretics, c.1330. Ugolini distinguishes between licit and illicit means of divining the future, and concludes that if any type of magic savours of heresy, it will come within the competence of the Inquisition. On p. 60, we read the following:*]

Divination, incantation, sorcery/fortune telling [*sortilegium*], idolatry, magic, divination by numbers [*mathesis*]. Workers of magic [*magici*] or astrologers [*mathematici*] are those who not only try to foretell the future and have a complete knowledge of things hidden, but by some magical practice – for example, making wax images – try either in some other fashion to torture and cause extreme suffering to someone's body, or in shameful fashion to bend some other person to their will.

4. Worshipping demons can be a good thing, Ramón de Tárrega, c.1370

Hansen II, no. 12 (p. 67)

[*Ramón de Tárrega (c.1335–1371) was a Catalan who was taught in Barcelona by Nicholau Eymerich. But later Eymerich prosecuted him for theological novelties, the kind of thing which can be seen in the following extract which appeared in his* De invocatione daemonum. *Ramón refused to retract and was imprisoned in Barcelona, dying there in gaol.*]

It is licit to worship and honour created things and beings with honour and the worship reserved for God alone [*latria*] without incurring sin. It is even meritorious in as much as they are representatives of their Creator.

It is permitted to worship and honour demons with divine worship, and to do so meritoriously, if they represent their Creator.

Not only can demons be worshipped with near-divine worship [*dulia*] without incurring the sin of heresy, but even without incurring any sin at all, unless it is forbidden by God.

Someone who sacrifices to a demon can be excused from idolatry just as much as, or better than, a Christian who worships an image of Christ or the saints.

It is in accordance with Nature that one should worship and sacrifice to demons.[31]

[Hansen II no. 13 comes from Nicolaus from *Jawor's* Treatise on Superstitions, 1405. Nicolaus was a Professor of Theology at Heidelberg and represented the university at the Council of Konstanz, 1414–1418. His treatise was very influential and seems to have been widely read in manuscript. On p. 70 we read:]

Although demons cannot by their own power and without an intermediary move or change things to a form found in Nature, they are able, by their own power, to move, change, and transport things to various places. Consequently, they cannot transform or change horses or anything in Nature into some other thing in Nature, or change human beings into horses – in a word, and as a general point, [they cannot] change anything for better or worse in its basic composition, and without an intermediary. They do so only in appearance; or else the [demon] presents himself as such a person or object by taking on its physical attributes.

[Hansen II no. 15 quotes from another Heidelberg professor, Johann from Frankfurt, who puts forward a question for debate on 9 January 1412: 'Do magical characters, drawings and utterances have the power to compel demons?]

[Hansen II no. 16, from an anonymous Treatise on Demons, *c.1415, asks, 'Do demons have the power to cure the sick or inflict illnesses? (p. 82); How do demons transform themselves into some other shape?' (pp. 82–3), and discusses incubi and succubi (pp. 84–86), the whole relying heavily on Guillaume d'Auvergne.]*

5. Actions which are superstitious and actions which are not, Heinrich von Gorkum, c.1425

Hansen II, no. 18 (pp. 87–8)

[Extract from his Treatise on a number of superstitious occurrences, *put together in the University of Köln where he was a student, by Professor Heinrich von Gorkum. Heinrich (c.1386–1431) actually studied in Paris before he came to Köln, but once arrived he stayed and became a well established scholar, best known perhaps for his commentary on the works of St Thomas Aquinas. See further, H.S. Schoot, 2001, 'Early Thomist reception of Aquinas's Christology: Henry of Gorkum', in* Aquinas as Authority, *ed. P. van Geest, H. Goris, C. Leget (Leuven: Peeters Publishing), pp. 30–8.]*

1. To inscribe these words – 'holy, willing mind' – on wax blessed on the Feast of the Purification, while Mass is being celebrated on the Feast of St Agatha, with the intention of remaining safe from fire, placing trust only in esteem for God

---

31.   In 1398, Jehan de Bar, physician to the French King, Charles VI, was arrested for practising ritual magic and for possessing a number of grimoires. He declared himself repentant, and confessed that 'in my books are several errors against our faith, such as saying that some devils are good and benign'. Veenstra, *Magic and Divination*, p. 354.

and St Agatha and hoping for assistance from their merciful kindness, does not appear to be illicit or superstitious.[32]

2. To believe that the words themselves, when written in this way, by that very fact have within them the power of preserving [people] from fire in every instance, and as a result of this notion to go on to perform [magical] operations is entirely illicit and superstitious.

3. To bring pigs' shoulder blades to church, or other types of food, or cups, with the intention of having God's name invoked over them, or having them blessed with certain specific prayers, and then using them reverently at the beginning of a meal, one's purpose being governed by these preliminary circumstances, does not appear to be illicit or superstitious.[33]

4. Secondly, if [religious] observance turns into [magical] practice in the way which has been described, it is illicit, fatuous and superstitious.

5. To write the names of the three Kings[34] on pieces of paper and hang them round one's neck out of reverence for God and the Kings, and out of confidence in them to hope for their help, is not illicit.

6. To make crosses on Palm Sunday in the frame of mind alluded to in no. 4 is deeply superstitious, since it proceeds from a frivolous intention.

7. When one considers the way they originated, one should not be surprised that superstitious practices will be different in different places, for it is generally agreed that Christians sprang from people who were once pagans devoted to idolatry and full of superstitious ceremonies.

8. A practice which is done after baptism in some places can be said to be more superfluous than illicit, and is capable of being interpreted as an act of piety. What I am saying here is clear enough. In some places after baptism, the priest brings the Body of Christ in the pyx to those he has baptized and takes a Host from it, lifting it up with two fingers so that the godparents can see it.

9. When it comes to the foresaid practices, people should be told not to do them with immoral intention, because if such a ceremony is completely unwilling to steer clear of impious intention, it should be exterminated by means of painful punishment – not that this [is intended] to get rid of right-thinking devotion or

32.   The Feast of the Purification is observed on 2 February, that of St Agatha on 5 February. The wax is that of the candles blessed on the Purification. 'Holy, willing mind' is a phrase from the antiphon of St Agatha's Mass. An eruption of Etna in *c.*252 is said to have been stilled by intervention of St Agatha: hence her connection with remaining safe from fire.

33.   The pigs' shoulder-blades seem to be out of place here, since objects such as these were often used in divination, itself a suspicious, if not forbidden practice. It is therefore more likely that the phrase refers to hams. The inhabitants of the Italian town of Fiuggi (formerly Anticoli), for example, had to pay an annual tax of 40 *scapulas porcinas* to the Pope until Martin V abolished it. These were certainly not just shoulder-blades, but choice cuts of meat.

34.   That is, of the Magi: Melchior, Gaspar, Balthasar. Their names were not infrequently used in magic. The celebrated Montpellier physician Bernard de Gordon (1260–*c.*1318), for example, suggested recourse to them in cases of epilepsy. 'When someone is having a fit', he wrote, 'if another person puts his mouth over that of the one who is sick and says these three phrases into the sick person's mouth, [the sick person] will undoubtedly get to his feet at once: "Gaspar brings myrrh, Melchior incense, Balthasar gold"', *Lilium medicinae* book 2, chap. 25.

to furnish active scandal. What I am saying here is that many people sin out of ignorance, [but] are ready to submit themselves to the instruction of their superiors, and so such people, who are eminently curable, are brought back to the right path by straightforward instruction. But if people wish to depend on their physical senses and are unwilling to dissociate themselves from superstitious intention, it will be necessary to employ a sharper medicine so that the disease may be cured and not gain strength. One must not, under cover of concealing one's real purpose, cross the line in those things which concern the Christian religion, either. But the specific way of proceeding in the punishment of such people belongs to the law rather than theology, and because no disorderly mind deserves to be called 'devout', since devotion is an act of religion, the result is that eradicating such pernicious errors is not to remove morally correct and genuine devotion. This is why it was prescribed that salt be included in every sacrifice of the Old [i.e. Jewish] Law, in consequence of which due distinction is signified in the worship of God. It was forbidden to offer honey, too, because pagans [used it] in their idolatrous rites, and so that there would be no likelihood of God's people converting to paganism, as Leviticus 2 makes clear.[35] From this same [chapter] it appears that those who forbid such superstitions do not rouse any scandal in their mind. But if misguided people take the opportunity to be scandalized on this account, the truth of religion should not be disregarded: witness our Saviour who did not stop teaching the truth, even though the Pharisees were scandalized, as Matthew 15 makes clear.[36]

6. Infecundity, eating children and repentance, Johannes Nider, 1435–1437

Hansen II, no. 19 (pp. 88–99)

[Johannes Nider (1380–1438) was a Dominican who played an important role at the Council of Basel. His Formicarius *('Ant Hill') is a treatise in five books dealing with contemporary philosophical and theological concerns. Book 1 discusses the exceptional precedents and actions of good people; book 2, trustworthy revelations which are likely to be genuine; book 3, false and illusory visions; book 4, the virtuous actions of those who have attained perfection; and book 5, workers of harmful magic and their deceptions.*

Hansen's extracts are taken primarily from book 5 and illustrate the definition (p. 90) from chapter 3, that 'a worker of harmful magic is so called because he does wicked things or observes the Faith in a wicked fashion; and one finds both in workers of harmful magic who damage their neighbour with their superstitions and their practices'. *The following is part of the reply by a 'theologian' to questions asked by 'a lazy man'.]*[37]

35.   Leviticus 2.11, 'No leaven or honey will be burned in a sacrifice to the Lord'.
36.   Matthew 15.12–13, 'Then His disciples came to Him and said: Do you know that the Pharisees were scandalized after they had heard what you said? But He replied and said: Every planting which my heavenly Father has not planted will be uprooted'.
37.   Hansen's extracts have been translated into French by Catherine Chène in Ostorero,

[Hansen, pp. 91–3] Theologian: In answer to your question, I'll give you anecdotes and some religious teachings which I know partly from teachers in our [university's theological] faculty and partly from the experience of a secular judge who is a respectable man and worthy of being believed. He learned many things of this kind from interrogations, confessions and public and personal experiences, and I have often had wide ranging and profound conversations with him.

There was, for example, Maître Pierre, a citizen of Berne in the diocese of Lausanne, who burned many workers of harmful magic, of both sexes, and made others take to their heels from the territory of the seigneury of Berne. I also had a conversation with Dom Benedict, a Benedictine monk. Although he is a very devout man from a reformed monastery in Vienne, 10 years ago he was still living in the world and was a necromancer, a great entertainer and trickster,[38] well known among the secular nobility and a man experienced [in his trade.] Likewise, I have been told certain things I shall discuss later, by an inquisitor from Autun, a member of our Order, and a devout reformer belonging to the monastery in Lyon, who had interrogated many accused in the diocese of Autun about acts of harmful magic.

Well now, there are (or recently have been), as the inquisitor and Maître Pierre[39] have told me and as common gossip has it, a number of workers of harmful magic, of both sexes, in the neighbourhood of the seigneury of Berne. These people, contrary to the inclination of human nature and, indeed, contrary to the disposition of all types of animal except the she-wolf, are in the habit of devouring and consuming the young of their own species. In the town of Boltingen in the diocese of Lausanne, for example, an illustrious worker of harmful magic [*grandis maleficus*] called Schedelli was arrested by the foresaid Pierre, the local judge, and confessed that in a nearby house where a man and his wife were living together, by his acts of harmful magic he had killed about seven infants, one after the other, while they were still in the foresaid wife's womb, and [had done so] in such a way that the woman would always abort them, year after them. He did a similar thing to all the pregnant animals in that same house and, as events proved, not one delivered a live birth during those same years. While this evil man was being interrogated about whether and in what way he was guilty of these things, he disclosed his crime and said he had put a lizard under the threshold of the door of the house, and he declared that if it were removed, fecundity would be restored to those who lived in [the house]. But when they looked for the reptile under the threshold and did not see it (perhaps because it had been reduced to dust), they removed the dust and earth from under [the threshold] and, that very year, fecundity was restored to the wife and all the draught animals belonging to the house. (He confessed all this, however, after

Paravicini Bagliani, Utz Tremp, *L'imaginaire du sabbat*, pp. 122–99. On the *Formicarius*, see further Bailey, *Battling Demons*, pp. 95–101, 111–17.

38.   In other words, he was what we should call an illusionist and conjuror.

39.   Hansen identified him as Peter von Greyerz, but see now Catherine Chène, *op. cit.* supra, pp. 223–31.

being tortured, not of his own free will, and was handed over to the fires by the foresaid judge.)

Next, I found out from the foresaid inquisitor (who mentioned it to me this year), that in the duchy of Lausanne, some workers of harmful magic had cooked and eaten their own newly born children. The way they learned to do such a thing, he said, was that workers of harmful magic came to a certain meeting and, as a result of what they did [there], they saw with their own eyes a demon who had taken on the appearance of a human being. His disciple was obliged to give him his word that he would renounce Christianity, never worship the Host and find the power to trample on the cross when [he could do so] without being noticed.

Furthermore, as the foresaid judge Pierre said to me, there was a widespread rumour that in the territory of Berne 13 children had been eaten within a short space of time by workers of harmful magic, and for this reason public justice burned pretty harshly against such murderers. But when, after her arrest, Pierre asked a female worker of harmful magic how they used to eat the children, she answered, 'It's done this way. We lie in wait for infants who have not yet been baptized, or even those who have been baptized, especially if they are not protected by the sign of the cross and prayers. We kill them by means of our rituals while they are lying in their cradles or beside their parents. Afterwards, people think they were smothered or died some other way. Then we secretly and stealthily take them from their graves. We cook them in a cauldron until the bones fall away and almost all the flesh becomes runny and drinkable. Out of the more solid matter we make an ointment appropriate to our wishes, our practices and our transformations. We fill a flask or bottle with the more liquid matter and, after we have performed a few rituals, anyone who drinks any of it immediately becomes privy to our sect and an expert in it.

Another young male worker of harmful magic who was arrested and burned even though in my opinion he was truly penitent at the end, disclosed this same method with greater clarity. (Not long before, he had escaped from the hand of the said judge Pierre, along with his obstinate wife, a worker of harmful magic.) This young man and his wife were arrested in the jurisdiction of Berne, and he was put in a tower separate from hers. He said, 'If I could obtain pardon for my wrongdoings, I should willingly expose everything I know about acts of harmful magic, because I see I shall have to die'. Now, when he was told by men of learning that, if he was truly penitent, he would be able to obtain complete pardon, he joyfully offered himself to death and explained the ways he had been tainted in the first place.

'The way I was led astray is as follows', he said. 'The first Sunday before holy water is consecrated, the future disciple has to go into the church with his instructors and there, in their presence, deny Christ, his faith, his baptism and the Catholic Church. Then he has to pay homage to *le petit maître*, that is, 'the little teacher', which is what they call the demon. (They use no other title.) Next, he drinks from a bottle' – (Nider: I mentioned this earlier) – 'and after he has done this, he immediately feels deep inside him that he is imagining and retaining images of our [magical] practices and the principal rituals of this sect. This is how I and my wife were led astray, [but] I think she is so obstinate that she would rather endure the fire than be willing to confess the slightest truth. But alas, we are both guilty.'

What the young man said turned out to be true in every respect. After he had made his confession, the young man was seen to die full of contrition. His wife, however, who had been proved guilty by [the testimony of] witnesses, was unwilling to confess, even under torture or at the point of death. On the contrary, once the executioner had got the fire ready, she cursed him with most wicked words and in this state was burned.

[Hansen II, no. 20. Martin le Franc, secretary to the anti-popes Felix V and Nicholas V, is best known for his immensely long allegorical poem, The Champion of Women, *composed in the early 1440s. Written in five books, and intended to divert as well as interest, it purports to be the account of a dream in which women and women's characters are alternately defended and attacked by a variety of allegorical figures, ending with the triumph of the Virgin Mary over her detractors. Le Franc's 'champion' takes the line that women are deceived by Satan (vv. 17641–56):]*

When the poor thing lies down to sleep and rest, the Enemy, who never rests, comes and lies down beside her. He knows how to manufacture illusions very subtly, so that she believes or convinces herself that she is merely dreaming. Inevitably, the old woman will dream she is going to the meeting on a cat or a dog. But in fact, none of it will be true, and neither staff nor stick can lift itself up one foot [from the ground]. That deceitful magician knows how to poke her eyes out in this fashion.

[Le Franc's manuscript also contains the earliest pictures of women riding through the air, one astride a broomstick, another on a long stick. A marginal note says, 'Some Waldensians go over Martin'. Hansen II, no. 21 is taken from a treatise by Johann Wunschilburg, 'On Superstitions' (c.1440), which argues that workers of harmful magic do what they do, not by the power of words but because they have made a pact with a demon and worship him.]

7. Can people sometimes be carried by the Devil through various places?
Alonso Tostado, c.1440

Hansen II, no. 22 (pp. 105–9)

[Alonso Tostado (c.1400–1455) was a Spanish theologian and exegete. In 1453 he was condemned for heresy, but this was immediately retracted and he went on to become Chancellor of Castile and then Bishop of Avila.]

Certain people say no, because in the Council of Ancyra,[40] the Church forbids belief in this, as is clear in *Decreta* 26, question 5, chapter 'Episcopi', where it is said that certain wicked women, led astray by the illusions and imagined fancies

---

40.   Reading *Anquirensi* for *Acquirensi*, as it appears in Gratian, *Decretum*, case 26, question 5, chap. 12. This chapter contains an extensive quotation from the canon *Episcopi* upon which Tostado here comments.

of demons, believe and assert that 'during the hours of night they ride upon certain animals with Diana, a goddess of the pagans, or with Herodias and a numberless crowd of women, cross over many expanses of territory during the silence of the dead of night on particular nights, and obey her orders, as those of a mistress'. It is said that these women are led astray by the illusions of demons, so when they profess to travel through the night, that is not true.

Item: It is said there, 'If only it were just these women who would die in their treachery instead of dragging many [others] with them to the height of faithlessness! For innumerable people, deceived by this false notion, believe it is true and, by believing it, deviate from the correct faith'. So not only are these things false; believing them leads to the sin of faithlessness.

Item: It is said there that these women undergo nothing in reality, but that it is a delusion of the demon in their imaginative faculty: 'in as much as Satan, who transforms himself into an angel of light, starts with some woman's mind and brings it under his control by means of faithlessness, and in there he transforms himself into the appearances and likenesses of various individuals, deluding her mind (which he holds prisoner) in dreams, giving her the sight of things which are sometimes happy, sometimes sad and at other times [showing her] people she does not recognize; and thus he takes her off along every kind of deviant path. Although only her spirit is undergoing this, she supposes that these things are taking place not in her soul but in her body'. It is also said there, 'This is like the woman who is led away in dreams and nocturnal visions, not outwith herself, and has seen many things while she is asleep, which she had never seen while she was awake'. Well now, who is so stupid and dull witted as to think that all these things which take place only in spirit also happen in the body?

These things notwithstanding, however, it must be said demons can take people, sometimes willingly, sometimes unwillingly, through various places by day as well as by night; and sometimes this actually does happen. First, it is clear that there is no doubt a demon has such great power that he can carry not just one person but many through the air at the same time and take them to various places in an instant, because demons have not lost those parts of themselves which belong to Nature, and they themselves are equal in those natural parts to good angels. Indeed, more demons are more pre-eminent in their natural parts than many good angels, because some are said to have fallen from one or other angelic rank. But good angels have such great power that they can move the heavens, because philosophers as well as the Holy Scriptures maintain that the heavens are moved by Intelligences which we call 'angels'. This is a power at which one must be astonished. So whoever can move the heavens will be able to move many people at the same time at whatever speed he wishes.

Item: It is clear that this has often been done, because on one occasion a demon carried Christ from the desert to the pinnacle of the Temple, and again from the pinnacle to a very high mountain, as is made clear in modern literature and in Luke 4.[41] So since a demon was able to carry Christ, he will be able [to

---

41.   Luke 4.5 and 9: 'And the Devil brought Him to a very high mountain ... . And he brought Him to Jerusalem and placed Him on the pinnacle of the Temple'.

carry] anyone else as well. For Christ's body was not lighter than those of the rest of humanity; it had a natural heaviness commensurate with the type of body He had, [and] a point worth noting, if the demon had not carried anyone from place to place before this incident, he would not have made the effort to carry Christ. But he had carried others before this, or knew his own strength, and he knew it because he was able to carry [them]. When it comes to good angels, it is clear that the angel of the Lord transported Habbakuk from Judaea to Chaldaea in an instant by a hair of his head: Daniel 14.[42] Everyday experience also illustrates this, even though this is not so well known; for we know many people who transport themselves from faraway places to others in an instant, with demons, who are the princes of workers of harmful magic, lending them their assistance. Consequently it is obvious that it would be unwise to deny it, since we run into a thousand witnesses who are aware of these things.

Therefore it must be said that a person can be deliberately carried by demons through various places in order to associate with them in doing what workers of harmful magic do. Sometimes some people are carried off by demons against their will and transported to out-of-the-way places, either because of their sins, or by God's ordinance as a result of some mystery. There are no witnesses to this [last]: that is, some people, with God's permission, and doing what workers of harmful magic do, compel others to come to them from very remote places, as if in an instant, and if God did not forbid it, many things of this kind would happen frequently. This is made clear in the *Life of Cyprian and Justina.* Cyprian who was at that time a pagan and a worker of harmful magic wanted to bring a virgin, Justina, to him and sent demons to her. But she defended herself by making the sign of the cross and invoking the name of Christ. It is also made clear in the *Life of St James.* Hermogenes began to send demons to St James's house to tie up James and his pupil Philetus, and bring them to him. But they were rescued by Christ. It is also clear in the *Life of St Peter,* where Simon Magus would fly through the air, borne up by demons. These things are therefore well known, and no one will be able to deny them if he has any sense.

What is said about women who range through various places at night is also true, because it has often been encountered and punished by the courts, and some of those who want to imitate their dreadful ceremonies run into great difficulties. Nor can it be said that this happens in a dream, because not only those who have undergone [the experience], but also many others were witnesses of it. There is no reason to have doubts about it. It is true, however, that simple-minded people have muddled what is false with what is true, because demons are keen to harm not only their morals but also their faith; and sacred teaching forbids belief in these things because very many of them are contrary to the Faith.

First counter-argument: It is not denied that the women can be carried by demons during the night and borne across various places, but one is forbidden

---

42. Daniel 14.35: 'The angel of the Lord seized him by the crown, and carried him by a hair of his head, and put him in Babylon on the shore of a lake, in a vigorous thrust of his spirit'.

to believe absolutely everything these women maintain – namely, that they travel with Herodias or Diana, a goddess of the pagans, and believe that she is a goddess, in the way a majority of gods were understood among pagans. So to say that Diana is a goddess is not only an error, but also faithlessness; and it is clear that that is intended [to be taken] literally, because when this error is censured, it is said that a numberless crowd, deceived by this false opinion, believe it is true and by believing it deviate from the correct faith and are caught up in the error of the pagans, since they think there is something of divinity or of godhead outwith the one God. But this Diana and Herodias are demons who get themselves reverenced in the form of goddesses, and although these women really do travel with them during the night, they are enticed into it because they think that [Diana and Herodias] are goddesses, when they are actually demons.

Item: These women used to say that they rode upon certain animals. But this is not true, because no animals can fly through the air so that they cross great stretches of territory in an instant. These were demons who change their shape, sometimes into that of livestock, sometimes into any other form, just as they please, as is clear from several written accounts.

Item: These women were in error, because they used to say they were summoned on specific nights to worship this Diana, goddess of the pagans,[43] and obeyed her as their mistress. For it is not in the power of demons to bring people along with them to these [meetings] unless they actually want [to be brought] and to enter into pacts with the demons. It is rare for people to be brought along against their will by demons, and [it happens only] in particular circumstances. Therefore it is not true that these women are summoned by Diana on specific nights and are compelled to obey her as their mistress.

Second point: When [the canon] says it is the sin of faithlessness to believe this and retreat from correct faith, one must declare that the error does not lie in believing that people can be carried by demons through various places, and that sometimes they are carried in reality, but [in saying] that what I have said earlier is believed, especially that Diana was a goddess, because the canon specifically condemns that error when it says they are caught up in the error of the pagans when they think there is something of divinity or of godhead outwith the one God. It does not say it is an error of the pagans to believe that people are carried by demons.

Third point: When [the canon] says these things happen in a dream because the Devil fools the imaginative faculty by showing sad and happy things, one must declare that it is true such things can often happen in a dream, and a person will think they really are happening externally, because a prophetic vision often takes place via the visual faculty of the imagination. But it is not denied that these things really can happen externally, as is shown by [the canon's] example of dreams in which in reality someone undergoes none of the things he or she thinks he is undergoing; and yet this does not do away with [the fact] that such things really do happen outwith a dream.

43.   Reading *gentilium* for *gentium*.

But it will be objected (because it is said [in the canon]), that therefore everyone should be told that the person who believes such things, and things like them, loses his or her faith, that to believe these things in this way is faithlessness, and that it is necessary to say that these things are a delusion of the imaginative faculty. It must be said that this brings us back to the errors mentioned earlier, namely, [that] anyone who believes everything these women were maintaining loses his or her faith. Because they used to say that Diana was a goddess with whom they travelled at night, asserting this is losing one's faith because it means one is erecting more than one god. It is clear that this is the meaning of the text when it is said that the person who believes such things loses his or her faith and the person who does not have the correct faith belongs, not to Him, but to the one in whom he or she believes, that is, the Devil. This is why these people are said, in the canon, to lose their faith – because they believe in the Devil. They believe Diana is a goddess, and yet Diana is the Devil. But to believe that a person can be carried through the air by a demon is not to believe in the Devil. Neither does it cause a retreat from the Faith when Holy Scripture maintains similar things – that is, that Christ was carried by a demon. Therefore it should not be denied that, after they have completed their dreadful ceremonies and anointings, women who work harmful magic [*mulieres maleficas*], and even men, are picked up by a demon and carried through various places, that many of these people meet in a single spot and that they show honour to demons and are free to indulge in lust and every kind of indecency.

8. Peasant beliefs and practices according to a hostile source, Felix Hemmerlin, 1444–1450

Hansen II, no. 23 (pp. 109–12)

[Felix Hemmerlin ('Little Hammer'), 1388/9–c.1460, was a Swiss scholar and an adherent of the reform party at the Council of Konstanz. He also took part in the Council of Basel. His De nobilitate, *from chapter 32 of which this extract is taken, was written in the form of a dialogue and is an attack on his fellow . countrymen, so it is scarcely surprising to find that he suffered at least one violent attack on his person (in Zurich) because of it. Chapter 32 is headed, 'The outrages of modern peasants'..]*

Nobleman: Aren't you like that race of people which summons clouds and disturbs the air with the help of demons in order to produce lightning, hail, snow, ice and storm spirits, with the result that not only the poor suffer but also the nobility, because you and people like you trample on the wonderful gifts of the earth, the crops and the shoots?

[The peasant offers wholesale objection.]

Nobleman: [In Job it mentions that] with God's permission and Satan's co-operation, the fire of God fell from the sky [...] and so St Thomas [Aquinas] argues with regard to these and other points that clearly demons can cause hailstorms, thunder and bad weather with the Lord's permission, and because people's evil deeds have provoked it.[44] Such people have united themselves with evil spirits and made pacts with them [*confederaverunt*], and [God] allows greater and lesser things [to be done] through a person's free will – in olden times through Simon Magus and Pharaoh's soothsayers [*ariolos*] and nowadays on single occasions. Hence it is clear to me that your wives are accustomed to put together the most poisonous and squalid concoctions and, along with roots, certain herbs which give off vapour. These they cook for the appropriate length of time in a cooking pot which they have been careful to cover, and then remove the cover and stand the pot in the brightest rays of the sun. At first, as one might expect, smoke rises, and soon a cloud thickens in the completely clear sky and, because of the [women's] traffic with demons, as I said earlier, unexpected storms are produced. Don't be surprised that I speak about your wives. It's not without good reason, because you search out and collect one of the principal ingredients only with the help of women.

Item: It happens when the sky is clear that the sun can attract vapour without hindrance beyond the second region of the air where snow is produced, and below the fourth region of the air whence come showers and rain, and where the third formation of the region of the air becomes settled, and where the coagulation of hail usually happens (according to Isidore, *Etymologiae* 3), where, if you want, you will be able to see hail being produced.[45]

Item: Artificial hail of this kind is often produced in valleys, according to the degree to which the ascent of this kind of vapour will be less impeded by the winds until it is lifted upwards from the ground.

Item: It often [happens] at the hands of mountain and alpine dwellers, because one particularly important type [of herb] is quite frequently found in the higher reacher of mountains [...].

It is generally agreed that in 1420, during the time of Pope Martin [V], a female witch [*mulier strega*] living across the Tiber had transformed herself into a cat and did things uncommon to human experience,[46] (indeed impossible), appropriate only to cats, and purely mischievous. Among everything else, she tainted children lying in their cradles with her acts of harmful magic and then afterwards she turned herself back into a human being and cured them and got her hands on her fee! [But] in choosing [to get hold of] this last profit of hers, she cast suspicion on herself and publicly confessed to these and

44.   Job 1.16, 'The fire of God has fallen from the sky and has destroyed the sheep it has touched, and the children'. Hansen refers the reader to Aquinas *Expositio in librum Job*, chap. 1, lectio 3. In fact, St Thomas here merely remarks that God sent fire from the sky 'to impress on [Job's] mind that he would be suffering persecution not only from human beings, but also from God'.

45.   St Isidore of Seville (c.560–636), *Etymologiae* 13.6. [The '3' in Hansen's text may be a misprint]. St Isidore says there are five zones round the earth, but those he gives do not correspond with Hemmerlin's description. It is more likely that Hemmerlin (or his 'Nobleman') is speaking from memory of 13.7 which discusses the behaviour of air. When condensed, it says, air makes rain; when its clouds are frozen, snow; when denser clouds freeze and are subject to turbulence, hail.

46.   Reading *usui* for *ritui*.

other things, ending her life by being burned according to the sentence of a court [...].

Be aware that the land of the country or diocese of Sion is full of this curse, and because of this innumerable people of both sexes, especially country folk and the lower classes, frequently make public confessions of what I have been describing, and by the authority of the law or the custom of the country have been seen to have been killed by the most bitter punishment of fire [...].

Not long ago, a peasant asked my advice. He had been directed to me by his priest who had refused him the sacraments of the Church on the grounds that it was his custom to cure animals subjected to harmful magic [*maleficiatas*] by other peasants. [He did this] by means of unnatural devices – which he revealed to me in detail – of words, signs and gestures, on particular days chosen by him for this purpose.

Item: It is clear to me from the account of trustworthy male eyewitnesses that certain peasant women, who denied they actually did their best to invoke storms, deflected a mass of clouds which was threatening disturbance in the surrounding area into another mountainous, wooded, barren, infertile region so that its fruit and wheat which had been acquired with a great deal of sweat might be destroyed completely [...].

So let's go back to peasants who have been full of these acts of harmful magic for many centuries – indeed, so accustomed to it that even when they are suffering from a natural illness, they think they have become the object of harmful magic [*maleficiatos*] from one of their own. For example, as frequently happens, a peasant is invaded by *Amorreus* (i.e. *amor ereus*),[47] which, according to Avicenna is an illness issuing from the excessive and immoderate fiery heat of love, [the heat] a man usually feels for a woman, or vice versa, in such a way that because of the bitterness of his heart, he finds it very difficult to sleep, and while he does sleep, his mind is restless and grows hot with his calculations of profit and loss and the deep sighs of his most bitter heart. Soon afterwards, not taking into account that this could be the natural heat of an infirmity, the peasant believes he has been infected and distressed by a woman's secret practices. He is the sort of person who, while he languishes for love of his absent companion, [finds that] this languor is as strong as death, this affection harsh and this jealousy like Hell. This is love (Song of Solomon 8);[48] and about this it is said, 'Love finds a way of not putting up with any limit'.[49] Pierre de Blois said that, at the Devil's instigation, certain women make images out of wax or clay so that by these means they can torture their enemies or set their lovers on fire, in accordance with that

47.   The adjective copper or bronze (*ereus*) may refer to a colour, either of the cold or heated metal, and thus to the redness of high temperature.

48.   *Canticum* 8.6, 'Put me as a seal upon your heart, as a seal upon your arm; for love is as strong as death, jealousy harsh as Hell, its torches are torches of fire and flames'.

49.   This is a gloss on Propertius, *Carmina* 2.15.30, 'True love knows no bounds'. It may have been mistaken for a genuine line from Propertius. See J.L. Butrica, 1997, 'Editing Propertius', *Classical Quarterly* 47, p. 199. Hemmerlin goes on to note that 'love' is a 'madness', possibly a comment on Propertius 2.15.29, 'He who seeks an end to frenzied love is making a mistake'.

[saying] of Vergil, 'As this clay hardens and as this wax melts'.[50] But I know that in permitting such things lie feebleness of mind and the worst kind of sincerity. For if it were possible to spread acts of harmful magic indiscriminately among human beings, the Duke of Milan would have been subjected to this kind of thing by the Venetians, Dionysius the tyrant by the Sicilians, Theodoric of Verona by the Lombards and infinitely more enemies of the universities.

But we have seen from experience that many couples of both sexes have been subjected to harmful magic in pitiable fashion during marriage and completely prevented from performing acts of the flesh together, [a situation] proceeding for the most part from people's poor faith and feeble hope.

[Hansen II, no. 24 is taken from Cardinal Juan de Torquemada's commentary on Gratian's Decretum *(c.1445). The Cardinal here considers five questions: (1) whether demons delude people's senses; (2) whether what is said about certain women – that they ride with Diana, goddess of the pagans – is merely an illusion created by the Devil and is thus fancy, not fact; (3) whether anyone who believes no. 2 to be true is guilty of departing from the Faith; (4) whether the popular belief that these elderly women can change their shapes with the help of pagan goddesses is true in fact; and (5) whether women are more guilty of this kind of stupidity than men.]*

9. The Sabbat, anonymous, c.1450

Hansen II, no. 25a (pp. 118–22)

[This extract comes from Errores Gazariorum, *'The errors of heretics or of those who are proved to ride upon a broom and a stick', which may have been written before 1437 in the Val d'Aoste in northern Italy. It is notable, among other things, for its antisemitic tone.]*

First of all, when some individual of either sex is led astray under the persuasion of the enemy of human nature, his or her seducer, while drawing his victim into the abyss [which awaits] evil doers, makes him[51] swear as often as he asks him [that] he will drop everything and hurry with him to the 'synagogue', for which purpose [the man's] seducer had to furnish him with the appropriate ointments and stick so that he could do it.

Item: When they were in the place [where] the 'synagogue' [was being held], the seducer busies himself with presenting the man he has led astray to the Devil, the enemy of [any] created being endowed with reason. This enemy sometimes appears in the likeness of a black cat, sometimes in the likeness of a human being

---

50.   Pierre de Blois (c.1136–c.1203), French diplomatist and poet. Vergil, *Eclogues* 8.80, reading *limus* (Vergil's text) for Hansen's *scimus*. The Vergilian context is one of love-magic as Amaryllis performs spells to make Daphnis fall in love with her.

51.   *Ipsum*, specifically masculine. The author consistently uses masculine pronouns throughout his essay, although one is not thereby entitled to assume either that only men were initiated into the society or that men played the major role therein.

(but one which is not quite right) or in the likeness of another creature: most often, however, as a black cat. The man who has been led astray is questioned by the Devil [who asks] whether he is willing to remain and continue in the society and obey the one who led him astray. He answers yes. When he has heard this, the Devil demands that the man who has been led astray swear an oath of loyalty after the following fashion.

1. He swears he will be loyal to the presiding instructor and the whole society.
2. He will recruit as many people to the society as he can.
3. He will not reveal the secrets of the society as long as he lives.
4. He will kill and bring to the 'synagogue' all the children he can strangle and kill. (This means children aged three or younger.)
5. He will drop everything and hurry to the 'synagogue' whenever he is summoned.
6. By means of sorceries [*sortilegia*] and other acts of harmful magic, he will obstruct to the best of his ability any marriage he can obstruct.
7. He will avenge injuries to the sect or to any of its members, conjointly or individually.

After he has sworn and promised these things, the wretched man who has been led astray worships the presiding [demon] and pays him homage; and as a sign of homage, he kisses the devil, who appears in his human or some other likeness (as I said before), on the backside or anus and, as a contribution, gives him a part of his body [to be received] after he dies. Once this is done, all the members of that plague-bearing sect hurry to celebrate the arrival of a new heretic and eat what they have with them, particularly children who have been killed and roasted or boiled. Once this heinous feast is finished and they have danced in a circle to their satisfaction, the devil who is presiding at that time douses the light and shouts, 'Have sex! Have sex!' After they hear his voice, they join themselves together in carnal fashion, a man with a woman, a man with a man, and sometimes father with daughter, son with mother, brother with sister, without the slightest regard for the proper order of Nature.[52] Having completed these wicked, heinous acts of disorder (as I called them earlier), they relight [the candles and torches] and drink and eat again; and when they leave, they piss in the wine barrels and even drop gross matter into them.[53] (When they are asked why they do this, they say they do it [as a sign of] contempt and derision for the sacrament of the Eucharist because it is made of the said wine). After they have done this, each person goes back home.

Item: After the man who has been led astray has paid homage to the presiding devil, [the devil] gives him a small box filled with ointment and a stick and everything else he needs to come to the 'synagogue', and teaches him how and in what way he must anoint the stick. That ointment is made, by a secret method

---

52. Utz Tremp and Ostorero mistakenly put a comma between *equo* and *ordine* and take *equo* to be *equus*, 'horse', instead of *aequus*, 'right, proper', *L'imaginaire du sabbat*, pp. 290–1.
53. I.e. faeces.

of devilish malice, from the fat of children who have been roasted and boiled, along with other things (as will be made clear).

Item: Another ointment [made] from children's fat is mixed with very poisonous creatures such as snakes, toads, lizards and spiders, all of which are mixed together at the same time in the foresaid secret way. If this ointment touches anyone just once, he or she will die a painful death for which there is no remedy, sometimes lingering in weakness for quite a long time, sometimes dying all of a sudden.

Item: They make powders with which to kill people. These powders are made from children's guts mixed with the poisonous creatures mentioned above. Everything is reduced to powder by a member[54] of the foresaid society and scattered in the air when the weather is foggy or misty. Those who are touched by these powders either die or suffer a long, serious illness. This is why people die in some towns and villages and why the air is very stormy in other neighbouring places.

Item: When these plague-bearing people can get hold of a red-headed man – not a member of the sect, but a faithful Catholic – they strip him naked and tie him to a bench in such a way that he cannot move his hands or arms or legs. Once they have tied him, they bring in poisonous creatures from all over the place and some people belonging to the sect, who are more pitiless and more cruel [than the others], force them to bite him all over in such way and to such an extent that the wretched man breathes his last during those torments and dies, suffocated by the poison. When he is dead, they hang him up by his feet and put a glass or earthenware vessel below his mouth to catch the impurities and the poison which drip from his mouth and other passages. They collect this and make another ointment, with the Devil's help, from the fat of those who have been hanged on the gallows, the guts of children and the venomous creatures which have poisoned the man to death. One touch of this kills anybody.

Item: With the foresaid help, they take the skin of a cat, fill it with pulses – barley, corn, oats and bunches of fruit – and put this filled skin in a running stream where they let it stand for three days. Then they take it, dry it, reduce it to powder, climb up a hill when the weather is windy, and scatter it over and round fertile areas and opposite land owned [by other people]. They say that this produces infertility and that, because of this sacrificial offering, the Devil destroys the crops of those opposite [whose fields] these powders are scattered.

Item: Some members of the sect who have already been burned have confessed that during storms, at the Devil's command, many of them have come together in the hills to break ice. (On many occasions, great masses of ice are found on the hills.) They also say that some of them – not all, because they don't all have the ability or the confidence to do it – ride through the air with the help of the Devil during stormy weather, carrying ice to destroy the fertility of their enemies' fields and those of the rest of their neighbours.

Item: According to some people's statements – indeed everybody's – all those belonging to the sect, who enter that damned society generally do so for three

54.   *Unum*, specifically masculine.

reasons. First, there are some people who cannot live peacefully, and accumulate many enemies. Their hands are against all the descendants of Ishmael [i.e. the Jews], and all [the descendants of Ishmael] are against them, and seeing they cannot, by human contrivance, get vengeance on those who are their enemies, they seek vengeance from the Devil. Now, because he is accustomed to lead astray the simple minded by means of their credulity, he soon sends the foresaid error into their minds via fantasies, and persuades some members of the sect to go to them, as though they were their close friends and neighbours, so that he can deceive them and lead them astray while [the members of the sect] make sure the deception is effective. So they come to someone on the excuse of offering him comfort (they say), and, maintaining this pose, ask him why he is in distress. According to the different reasons [they are given], they plunge him into a pit of sin in different ways and, promising him vengeance, induce and persuade him[55] to come into their society. They also promise they are willing to give him a life dazzling and free from restraint, and when he hears this, he gives his consent at once.

Item: There are some people who have been accustomed to live a life of comfort and self-indulgence and have used up all their property in living this way. There are also others who want to be gourmets all the time. The Devil pays close attention to these and (as I said earlier), persuades some members of the sect to bring him or them to the 'synagogue', after telling them about the practices of the sect which are relevant to their desire. Once they have been told about this, the Devil brings them at the appointed time to the houses of influential people in authority – noblemen, burgesses and others – where he knows there is the kind of food and wine to satisfy their want and desire. He opens the cellars of these influential people at about the third hour of the night and brings [his victims] in. They stay there until midnight or thereabout – but not longer, because this is their [special] time and the darkness is full of power – and after they have eaten and drunk, each person goes back home.

Item: The third reason they enter that damned society is because some people want, more than anything else, to take wanton and casual pleasure in the act of sex, and there they do so as much and as wantonly as they like. (Note that the Devil forbids any member of the sect to steal gold, silver or vessels made of precious materials, so that the sect won't be exposed because members have a large number of these precious objects.)

Item: Confessions reveal that when anyone does something contrary to the sect's rules, he or she is given a good whipping by a member of the sect on the orders of [his or her] instructor. Because of this, they are absolutely terrified of offending their instructor or the adherents of the sect.

Item: According to the confession of Jean from Etroubles[56] and of others who have been burned, when a person[57] enters the sect for the first time, after he has

---

55.   The author has forgotten that the focus of attention is a 'him', and now uses plural verbs, *intrent* and *praebent*. For the sake of consistency, I have chosen to keep the singular.

56.   A town in the Val d'Aoste.

57.   *Unus*, specifically masculine.

taken the oath of loyalty (as mentioned earlier) and done homage, the Devil draws blood from the novice's left hand, using a particular device, and with this blood writes some words on a piece of parchment which he carefully keeps in front of him. (Quite a few members of the sect had seen this and gave testimony to that effect.)

Item: When they want to strangle children while the father and mother are asleep, they enter the parents' house, with the Devil's help, during the silence of the dead of night, take the child and throttle it or constrict its chest until they have killed it. In the morning, while [the child] is being taken for burial, the man or woman or people who have strangled and killed it rush forward together and, along with the parents and their friends, bewail the child's death. The following night, however, they open the pit and take the child although sometimes they leave its head, hands and feet in the pit because, unless they want to make some kind of magical object [*aliquod sortilegium*] out of the child's hand, they never take it with them. Once they have removed [the body] and filled in the pit again, they take the child to the 'synogogue' where it is roasted and eaten (as I said earlier).

Note that there have been some people who have killed their own sons and daughters and eaten them during a 'synagogue'. An example is Jeanne Vacanda who was burned in the place called Chambanaz on the feast of St Lawrence [10 August]. She admitted in front of the whole population that she had eaten her daughter's son and had killed him with the help of another woman who was named during Jeanne's trial.

Item: From the confessions of those who have been burned, it is clear that members of the sect give the appearance of being better [Catholics] than the rest of the faithful. They generally hear Mass, often go to confession during the year and frequently take Holy Communion (like Judas who [received it] from the Lord's hand).[58] They do this so that they won't be detected if they stop taking the sacraments, or so that their error may not be exposed.

10. The extent and limitation of demons' powers, Jean Vineti, c.1450

Hansen II, no. 27 (pp. 124–30)

[Jean Vineti, a Dominican, was Professor of Theology at Paris in 1443 and Inquisitor in Carcassonne for 25 years between 1450 and 1475. His book, Tractatus contra demonum invocatores, *'Treatise against those who invoke demons', was notable for suggesting that magic which involved the Devil was a new heresy, and although Vineti was not the first to say this, his treatise shows that this particular interpretation of magic and magical practice was gaining ground. Hansen excerpted it by referring to folio pages. Folio 6 notes that demons can clothe themselves in a real body. This, says Vineti, does not contradict the canon* Episcopi, *and the canon itself is not talking about modern heretics who invoke demons, worship them, and pay them tribute.]*

---

58.   John 13.26: 'It is he to whom I shall have given bread dipped in sauce. And when He had dipped bread in sauce, He gave it to Judas Iscariot, son of Simon'.

Folio 10v. Can demons procreate while they are in the bodies they have assumed? There are two opinions [about this]. Some people say that demons are unable in any way to procreate while they are in the bodies they have assumed, but others think they can – not, of course, by means of semen detached from the assumed body or through the power of their own nature, but by a man's semen brought from elsewhere for the purpose of procreating by this mean – and that one and the same demon may be a succubus with respect to a man, and that he transfers the semen he has got from him into a woman to whom he becomes an incubus. This can be upheld quite in accordance with reason … . From which foregoing [remarks] it is adduced with a degree of probability that the depositions and confessions of certain women who admit they have sex with demons are not what one might call 'false', and should not be regarded as impossible.

[Folio 14. Can an angel by his own natural power translate a person physically from place to place? *Vineti runs through the usual arguments, such as those we have seen already employed by Tostado, and comes to the conclusion that the depositions and confessions of those who admit they are translated physically by demons from one place to another by night as well as by day are dependable,* 'unless anything to the contrary stands in the way'.]

Folio 15. Can an angel completely overturn cities and towns, kill people and call up thunder, brilliant flashes, hailstorms, rain and extremes of weather? No matter what things can happen through local movement alone, these things can be done by good spirits and by evil, [using] the power of Nature, unless they are stopped [from doing so] by God. Consequently, one must reflect, with Thomas [Aquinas] in his *Commentary on Job*, that while every kind of adversity was inflicted on Job by Satan, one must acknowledge that with God's permission demons can induce disturbance in the air, stir up winds and cause fire to fall from the sky. But although physical matter does not do as it is told at the nod of good or evil angels with regard to taking on forms, but only [at the nod] of the Creator, yet a physical nature is naturally suited to obeying one which is spiritual (where local movement is concerned), as is evidenced by the following: limbs are moved at the sole command of the will, so that they may proceed with the piece of work assigned [to them] by the will. Therefore no matter what things can happen by local movement alone, these things can be done by good spirits and evil spirits as well, [by using] the power of Nature, unless they are stopped by God. Winds, rain and other such disturbances of the air can happen simply as a result of the movement of vapours as they are being released from land and water. Hence, the natural power of a demon is enough to create movements of this kind. But sometimes they are stopped by divine power from doing this kind of thing which they are able to do naturally. (This is not contrary to what is said in Jeremiah 14.22: 'Is it really possible that the tribes have graven images which cause rain?') It is one thing to rain because of the natural course of events. That comes from God alone, who arranges natural causative agencies for that purpose. It is quite another sometimes to employ these natural agencies arranged by God in a way which owes more to craft than Nature[59] in order to produce

59. *Artificialiter.* This has a double implication. (a) It may refer to the *ars magica* which

rain or wind – sometimes in a manner which goes beyond the rules.[60] This is
what St Thomas says, for in his *Quaestiones de malo ('Questions about Evil'),*
article 9, solution to article 2, he says, 'Everything one can see taking place in
this world takes place as a result of demons, not only by means of the power
which belongs to them, but also by the intermediate active [powers] of Nature'.[61]
Thus St Thomas. From this it is perfectly clear that an angel, good or evil, can
bear a human being physically from place to place, and in consequence I think
one should trust the depositions and confessions of those who confess they are
carried physically to demons' assemblies.[62] The power of demons these days is
the same as it has been from the beginning, and they are able to do the same
things they have been able to do from the beginning, unless God forbids it.

[*Folio 15v asks whether a demon can of his own natural power take his
confederates (i.e. witches) into a house through closed doors and take them out
again while the doors remain closed. Vineti concludes, on the ground that one
cannot be in two places at once, that, in spite of witches' confessing they have
actually done this – entering houses to kill children or locked cellars to drink
their contents – confessions of this kind cannot be believed.*]

Folio 26v. Can elderly female fortune tellers[63] cast the evil eye on people?
Elderly female fortune tellers can, with the Devil's assistance, cast the evil eye
on very young children. For its occurrence, one should note St Thomas, part 1,
question 17, article 3 [where he says] that St Augustine 'attributed the cause of
the action of the evil eye [to the fact] that physical matter is naturally suited to
obeying a spiritual entity rather than its opposing agents in Nature.[64] So when
the soul's imaginative faculty is strong, physical matter is changed in conformity

will therefore make the *artifex* who employs these causative agencies a magician. Hence the
reference to 'craft' (*ars*) contained in *artificialiter*. (b) God is the *artifex*, 'the craftsman', of the
universe, and by acting as an *artifex* (i.e. *artificialiter*), the magician is usurping a prerogative
belonging to God alone. Both implications are thus condemnable.

60.   *Extraordinarie*. Vineti has been using the verb *ordinare*, 'to arrange in a particular
order or pattern', to describe what God has done with the causative agencies of Nature.
Extraordinarie thus says that the magician is going outwith the arrangement made by God,
and so implies that he is deliberately flouting God's order – an action of sacrilegious arrogance
and hence a sin.

61.   *Quaestiones disputatae de malo*, article 9. Vineti appears to have taken two separate
sentences from the beginning of article 9 and welded them together after a fashion. St Thomas
is here actually discussing whether demons can change their appearance or not. 'One can
believe without being foolish that everything one can see taking place happens through the
lower powers of the air .... . But if demons can change their bodies only by virtue of the active
[powers] of Nature, they cannot make other transformations'.

62.   *Synagogas*. The Jewish term is not infrequently used during this early period to refer
to meetings of witches and demons.

63.   *Vetule sortilege*, which may also be translated as 'sorceresses'. *Fascinare*, 'to cast the
evil eye', may be the Latin equivalent of the Greek *baskainein*, 'to slander, to envy, to cast the
evil eye'.

64.   *Summa theologiae* Part 1, question 117, article 3. (Hansen's '17' may be a misprint).
Aquinas's reference to St Augustine at this point says simply, 'Augustine says that physical
matter obeys God's nod of command alone', and in fact in this passage, Vineti is quoting St
Thomas's lengthy quotation from Avicenna's commentary on Aristotle's *De anima* 4.4.

with it,[65] and this, he says, is the cause of the evil eye. But it has been shown above that physical matter does not obey a spiritual entity's nod of command except for the Creator alone,[66] and therefore it is better to say that the spirits of the body with which they are connected are changed by the soul's strong imaginative faculty.[67] This change of spirits happens principally in the eyes to which spirits composed of finer particles penetrate. But the eyes tarnish the air uninterruptedly up to a specific distance. This is the way mirrors, if they have started by being new and uncontaminated, contract contamination from the glance of a menstruating woman, as Aristotle says in his book *De somno et vigilia* ('Sleep and Wakefulness').[68] Therefore when some soul or other has been very strongly stimulated in the direction of wickedness, as happens particularly in elderly people, his or her glance is made poisonous and harmful in the way described earlier, especially to children who have a delicate body which takes a mark or impression rather easily. It is also possible that, with God's permission, or even some kind of secret pact, the malice of demons, with whom elderly female fortune tellers have a formal agreement, may work to that end'.

[Hansen II no. 28 is taken from a work by Johann Hartlieb (c.1410–1468) who was physician to several noble clients, including Albert III of Bavaria. His short treatise, 'Book on all the Forbidden Arts, Heresy, and Magic' (1456) was not intended for publication, but for the eyes and interest only of Margrave Johann von Brandenburg to whom it is addressed. Chapter 32 contains a recipe for witches' ointment:]

How to enable oneself to fly through the air. For journeys such as this, men and women, that is, the witches [*die unhulden*], have an ointment called *unguentum phaleris* ('horse-brass ointment')[69] They make it from seven plants, picking each of them on the day belonging to that plant: so, on Sunday, they pick and dig up heliotrope; on Monday, lunaria 'annua' or 'rediviva'; on Tuesday, verbena; on Wednesday, mercurialis; on Thursday, anthyllis barba Iovis; on Friday, adiantum

---

65. Reading *eam* for *eum*.

66. Here Vineti seems to be remembering a quotation from St Augustine given in *Summa theologiae* Part 1, question 110, article 2: 'One must not think that the physical matter of things one can see obeys these rebellious angels' nod of command. [It obeys] God alone'.

67. 'Spirits' were part of contemporary and ancient medical theory. The spirits were particles in the bloodstream and thereby carried to various parts of the body. 'Natural' spirits arising in the liver became 'vital' spirits in the heart and were again changed by the cerebellum into 'animal' spirits. Among other tasks, the spirits transmitted sense perceptions to the two anterior lateral ventricles of the cerebellum where the imaginative faculty was lodged.

68. Book 2, chap. 2 (459b.27–30): 'In the case of mirrors which are completely spotless, whenever menstruating women look into [such] a mirror, the surface of the mirror takes on a blood-coloured cloudiness'.

69. *Phaleris* is difficult to account for. I have taken it to be the dative plural of *phalerae* = 'ornament worn by horses', on the grounds that the broom or stick on which the ointment is to be smeared is the witch's 'horse' and thus indicates riding, and because the ointment is smeared with, presumably, more than one application, the smearings serve as the stick-horse's 'ornaments'. The explanation is somewhat strained, but there does not appear to be any other more acceptable.

capilli Veneris.[70] From these, they make [it] and add birds' blood and fat from animals. (I shan't write these down to avoid giving anyone offence.) Then, when they want to, they smear it on benches or stools, rakes or oven forks and fly on them. This is genuine negromancy and is strictly forbidden.

[Hansen II, no. 29 comes from the Flagellum haereticorum fascinariorum *('The Whip of Heretics who cast the Evil Eye and work other Harmful Magic'), written in 1458 by Nicolaus Jacquier, inquisitor successively in Tournai, Bohemia, and Lille, covers familiar ground in discussing the canon* Episcopi, *although he is clear that there is a difference between the women described here and those who constitute the modern sect of witches; and he also devotes space to informing his readers what happens at a Sabbat. His term for a witch,* fascinarius, *appears in its masculine form, although grammatically the plural will not necessarily be gender specific and will thus include both sexes. The word has its root in the concept of casting the evil eye, but here clearly embraces other forms of harmful magic, too. Details about the Sabbat are given later and at greater length by another author (see no. 11). The short extract which follows is an illustrative anecdote showing that Jacquier, like most writers on these subjects, included the most up-to-date information he could.]*

(Hansen, p. 137) This year – that is, 1458 – a man confessed in legal form and of his own accord that when he was young (five or six years old), his mother took him and his little brother, whom she carried in her arms, and his sister to a convention of witches [*synagogam fascinariorum*] and offered these three children to a demon who appeared in the shape of a goat. She told them he was their lord and teacher and would do them much good. The mother made her children touch the demon on the head of the appearance he had assumed, and the demon, whom they called 'Tonyon', touched all three of them on their hip with his forefoot and imprinted thereon an indelible mark. The man making the confession had this mark on him. It was quite visible and was the size of a bean. After his initiation, he, his brother and his sister continued to attend this sect for several years. He was about 60 years old when he made this confession – of his own accord, as I said.

[Hansen II no 30 is taken from book 5 of Fortalitium Fidei *('The Fortress of the Faith') by Alfonso de Spina, a Spanish Franciscan, died c.1491. The work is divided into five books, each of which deals with a separate enemy of the Christian religion, thus: book 1, those who deny Christ's divinity; book 2, Heretics; book 3, The Jews; book 4, Muslims; and book 5, Demons and other enemies from Hell.]*

(Hansen, p. 146) 'Magical practices and divinations cannot be carried out to seek advice or help from demons without sin unless, by chance, as we are told by some holy men, in a situation where God would be bringing the Devil to the attention of a person of merit. But it cannot be done as a voluntary transaction without sin'.

---

70.   The text contains only these six plants and six days. The plants may have been chosen because their Latin names correspond to the Latin names of the weekdays.

(Hansen, p. 147) 'There are some wicked people, men and women, apostates from the Faith, heretical creatures and deceitful, who give themselves to the Devil of their own accord. The Devil receives them and grants them (i) that he appears to them by means of his deceiving practices; (ii) that they walk 200 leagues and back in the space of four or five hours; (iii) that they destroy living things and suck their blood; (iv) that they and those who believe them are greatly deceived and deluded by the Devil'. [They use ointments and their 'second self' (De Spina calls it an image and an imagined picture), goes where they want while their body lies in a state of insensibility.]

(Hansen, p. 148) 'There is an immense number of these women in Dauphiné and Gascony, where they allege they meet at night on a deserted stretch of ground where there is a boar on a crag – it is called *E boch de Biterne* in the local tongue – and that they meet there with lighted candles and worship that boar and kiss him on his backside. This is why several of them have been arrested by inquisitors of the Faith and, after conviction, burned. In the inquisitor's house in Toulouse there are paintings of those who have been burned, showing them with their candles, worshipping the boar and [wearing] a large variety of smocks, as I have seen with my own eyes'.

11. *The Waldensians, their Sabbat, their evil deeds and how to prosecute them, anonymous, 1460*

Hansen II, no. 31 (pp. 149–81)

A recapitulation of the condition, state and situation of Waldensian idolaters, drawn from the personal experiences and commentaries of several inquisitors and other people of tried experience, and from the confessions of and legal proceedings relating to the Waldensians in Arras, made in 1460. [Zeal for the Catholic faith has been the stimulus for this account, which can be divided into separate sections.]

Section 1: The possibility, and even the reality and truth, of Waldensians' physical translation to their meetings whither they are carried by demons

[It is very well known that demons can do this kind of thing, although a demon's power is restricted by God's will. His remaining natural abilities let a demon act as it were in an instant. All learned men are agreed on these points, and St Thomas Aquinas, Peter Lombard, Duns Scotus, St Bonaventure and Dionysius the Areopagite are all adduced in support of them, along with the examples of Christ's being carried to the pinnacle of the Temple, and the aerial flight of Simon Magus.]

(p. 151) The reality and truth of the translation of human beings in body and soul while they are awake to the assemblies which Waldensians hold depends on the confessions and legal proceedings of Waldensians themselves. But this reality is well founded and firmly established ... [71] and in many regions the Church

---

71.   I omit here a reference to 'the previous little essay', since we do not have it in Hansen's text.

punishes Waldensian idolaters not because of dreams or fantasies or illusions, since we deserve or earn nothing in sleep or in a dream, but because they agree to let their demon transport and translate them in reality to their assemblies, and because of the very serious offences they commit there or elsewhere on that occasion, at the urging and command of the demon. In his book, *De doctrina Christiana*, St Augustine appears adequately and briefly to touch upon the possibility and circumstances, or reality and truth, of Waldensian idolaters' being translated, about which there is discussion at the present time.[72] If one studies these things in greater detail, [one finds that] in his *Speculum historiale* (*'Mirror of History'*), Vincent takes an example from Hélinand, which deals with Waldensians' meeting each other about 300 years ago in a wood near Arras. The Archbishop of Rheims and the Provost of Aire are mentioned.[73] In the second part of the book, *De [septem] donis Spiritus Sancti* (*'The Gifts of the Holy Spirit'*), chapter 5, 'The power of Christ's holy cross to put demons to. flight', there is briefly mentioned a priest who gives a full explanation of this sect of Waldensian idolaters; and in the *Legenda Aurea* (*'Golden Reading Matter'*), mention is made in the 'Life of St Basil' of a girl given in marriage, etc. where the Waldensians' declaration [of faith] is made perfectly clear.[74] Other people at various times in the past have been Waldensian heretics, or 'Poor People of Lyons',[75] and Albigensians who enjoyed power for about 270 years. But they were different from [Waldensians] because they were clearly heretics (as is said in the book *The Gifts of the Holy Spirit*), whereas [Waldensians] are, properly speaking, not heretics but worse, since they are secret idolaters who keep themselves hidden, apostates and faithless, sacrilegious people, etc.; and judges remark that if female

72.   St Augustine does not here discuss the physical movement of humans by demons, but rather mentions a pact between them, basing himself on 1 Corinthians 10.20, 'I do not want you to become associates of demons'. See *De doctrina Christiana* 2.89, 74, 94, 102, 139.

73.   Vincent de Beauvais (*c*.1190–*c*.1264), Dominican historian. His *Speculum historiale* was actually part of a much larger work dealing with creation and the enormous range of human knowledge and activity. The historical volume describes the history of the world from its beginnings until Vincent's own time. Hélinand of Froidmont (died 1229) was the author of a *Chronicon* (1211–1223) upon which Vincent based his own history. As Hansen observes, the references made by 'Anonymous' here do not seem to be in Vincent's work.

74.   The text of *Gifts* is given in A. Lecoy de la Marche (ed.), 1877, *Anecdotes historiques, légendes et apologues tirés du recueil inédit d'Etienne de Bourbon*, Paris. The priest appears in Part 4, title 7, para. 342: 'This is how that sect began, according to what I have been told by several people who saw their former members, and by the priest, a wealthy man, who was held in respect in the city of Leiden, and was a friend of our [Dominican] brethren. His name was Bernard Ydros'. What follows is a brief account of the origins of the sect. *Legenda Aurea* was compiled by the Blessed Giacomo da Varezze (*c*.1230–1298), a Dominican and Archbishop of Genoa. The *Legenda* consist of lives of the saints, and in the 'Life of St Basil' there is a lengthy anecdote describing how a slave fell in love with a respectable man's daughter and turned to magic to achieve her love. He made a bargain with demons, and although his wish was granted, he repented and was finally released only by his own sincere contrition and the prayers of St Basil.

75.   See further G. Audisio, 1999, *The Waldensian Dissent*, English trans. (Cambridge: Cambridge University Press), pp. 6–11.

or male fortune tellers and male or female invokers of demons are questioned correctly, for the most part [it turns out] they are Waldensians and belong to that sect. Nevertheless, all Waldensians, from the moment they profess [their faith] and are received into the congregation are looked on thereafter as invokers of demons, although not all invokers of demons are Waldensians. But fairly often invocation and Waldensianism do go together.

One should note first of all, before anything else and as a general point when it comes to the business of Waldensians, that in it there are three specific topics.

First: as regards travelling to meetings and everything else which is concerned with this sect, the possibility that it is real, and also that [what is said of] this damned sect is real and true: that is to say, is it true that people of both sexes are transported from one place to another to their damned meetings in body and soul, while they are alive and wide awake and able to exercise all the faculties of an animate, human, living creature? To demonstrate that this possibility is real and genuine, well-educated men, particularly those skilled in interpreting the Scriptures, are required. But these days in that place about which everyone is talking at the moment [i.e. Arras], since the real existence of this [mode of travelling] has started to be clear – clearer than the sun – to those who give it careful thought and to every other serious-minded, learned man of estimable zeal and correct judgement, there is no need of learned men and theologians when it comes to this first topic. To establish that it is real, and to persuade people of it, an unambiguous piece of evidence free from deception of the senses ought to be sufficient: or a confession, made by Waldensians themselves, that they have been genuinely and truly transported, alive and wide awake, in soul and body, to such and such a place by a demon – not saying they were *dreaming* they had been translated from place to place to such and such a location, in the way someone who had been dreaming he had been in some place would not say he *had* been in such a place, but that he *dreamed* he had been in such a place, but had not actually been there. Nor do the canon *Episcopi* and the chapter 'It is not extraordinary', etc.[76] contradict this, because their situation is different, and the result is that the person who looks into and considers both sides [of the argument] can take a firm stand on something which is perfectly clear. That is to say, seeing he is not worshipped and venerated in Christianity openly and manifestly in [the form of] idols or in other ways as he used to be in pagan times, because of the punishment inflicted on such people who do worship him openly, the demon, with God's just permission, transports these 'Christians' by night to very remote places so that they can worship and venerate him in secret, without being seen.

The second topic in this business is the investigation and legal proceeding with regard to a specific individual, right up to the verdict of the court, [to find out] whether he or she is a member of the sect or not. For this, theologians are required, as is a small number of suitable men of faith and also of

---

76. The canon *Episcopi* argued that women who claimed they flew through the air had been 'led astray by the illusions and fantasies of demons', and Gratian's *Decretum*, causa 26, question 5, chap. 14 which begins 'It is not extraordinary' has the heading, 'the things magicians do by trickery are not true but are proved to be absurd fantasies'.

the most commendable zeal – men who have practical experience, especially in this business in which a few men of practical experience are of more use than many of no practical experience, however learned they may be. The reason is that this business is atypical, as are the method of proceeding and everything else [connected with it], and one cannot look for guidance as one can in other cases, primarily because the specific case of Waldensians is one which involves concealment, keeping hidden and being extremely secretive, and one cannot normally get a grip on it except through their own confession or through accomplices who alone can and should be accusers and witnesses in this case. Neither reputation nor behaviour (pretended outward signs of devotion, and anything else like it), which are given weight in other cases and increase, diminish or lift suspicion, have much of a place in this instance. A second reason is that among Waldensians the demon has very great power because they have been almost entirely abandoned by God. To no small number of these, out of his own malice, guile and power, [the demon] provides every assistance, being justly allowed to do so by God whom [the Waldensians] have completely deserted. What is more, the demon himself suggests answers, puts them in people's mouths, or stops [people] from accusing themselves or others, as will be made clear at greater length later on.

The third topic is assessment of blame, more of it or less according to the nature and extent of the crime, and appropriate to whatever the specific case [may be], once the large number of accomplices has been taken into account, the example to be given the people for their edification has been considered, and (to be brief) all the things which need to be pondered have been weighed and measured; and for such[77] an assessment, learned men are required, especially those who have practical experience in this business. But when it comes to punishing [offenders], it is not a good idea that they come from outwith the district, because they would return to their congregations and (what would be worse), infect other people. Those who are sentenced to perpetual imprisonment (even though they can be recidivists and backsliders by leaving out something from what they say, or denying it, or omitting something about themselves or others from their confession, in which case they should be handed over to secular justice), cannot generally infect others. On this subject, Reader, note that in the case of Waldensians generally speaking and for the most part only, experienced commentators tell us that demons produce two illusions in [the form of] deceitful tricks or by some other possible way – that is to say, in [the form of] money which seems to be real and isn't (although sometimes a demon does give real money, as in the confession of Belotte Mouchard),[78] and sometimes [in the form of] food which appears other than it is (although sometimes during their meetings there is very good, genuine food which actually is what it appears to be). They do not

77.   Reading *tali* for *talis*.

78.   Belotte was due to be burned for heresy, along with other citizens of Arras, on 7 July 1460, but failed to complete her task of drawing the Devil on the paper mitre she would wear at her execution. In consequence she remained in prison to finish it and so escaped the fire that day.

stop meeting in cold weather, such as during winter, but celebrate just as they do in hot weather, but without a fire, because the demon quickly brings things which create heat into contact with the surrounding air so that people at the meeting do not endure the intense cold, and he somehow inflames and heats their bodies with the food [he gives them], and by stirring up their blood, although sometimes people at the meeting do have a fire which, by the demon's cunning and agency, makes them warm.

Secondly, with regard to the mode of proceeding against some individual, and taking for granted he will be admonished in a salutary fashion and will have sworn to tell the truth during the inevitable interrogatory sessions up to the point where he reveals what he has to say without leaving anything out, one should note that however much the person being interrogated will have sworn to tell the truth, he will rush into many perjuries during the whole legal proceeding and will fabricate many lies by constantly leaving things out, or by denying what he is accused of doing; and with many oaths and calling down of curses, he will employ charming words of the noblest kind – one takes for granted he protests to his demon, 'Don't be annoyed, sir!'[79] – and will say he submits himself to an investigation to be undertaken about him, with respect to his reputation, etc. All this does him little good in this business, as will be plain in what follows. He will also call upon God and the saints (especially the saint to whom people in his locality turn most), saying – imploring them to be willing to deign to come to his aid and help him as he deserves. In addition to this, he will say he hates Waldensians more than anything and would like them all to be burned to a frazzle. The assistants, however, should not be moved at all by what he says and his persistence [in saying it], but should proceed as one immediately to question him, whatever he may be saying. The witnesses or accusers should not be present unless it is known in advance that their inclinations are sound; and yet even though it is known in advance that the inclinations of those who are present are sound, there is danger in their being present, because they have some sign among them with which they sometimes signal their changes of mind or mood in the presence of the accused. But if it seems to be helpful, he can be asked whether he is willing to confront the witnesses. He will often say no, and that they are contemptible – which will be a sign he is guilty. If he were to say yes, he would not confront those whose [evidence] had been heard, and time as well as that session would be lost. While he is going to be questioned,[80] he will call on God to judge him and will say to those present that he will not say what he does not know, whatever they may want him to say. But before he is questioned, he should be completely undressed, shaved and have every part of his body examined. His fingernails should be split in case there is some sign [of his having made a demonic] pact or some small physical object he has been given by the demon – a seed, a hair, a ring, a thread or something of that kind – whose existence gives them[81] hope that the

---

79. These words are in French.

80. *Dum quaestioni dabitur.* 'Quaestio' simply means 'interrogation', but 'he will be given to interrogation' implies he is going to be tortured, as later remarks make clear.

81. The narrative switches without warning between singular and plural.

demon will help and succour them. As long as they have this sign, they will not speak the truth because of [this] assurance from the demon; or if they do speak, they will say at once that they have confessed because of the severity of the torture.

Above all, however, once the assistants have gone into every detail of the accusations or accusation, and if after questioning and interrogation he does not begin to confess on that occasion, let him be warmed up, given time to recover and revived. Once this has been done and he has been revived, [and] while the pain is still fresh, he should be sent back for questioning or shut up in a foul prison again and given not much food (and that sour and unpalatable), because a dark prison and short rations and sour food do much to make someone realize his situation, as well as having some people speaking to him harshly while they urge him to tell the truth, and others with kindly gentleness. So if he starts to confess what has happened to him, let the assistants ask questions:[82] '[Tell us] about the place you were in. Who was with you? [Did you go] in order to take part in intimacy?[83] Who instructed you? Who brought you there? Who was in charge? What shape did he have? What was his name? Where are the ointments and the stick?' (He should have it taken off him beforehand). '[Tell us] about the exchange of gifts'. Let him give his account in such a way that it seems conformable with the accusation [against him], and let all examinations relating to his account be kept short. (Those who have practical experience of this business are familiar with these examinations from legal proceedings and this present essay.)

As soon as he has admitted and agreed that they had held three or four meetings, or thereabout (because at first he will confess only one, when they will actually have taken place on a thousand occasions, in order to distance himself from his situation and in hope the Church will show him mercy), and once places, time and so forth have been set down in writing so that the assistants may realize he has frequented meetings over a very long period, let those to be accused be interrogated, generally without limit of time being put on interrogation – this is something to be avoided at all costs – and let a straightforward, agreed, written record be made of all those who are to be accused, without details of intimacies and without disclosing evidence on this first occasion. Once all this has been put down in writing, he should be interrogated about the details of each intimacy, giving every bit of evidence – that is, the names, clothing, etc., of each partner in the intimacy – so that the accusations made by and coming from other people may correspond and concur [with each other]. Then interrogations should settle where, when and at which meetings the accused have been present; and have they been at some meetings and not at others?

None of the assistants should say anything to excuse those who are being or have been accused, because [there are those] who ask nothing more than to excuse or have an opportunity of excusing [the accused] in accordance with their service to the demon and in expectation of pleasing those who have been accused

---

82.   I have changed the rest of the sentence from indirect to direct speech.
83.   *Pro parte copule.*

and thinking that by doing so they will please the assistants as well. For they accuse [people] grudgingly and unwillingly, as will be described in detail later on. So note, Reader, that often they are not willing to accuse anyone, thinking they *ought* not to accuse them, or pretending they have made a confession about the sect to a priest. Prompted by the demon and people in their assemblies, they accuse, reluctantly and very unwillingly, important people and those who do not belong to their social category or class; and they are unwilling to be the first to accuse their friends or important people, saying, in accordance with their own malice and that of the demon who speaks plausibly in their persons, that in those meetings there were none but pitiful women and wretched individuals. They also reckon among themselves (instructed by the demon and his accomplices – or pretending to have been so instructed), that they ought not to reveal the sins of others or to accuse other people, and the assistants need to be warned about all this in advance.

I must not neglect to mention that while they are speaking about themselves or others, if they anticipate interrogation by saying they don't know anything (because they are afraid of being interrogated), this is a reliable sign that they do know it; and, Reader, do realize that those who are newly arrested these days have in all likelihood thought things over during their daily assemblies [and decided] that, out of malice they will deliberately name and accuse all those whom the assistants want them [to name and accuse] or those whose [names] first occur to them. This they do in order to bring the accusations into disrepute and spoil them and every fact in them – for example, out of their own nastiness they say that the angel of Satan can transform himself into an angel of light and represent human beings in those meetings, as [will be described] at length later in [its own] section. Neither judges nor assistants, however, should be disturbed by this in any way, but listen patiently, take countermeasures, and, with well-grounded discernment, take what precautions they can; for there is no malice greater than that of the demon and Waldensians.

You should also bear in mind that they often describe an individual who is very well known to them and accuse him or her with many disclosures of evidence. They know his or her name but, out of their own malice and that of the demon, are not willing to give it; or, if they do give a name, they give some other name in order to spoil the accusation and bring it into disrepute, or [they mention] a piece of evidence which does not apply to the person they have described. Frequently, however, either from malice or by particular design, they have shortcomings in age more than in other pieces of evidence.[84] A man and wife can belong to the sect for the same reason or for different [reasons] – the wife because [she wants] physical pleasures, the man because [he wants] a lot of money – or vice versa, or because of something else; for when anyone has been given to the demon, he[85] wants everything which is illicit, and all respectability and every limit is removed from him, as though everything were permitted to him. Also, the man can go to one meeting, his wife to another, and so sometimes they don't know what the

84.   That is, they are too young for their evidence to be heard and accepted legally.
85.   Specifically masculine in the Latin text.

other was doing, [although] sometimes they do. Perhaps I should also say that in the sect permission, help and opportunity have been afforded some people to marry someone else. Sometimes the husband is a member of the sect and his wife is not, and the wife will not notice anything in connection with her husband because [members of the sect] go to meetings in the most secret hour of the night, while sleep is strong (that is to say, about 11 p.m.), and quite often come back at about 2 or 3 in the morning. The assistants and judges should not be disturbed at all if one accusation says of one man that he has been with one woman, and another accusation says he was with another, because this happened at different meetings, and they go to meetings several times and for very many more years than they confess. Sometimes, too, one man has several women during the same meeting and moves on from one to another. Substantially, the accusations are about the same thing.

Finally, let them be interrogated about acts of harmful magic [*de maleficiis*] and also asked how many people they instructed and who these people were. The proceedings should continue without interruption, if possible in a single session, because in general inquiries should be followed up while [the accused] are disposed to tell the truth; for if [the session] is postponed, those one has let go will be found on another occasion, transformed by the demon or changed by human beings. Note most particularly, Reader, that in order to eliminate this cursed sect, those who conduct trials and the investigation have to concentrate absolutely on those who should be accused and concern themselves with accusations by other people, more especially concerning acts of harmful magic perpetrated by these Waldensians (because therein lies one's whole satisfaction in extirpating and eliminating the sect), with the result that, for example, they name and accuse anyone they have recognized with certainty [as a participant] in their meetings. Otherwise Christianity will be destroyed in no small part and the Faith will perish.

Section 2: The method of introducing people for the first time to the sect of idolatrous Waldensians and how they are given instruction

For the most part there can be no doubt[86] that they are brought into the sect and congregation by a demon rather than by a human being, since clearly anyone who, from greatness of mind or any other reason, aspires to heights which it is more or less impossible for him to reach, falls into a state of hopelessness and desperation, or has a violent, excessive and disordered passion for someone, and is mentally disposed to do anything illicit as soon as he becomes useless or, made hopeless, is agitated by any kind of disordered emotion. To such a man made hopeless and, as it were, desperate in such a fashion, the demon appears, describing his bad luck to him and promising him a remedy provided the man obeys him and gives him his soul (because otherwise the demon does not do business). At length he brings him to an assembly, gives him instruction, teaches him everything and gives him ointments and powders, a stick and all [the usual apparatus], provided they are both of the same mind, since consensus alone, without resistance, meets the needs of the case.

---

86. Reading *vero* for *raro*.

But quite often one human teaches another, explaining to him (when he has been given the chance to speak), that if he is willing to believe him he will live his days in prosperity, he will have at hand every desirable thing he wants, he will lack nothing and he will see lovely, extraordinary things (and one should be on one's guard about this during legal proceedings), especially if on a particular night (that is, [the night] of the next meeting), he is willing to leave his village to see 'the lovely society'. Such a man gives a full description of all these circumstances and particularly the reality of the situation. When the person who is listening to him gives his consent, his instructor gives him ointment [wrapped] in a bit of cloth or paper and a little stick which he is to put between his legs. He tells him when he is to go to the assembly and promises he will be there to look after him when it is time to come home, if he is not prevented [from doing so]. Should he be prevented (he says), a man will come to look after him. That 'man' is a demon, who appears in the shape of a man for the initial assemblies and forces him to go, saying, 'Such and such a man says such and such things to you', etc.[87]

On other occasions, as the night and hour are advancing, there appear the instructor and a demon-familiar, quite often in the shape and likeness of animals,[88] and [the demon] tells him how, on a particular day, such and such a person spoke with him. They leave by the door on the first occasions, or by some hidden [place], or through the window or chimney. Unseen by us, the walls of parts of the chimney suddenly come apart to accommodate the size of their bodies, and then come together again. This is the work of the demon who is an extraordinary artificer – as one knows from his [ability to] open anything which has been closed and bolted. They lean forward, put their sticks which have been covered in ointment between their legs, and say, 'Go, by the Devil, go!' or 'Satan, don't forget your lady friend!' or some such thing.[89] [Then] they are raised very quickly indeed into the lowest part of the middle region of the air, which is cold. (For this reason, they suffer pain in the heart and chest, and even feel pain in their eyes because of their sudden, violent cleaving of the air, especially when they are carried a long way, even though the demon applies things [to them] to protect them and keep them safe.) They also anxiously notice, especially when they go along way, the great distance and the places over which they travel. This novice is also prevented from calling to mind God and the saints and is told not to make the sign of the cross, otherwise he will fall. When they arrive at their destination they do the things which are included in the following section; and when they have done and completed them, they replace the sticks covered in ointment as before, and return where they wish, or where the demon wishes; and while going and returning, throughout the whole journey they have those sticks between their legs.

87.   This is the beginning of a dactylic hexameter. I have not been able to identify the poem.
88.   *Bestiarum.* 'Bestia' may mean (a) an animal, as opposed to a human; (b) a beast of prey; (c) a farmyard animal; or (d) a beast of the chase.
89.   These two phrases are in French in the text.

Notice, Reader, that sometimes in the first assemblies (by which I mean, of course, throughout the whole course of events), the demon appears to them in visible form. In others, however, and more frequently, he is invisible while he brings them together. Sometimes, too, one stick is enough for two people, and quite often the instructor and his pupil travel to the assembly and come back from it together.

Section 3: How the assembly and synagogue[90] is conducted on the first occasion

When a woman (and the same is true of a man), is brought in her own fashion[91] to the assembly for the first time by a demon-carer or demon-familiar, and by a man and woman who bring to and provide the assembly with people she knows, she is presented to the presiding demon who always appears as a man, although [her friends] are allotted various names and different visible forms of a human and brute beasts. There is also sometimes more than one presiding demon. But if the person presented comes from the lower classes and the humblest social rank, the presiding demon scarcely deigns to speak, thinking that such a wretched person is unworthy of being received into that gathering – the sort of woman (says the presiding demon in his hoarse voice when he does begin to speak after a short pause), who could not carry out any notable crime or great evil in the world in obedience to the said presiding demon. At length, however, he is persuaded by her demon-carer and human instructor, and she is received into the assembly, and renounces God and Christ, the glorious Virgin, all the saints and their intercessions and protection, holy Mother Church and the sacraments. She renounces the Faith completely, and promises particularly not to go to church, not to take holy water and sprinkle it over herself when people can see, except in pretence, and, by way of protest, saying to herself, 'Monsieur, don't be annoyed',[92] (speaking to the demon). [She promises] not to confess in future, except in pretence, and especially not to confess about this damned sect, nor to look up at the consecrated Host when it is lifted up in the hands of the priest, except with the protestation, 'Monsieur, don't be annoyed', while spitting on the ground in contempt, provided she is not seen by those standing round her. The presiding demon also allows such a person to turn her back [on it], or throw holy water on the ground and stamp on it. Likewise, the presiding demon throws a cross on the ground, spits on it and scuffs his feet over it, or defiles it with his feet in contempt of Christ; and he teaches the novice] how to make an imperfect sign of the cross in future by jabbing herself under the chin. He also tells the person received [into the sect] in this way to bring the Body of Christ

---

90.　This terminology for witches' meetings was in use at least as far back as *c*.1180 when Walter Map employed it in his *De nugis curialium*, chap. 30 of heretics' assemblies. 'About the first watch of the night, when gates, doors, and windows have been shut, the groups sit waiting in silence in their respective synagogues, and a black cat of extraordinary size climbs down a rope which hangs in their midst'.

91.　That is, using her own mode of transport, not a magical one provided by a demon.

92.　These words now and later are in French in the text.

to a meeting, where it is defiled and trampled on by those taking part; and in contempt of the 'great Teacher of the World', as the presiding demon says, the newly received bares her backside and displays it to the sky.

After all this has been done as a preliminary, she falls on her knees, worships the demon and does homage, first by fervently kissing his hand or his foot and offering him a lighted candle made of black wax (usually handed to her by a demon-familiar called N), or some money. This candle is then extinguished by the presiding demon or those next to him. After this, the presiding demon turns round and the novice kisses him fervently on the backside, and then she gives him her soul which he is to have when she dies, although she swears unreservedly not to reveal this in a court of law. (Members of this sect confess this rarely and very unwillingly.) However, the demon, as I mentioned earlier, never does business or makes a pact, especially one which is clearly defined, unless he is given the soul, and as a deposit and as a sign and pledge that she does give [him] her soul, the novice gives him a part of her body – that is to say, a finger, hair or fingernails – quite often along with some of her blood because (as St Augustine says), the demon loves human blood which has been shed.

By way of recompense, the demon first gives some particular favour or special opportunity either of having money which he promises to give [her] and sometimes does give (since he knows where treasures are hidden and, with God's permission, has some of them at all events under his control, and because, by that same permission, he is a great thief: or he reveals the exact methods of squeezing the poor by plundering, usury and carefully calculated actions of that kind); or he grants the ability to enjoy sex with women or men; or he grants the favour of [being able] to cure quickly and in superstitious fashion, the demon himself, with the just permission of God always playing its part, sometimes working the cure. [This he does] quickly, secretly and unnoticed, either by removing impediments to health or by making use of some seeds from physical things, which bestow physical health and are breathed in with food or drink or via secret channels. [He can do this] because of the faithlessness and sins of those who are to be cured, who agree to it carelessly and, to the danger of their souls, treat divine and human assistance as though they were of secondary importance. Sometimes, too, the body in question for whom the cure is intended is on the point of getting well, and this then follows. But the demon does not work [this cure], although he had foreseen, by sharp-witted guesswork, that it would happen. Quite often, too, the demon fails to carry out his promises, and tells lies. He is a liar and so is his father. Sometimes he knows that the things which are applied [to the patient] are capable of effecting a cure and have the power to do so.

Instead of this, he may grant the power to avenge oneself on those one hates, by bestowing 'a wand of retribution' to bring death to them by this particular mean, a death the demon himself, with God's permission, administers to good and bad people at random; and he does this by applying things which do harm and bring death in the way [I said] earlier he used things to bring about a cure. But sometimes he fails to do what he has promised and tells lies, because that is what he wants or because God does not allow him [to do it]. Sometimes, too, as though he were using divination, he predicts, by sharp-witted guesswork, that a death will happen from a natural cause and providence, or from some misfortune, and on that occasion he is not the one who causes it.

He may grant the favour of being able to reveal things which are hidden and lost, or concealed, and of finding hidden treasures; or the power to resist four or five human attackers, or to attack and overcome the same number; or the favour of being able to foretell and predict the future in a way beyond common human [ability], especially anent the state of the weather – will it snow, be fine, rain, hail, thunder and pour down, etc.? The demon frequently speeds up these [changes], doing so (with God's permission) by causing things to rise, or applying a cloud and some kind of physical matter by moving [them] quickly from one place to another; and with this same permission, he can move and change bodies he has created so that things turn out as predicted, as if [they happened] in no time at all. The result is that he keeps hold of the people in his cursed sect, and they invariably hope in him; and for this reason he fulfils his promises – sometimes, at any rate. But quite often, because the demon is treacherous, deceptive and a liar and cannot do anything without God's permission – (and sometimes God does not permit him to do things of lesser consequence, whereas under different circumstances He allows him to do things of greater consequence) – he tricks people and deceives them, and does not fulfil their expectation and hope. For the most part, however, the clouds behave naturally and are arranged according to chance and the way they [happen] to turn out on that occasion.

He also grants the opportunity and weird and wonderful means of acquiring secular offices and lands, or ecclesiastical dignities and benefices, by flattery and simony, so that [his followers can] amass money or [fulfil] some other damnable purpose; or he promises [to give them] the ability to hold on to the favour of magnates, princes and important men by means of the love powders he hands out, or love drinks, so that [his followers] obtain whatever they demand from princes and control them for other reasons which will be explained later. For in this situation, the demon works indirectly, making one thing follow on from another. First he influences the lords' minds by interfering with their blood and humours; then he puts stimulants in their food, or (using methods I touched on earlier) he adds things which arouse that part [of their minds] concerned with sensation and things which propel them into ardent love of those people for whom [the demon] is working or to whom he is giving any kind of similar favour.

In addition to the forementioned favours, however, the presiding demon then gives something personal to the woman who is received into the assembly – an identifying trinket perceptible to the senses, such as a gold, copper or silver ring, or a thread, or a small paper scroll with unknown letters painted on it, or some such thing – and because of the favour [the demon] has granted, if [the novice] touches someone with it, or makes use of it, it has an effect. Moreover, generally speaking, in addition to the two particular forementioned gifts, he promises the novice every good thing in abundance, and [says] he is never absent and [never] fails in his support, especially if he is invoked in [a moment] of necessity, (although the truth is he often fails in the moment of necessity because he is a liar and a deceiver, and because God justly does not allow him to be present all the time.) In particular, he does not come to assist when it is time for such a person to be taken into custody by the law, and he does not come to help when she is [actually] arrested, either. He is able to do nothing for her at that moment, although sometimes the demon appears in visible form to those locked up in prison and talks to them. Consider this, Reader: the demon, when invoked, is often present for Waldensians when they are at liberty, in order to keep them in the sect, and he frequently thrusts himself upon them, even when he has not been invoked. Consequently, all Waldensians are invokers of demons, although they often deny it.

Repeatedly, as though he were a preacher or something of the kind, he persuades the novice and those who are present at any of the meetings that (as he says), they may tell any kind of lie and, as scholars, proclaim falsely to preachers in the [real] world that there is no other god except their prince, Lucifer, who is God on high; that they themselves are gods and immortal; that the human soul crumbles away with the body, like that of a dog and of any animal; and that after death there is neither hot nor cold, delight or suffering, Paradise or Hell. The only Paradise (so he says), is the one he shows them in his meetings where every sensual pleasure is had at his nod of command; and during such a meeting at which those who are present feast and have a good time, men go from woman to woman in search of pleasure, and women go from man to man in similar fashion. Nothing they need is lacking.

After he has said this, the presiding demon leaves his lofty seat which is raised above the ground in front of everyone else and situated at the head of the congregation. He drags the novice to a place in a wood so that he can embrace her after his fashion and know her carnally. But, out of malice, he tells her she must take up a position facing the ground on her hands and feet, otherwise he cannot copulate with her. Whatever shape the presiding demon adopts, the novice touches his penis which, she discovers, is cold and soft (as, quite often, is his whole body). Then he goes into her, first by the natural entry, leaving behind rotten yellow sperm which he has caught from a nocturnal emission or from some other source, and secondly by the place of expelling waste, and thus abuses her in irregular fashion, whereby the novice commits a sin against Nature with the demon. Afterwards, the presiding demon goes back to his seat and the novice crosses [the floor] to sit with the other men and women who do not sit in a circle, but in long drawn-out rings,[93] some face to face, others back to back, others face to back.

Sometimes the novice makes her way to the dances[94] which are done there in every respect like those in the [real] world, but with greater liveliness; and she is really and truly there, not in dream or imagination (i.e. with someone standing in for her or in the form of some illusory figure), but in body and soul – just like, it must be said, the rest of those who are present. Living and fully awake, there stand nearby people who play the harp, drummers, actors, etc., and sometimes

---

93. Reading *ringas* or *rengas* for *reugas*.
94. *Ad tripudia.* The *tripudium* was a ritual dance consisting of three steps forward and one back.

there are cooks to prepare the food, as well. Before she eats, the novice may go to copulate with some man, or she may stay in her seat until the meal is over. [At this point][95] the presiding demon sometimes touches the earth or a tree with his stick and napkins appear on the ground.(But sometimes they have been brought beforehand by people coming to the meetings, or by demons.) There is meat and fish in abundance there, and quite often the flesh of a roasted calf, and red and white wine in jugs, earthenware vessels, water flasks and earthenware pots. They dine in fine style, enjoy themselves (sometimes to excess) and amuse themselves at table by conversation, any man with any woman. The demons, too, pretend to eat and give the appearance of doing so (though not very often), and it is well enough known by those who attend regularly by what means they eat.

Note, Reader, that there are three types of food there – or things which appear to be food – and the same may be said of what they drink. The best food has been donated to them by Waldensians, fetched from their own homes and brought there by demons, or secretly fetched from all over the place and put at their disposal by demons (with God's permission); or food which seems to be real has been brought by Waldensians on their journey to the meeting; or thirdly, food which is not what it appears to be because the eyes have been subject to trickery (just as sometimes demons give real money and sometimes apparent). At the same time, demons make what appears to be wine out of beer or water, and [similarly] with meat and fish. Frequently while they feast, a large number of male and female devils serves them at table and then, when [the diners] have finished eating, the candles (if there are any), are extinguished, the presiding demon issues a command that each man do his duty, and each man drags his [woman] to one side and knows her carnally. Sometimes unspeakable departures [from the norm] are committed during the exchanges of women at the command of the presiding demon while they are going from woman to woman and from man to man. [This involves] the unnatural abuse of women, one after another, and similarly of men abusing each other, or a man's [abusing] a woman by not using the vessel he should, but another part [of her] instead. Waldensians say they derive as much or indeed more pleasure from this, and that they are more potent and burn with greater lust than in the [real] world, because the demon sets their body afire and because of the powders and other stimulants the demons put in their food and drink with a view to inflaming and heating the passions which make them burn with carnal lust, so that [thus] they may be the more enticed and inclined to keep holding their assemblies because of the greater pleasure and licence with which they have sex there. (Yet a man experiences no enjoyment with a female devil, neither does a woman with a [male] demon. They agree to copulate out of fear and obedience.)

Afterwards, they return to the triple dance, and once that is over the presiding demon reminds the assembly of the precepts and prohibitions I mentioned earlier, along with others I shall list below. He says that if they keep his commandments, they will never lack anything they desire and need, and that he will not let them be arrested by the law. If, however, it turns out otherwise, he says (by way of

95.   This I take to be the sense of *itaque* here, since a bald 'therefore' does not seem to fit.

an example), 'N from this assembly was arrested because he did not obey me in every particular';[96] and if any of them have been delivered to the fire by sentence of the law [while they are] on the road to salvation (which is very rare indeed), he says they died because they did not observe his commandments, and then in a frightening manner he thunders, threatening them with death if they do not painstakingly observe his commandments. But if they died a natural death [while they were] on the road to perdition, or were impenitent (as quite often happens), he announces their death with greater restraint, as though he were happy. After this, he repeats his former precepts and adds some new ones as follows.

(i)   As earlier, they are not to confess or speak to priests.
(ii)   They are not to speak to each other in the [real] world about this sect of theirs, but keep it absolutely secret.
(iii)   So that the law will take no notice of them, they should make it generally known that [their meetings] are dreams and fantasies.
(iv)   If the law arrests any of them and realizes the actual reality and truth, they should not turn a blind eye or allow these [people] to go away unpunished. Those who have not been arrested should whip up rumours and popular calls for them to be burned quickly. [This is] to stop them from accusing others, and also so that the demon may the more quickly drag to Hell the souls of those who have been arrested, and thrust them into it – something he is waiting to do.
(v)   He enjoins [upon them] most particularly that if they are arrested by the law, they be willing to choose to die rather than accuse any of their accomplices, and [he says that] if they do this, the demon himself will come to their aid and they will not die. (They promise the demon and the rest of their accomplices at the meeting to fulfil this to the letter.)
(vi)   They are to prepare and bring to the meeting as many people as they can so that they may get more for the demons, otherwise they will be severely flogged, as they are when they fail to obey his other instructions. (Sometimes they suffer worse things because the demons flog them with cows' sinews, or they are stabbed with shoemakers' awls or [beaten] with sticks which the demon has near him.)
(vii)   As earlier, they are not to confess they have given their soul to the demon.
(viii) They must frequently and willingly come back and return to the meetings as often as they are given notice of them.
(ix)   They should not be present when Waldensians are burned.
(x)   They are to promise they will not reveal in any way their acts of harmful magic [when they are] in a court of law.

After this, he tells them the time and place of the next meeting, and once this is done, as I said earlier, they say goodbye to the presiding demon and go back home, sometimes on foot if it is nearby. But more often they anoint their brooms or sticks or straws, mount them and go back home very quickly, carried by the

---

96.   N is designated masculine in the Latin text.

demon through the lowest part of the middle region of the air. Note, Reader, that because of the violent, rapid motion, they experience hunger on the way back, quite often even after they have had a good meal. [This may also happen] because of their great physical exertion and jolting and weariness from having sex and dancing after eating, and thirdly, because of their journey through a very cold place where their natural heat is drawn back to a single spot inside them in order to effect digestion by surrounding and compressing [the stomach] when the surrounding cold is near it.

During her second meeting, however, the female novice is known carnally by her demon-familiar and carer in the way [she was known] on the previous occasion by the presiding demon. He does not have sex with her in any of the subsequent meetings unless there are too few men to accomplish the copula-tions – (and for the most part there are more women there than men) – because demons take the place of men in the copulations, just as sometimes (but rarely), when there are fewer women than men, female devils make up the deficiency. So quite often in meetings other than the first two, the first time the female novice comes back after her [initial] reception into the congregation, she is known carnally by the presiding demon and a male novice[97] is known carnally by a female devil who drags him to one side before he sits with the others; and in the second [of these subsequent meetings], he is likewise known carnally by a female devil after the offertory which all members of the congregation make at every meeting. Occasionally (but not at all often), it is found that a man adopts the top position during sex with a female devil. This is a sign of very great wickedness in him. Likewise, at every meeting. a woman always has a man or a demon.

Be aware that some meeting is held almost every night in that area[98] or region, and sometimes [meetings are held] that same night in separate woods or localities, although not every single member of the sect from that area comes to the meetings every single night. They attend less frequently, [but] come at least once a fortnight, sometimes coming from another area and very distant parts. On a busy night, as happened last year on the eve of St Martin in winter,[99] at one and the same place and at one and the same time there were (and it was possible for there to have been), several presiding demons and several meetings – for example, the meeting of Guillaume Tonnoir in the shape of a black man, [which took place] in the wood of Neufvirelle, and that in Tabary [where he was] in the shape of a dog and a bull, etc. – and men and women were wandering from one meeting to another. Meetings happen more frequently at night, after 11 p.m. Meetings which take place during the day are not so frequent, although they are held at every season of the year, just as are those which are held at night. People who come from far away are brought and taken back high in the air by demons. Those who live close by are rarely brought this way, although sometimes they are; but no one sees them, sometimes because the demon puts obstacles in the

97.	Supplying *vir receptus* which appears to be missing from the text.
98.	*Patria*. In these contexts the word refers to the district in which someone was born and in which he or she has lived since birth or childhood.
99.	I.e. Martinmas, 11 November.

way [of their being seen] – just as on occasion those at the meeting are not seen by those who are coming to it, although now and then they are heard – and sometimes because of the amazing speed at which they move. They might be able to see those who are on the point of departure if they were there, but [participants] leave from a hidden place when no one is present except the demon who is present to them and not to others. Those who live nearby more often come by day and go home on foot. (Note at this point that the demons have the same names as the people who come from the locality in which they find themselves.)

From what has been said so far, and quite apart from the acts of harmful magic which I describe later on, and their many perjuries in front of the judges during interrogation (because they don't care about perjuring themselves and drawing down curses upon themselves and swearing on a stack of Bibles),[100] it is clear that, because of their essential nature and formal profession of belief and reception into their congregation, these Waldensians are apostates from the Faith, idolaters and guilty of the crime of treason against God; that they have an openly expressed pact with the demon, and have a demon-familiar; that they are invokers of demons and behave in a disgusting fashion contrary to Nature with demons in various shapes of humans and animals; and that sometimes,[101] apart from this, if they bring others to the meeting, as they promise (a promise which, in fact, they do all alike fulfil), they are considered to be prime movers and zealous members of that cursed sect of Waldensians. So it follows they are, male and female, idolaters. Furthermore, it is clear that all Waldensians commit the same crimes equal [in magnitude] in that assembly of theirs, because they have one and the same form of professing [their belief] and a similar mode of behaviour in Waldensian assemblies, especially in their own locality, although some carry out more acts of harmful magic [*maleficia*] than others because, as is to be expected, Waldensians have existed for quite a long time, or rather, they have given themselves to the demon and have been abandoned by God.

Section 4: The acts of harmful magic which they, as a group, carry out by order of the demon whom they obey because sometimes they work together to fulfil their wicked desires

More than anything else, they obey him in every situation out of fear, since the demon is carrying out divine justice. They also commit many crimes because they are incited to do so by their human instructor. They burn houses and homesteads and set fire to those belonging people they know, people they don't know and people they haven't heard of, and to those of good people and of bad indiscriminately, with God's just permission, in order to test the patience of the good or for some reason hidden from us and known particularly to God alone. At the demon's prompting, they cause frequent and very great loss and destruction to the farm property – vines, for example, corn and meadows, etc. – of people they know and people they don't know. [They do this] by casting into the wind

---

100. *Iurando supra modum.* I have used this modern expression to convey the force of the original.

101. Reading *interdum esse* instead of *interdum sese.*

certain powders they have been given by the demon or their human instructor or which they have made themselves. (Information about this appears in court proceedings.) Once these [powders] have been thrown up this way, or because Nature has arranged clouds in order to cause such an outcome, [clouds] are brought near [the earth] by the demon's action [in moving them] from one place to another, or the demon stirs up some vaporous matter which rises and appears as if in an instant, whereupon a whirlwind mixed with hail, frost or some kind of storm grows up from below, and for that reason the fruits of the earth are damaged and dried out.[102]

They acquire consecrated Hosts for themselves on Easter Sunday or on other days. After making feigned confession,[103] they come to the altar with a very great show and sign of outward devotion during Masses they have had said, or else they take the Host from their mouth which they cover with a towel, and transfer it from one hand to the other and then into their sleeve. They take these Hosts home to give to toads which they rear in earthenware pots, and which they kill to make their ointments (mixing them with certain other things which are recorded in court proceedings). These ointments are made to take them to meetings – not that the ointments themselves have power to transport people, but that by order of the demon people arrive at such a great state of moral ruin that, in contemptible fashion, they give God, their Creator, Saviour and Redeemer, to a creature which people commonly think of as rather worthless and abominable. So the demon induces people to carry out such execrable sacrilege and such a colossal crime; because after those hungry toads have eaten the consecrated Hosts, their blood is drawn to make a compound of blood. Afterwards, the toads themselves are burned and reduced to powder for the same purpose – so that one person may have the method and procedure of instructing another how to do this. For it is the demon who, sometimes but not very often visible to humans throughout the whole journey, transports them to meetings. (More frequently, he is invisible for the whole journey, although [he may be] visible on the way back.) Neither the anointed besoms nor the sticks have power to transport [people], but this kind of procedure is followed so that once people arrive at an agreement, one man may have the method and procedure of instructing another and bringing him to the synagogue and assembly, and the demon may work in greater secrecy and transport people under [cover of] the form of those perceptible signs.

They procure and administer revenge and death against those they hate, using the 'wand of retribution' or something else given to them by the demon, in the way I described earlier; and midwives especially, since they belong to the sect, kill many infants before they have been baptized by throttling them, etc.,[104] as indeed

---

102. Presumably this means they are drained of their nourishing qualities, but it is an odd verb to use in conjunction with hail and storm.

103. The Latin makes it clear that this refers to both men and women.

104. *Stringendo*. This refers, among other things, to drawing something tight, and one of the simplest ways of dispatching new-born babies would be to strangle them with the umbilical cord. Sixteenth-century cases show that children only a few hours old might be

when priests belong to the sect, they too commit many faults [while celebrating] the sacraments of the Church. Waldensian men and women do the same either by driving pins or needles into [the infant's] brain, or binding fast the tender parts of their body, or by other well-tried methods, such as secretly drawing off blood by opening up the [babies'] umbilical cord or getting it some other way, in order to make their ointments by mixing it with [other ingredients]. Sometimes they bring to their meetings the bodies of infants they have already roasted, [ready] for eating – (this is clear from some of the records of legal proceedings from the area round Leiden in particular) – or [they bring] the infants to be roasted during their meetings.

They practise many sorceries [*sortilegia*] or acts of harmful magic [*maleficia*] and witchcraft [*fascinaciones*] by means of love powders or drinks or love tufts given to then by the demon, or Nicart bread,[105] or some such thing; and they cause a very large number of poisonings.

They poison wells and streams in a more or less similar way, and (to be brief), perpetrate disgraceful enormities without number which this document cannot deal with at length; and in any case it is not necessary to disclose them all.

Section 5. The various opinions of Waldensians about Paradise, Hell and the immortality of the soul

Some Waldensians admit that the soul is immortal and that Paradise and Hell last for ever, but when it comes to many other things which are grave sins, according to them in the false way they think, sins do not exist. Thus, they don't think they sin by going to a meeting and doing what they do there, principally because their forebears who, they believe, had a good reputation among their contemporaries, thought this way and passed it on to them. Others think that what the presiding demon urges upon them is true – namely, that a person's soul dies with his or her body, that neither Paradise nor Hell exists, etc.; and if they are questioned and reply in this way and persist in their stubborn [replies], they should be regarded as heretics. A third group, like the first, thinks that the soul is immortal and that Paradise and Hell [last for ever]. But they are impenitent, have no hope, are obstinate and obdurate and care nothing about [their] salvation even though they know they are committing a very grave sin, and it is enough for them that, however long they live, they enjoy physical pleasures to the full and live in a way which will give them fun, sensual pleasure and self-satisfaction. They also say that if they don't go to one place (that is, Paradise), they'll go to another. A fourth group thinks that the soul is immortal, that Paradise and Hell exist, and that they do commit grave sins, but hope to repent and confess in the

---

stabbed, strangled or allowed to bleed to death because the umbilical cord was not tied off. See M. Wiesner, 2004, 'Early modern midwifery: a case study' in E. van Teijlingen, G. Lewis, P. McCaffery, M. Porter (eds.), *Midwifery and the Medicalization of Childbirth: Comparative Perspectives* (New York: Nova Science Publishers), p. 71.

105. *Houppellos amatorios.* If *houppellus* is the Latinized form of 'houppel', it refers to a tuft or pompom such as might be worn in a hat. *Gastellum = wastellum*, bread of cake made from very fine flour. 'Nicart' seems to be a family name.

end before they die. They are, however, deceived because quite often they are overtaken by death or decide to get themselves ready much too late, [and so these] Waldensians die like the rest of them.

Section 6. Formal interrogation with torture in the case of indicted Waldensians[106]

After gentle admonitions and salutary exhortations, etc., which accord with both law and reason, when the accused keep on denying what they have done, with oaths and perjuries, as they are almost always accustomed to do, not to make use of formal interrogation with torture, by means of which one can get something from them, [if] only in general terms, would be nothing other than to wipe out this business and bury it, prevent its being brought to light, along with what stems from it, show favour to the demon and treat the true and living God with contempt. What is more, it would be openly to encourage this damned sect which is excessively secretive and keeps itself well hidden, as is clear from what I have said earlier. Nor can this family of demons be driven out except by torture and formal interrogation. So those who procure a cessation of torture and harsh interrogation in this business – and by 'harsh', I mean that which stops short of death and mutilation, [or] loss or crippling of limbs, [inflicted] because of the unusual nature of the case – are strongly suspected of [belonging to] the sect because they try to put obstacles in the way of one's duty to investigate – for which they should be considered excommunicate. In all likelihood they are afraid of being accused and implicitly excuse themselves from their duty before that happens. Consequently, it is quite clear that when they excuse themselves like this, they accuse themselves as well. The unusual nature of the case demands unusual forms of torture because during torture and formal interrogation an unusual struggle is taking place – not against the human being but against the demon whose word is law among Waldensians, who have justly been abandoned by God because they have unjustly abandoned God, the Maker, etc.; and it is [the demon] who suggests and gives replies as though he were speaking in them, the way the Holy Spirit used to speak in the Apostles when they spoke to kings and princes after the Holy Spirit had been sent to them in tongues of fire.

Now, the demon, who is sometimes visible to those who have been interrogated and tortured [*questionatis*], although the people standing nearby cannot see him, or who is invisible to both parties, also impedes their tongue, the entrance to their throat and the other parts of the body which give shape to the voice – sometimes, in the opinion of assistants, perceptibly and visibly – by diverting them and turning them aside in another direction. He assists them

---

106. *De quaestione et tortura*. The sixteenth-century French jurist Jacques Cajus, who was particularly well-known for his summaries of Justinian's *Digest* and *Codex*, defined 'quaestio' as *interrogatio quae fit per tormenta*, 'interrogation which takes place through torture'. 'Quaestio' is thus the whole judicial process of such interrogation, and '*tortura*' the actual infliction of pain by various methods. Hence I have chosen to translate the combined phrase, which appears frequently in this document, as 'formal interrogation with torture'.

a great deal, because he has remarkable power over them when they belong, so to speak, entirely to him. He stops them from speaking so that he may not lose his reward if they make a complete confession of their situation and accuse others, especially if they accuse important people who commit greater crimes in obedience to the demon and, with his authority and active encouragement, promote this damned sect. When it comes to this case, real benefit and advantage comes when they open up in a really satisfactory way, above all and principally when they accuse important people, because the result of punishing a few men and women of the lowest social class is simply to warn the faithful belonging to that class or to a similar category not to join that sect. Waldensians of lower or higher social rank, however, are not genuinely freed from error thereby, because of the character of that damned sect. Once they have given themselves to it, fear and the demon's threats prevent them from repudiating it and, except on very rare occasions and almost, as it were, by a miracle, they do not return to the bosom of the Church of their own accord unless they are arrested by the law; and for the most part, under those circumstances, Waldensians hold out to the end because they relapse or for some other reason, wherever they may go. This [whole] situation is very unusual. As a result, almost everything which distinguishes it [from other cases] is unusual and one does not find [these distinguishing characteristics] in any other situation. But if important people are left untouched, the demon will ascribe this to his assistance and the Waldensians themselves will ascribe it to the help the demon has given, bring more people to the sect, carry out more serious acts of wickedness, and thus, as time goes on, that wicked, vile sect will be the more increased.

Section 7: How much accusations of other people, made by Waldensians themselves, are worth

Suppose that accusations [obtained] not only during torture, but also outwith torture and formal interrogation have been upheld and ratified, and that they have come entirely from Waldensians themselves who have deponed without having words put into their mouth by leading questions or by any other method, just the way things should be done – (because they should not be asked leading questions at all, and nor should any words be put in their mouth); and suppose the accusations are affected by circumstances, spring from many accidents of time and place, and from signs of the accused person's [guilt] – (and specifying the role played by the accused person, and naming names, along with evidence regarding their carnal behaviour, would add greatly to the value of the accusation) – such accusations, I say, are of great importance. Moreover, no one who has had a great deal of experience [in these matters] and no one who has read the relevant literature has, for the most part, come across false accusations levelled out of hatred for the accused persons, or out of any excess of emotion, etc. This, perceptive judges can find out while they are collecting evidence and conducting their interrogations, because they accuse only those members of the sect who are guilty, for reasons I shall give at once. For example, not long ago there was an 'abbot of small judgement'[107] who, according to what he used to say, had an immense hatred for one particular man who lived in Tournai. [This man] had deprived him of his wife over a period of 22 years, [but] although the 'abbot' longed for the other man's death more than his own, he always said the man was not a member of this sect and that he would not accuse him [of being one]. One finds the same kind of thing with regard to others in the trial records and confessions of Waldensians. Therefore, given the existence of the suppositions I mentioned earlier, their accusations carry a lot of weight and have a great deal of force, except when it comes to concurrence about the nature of their carnal behaviour, because Waldensians are very restrained when it comes to making accusations and they always do so unwillingly and as little as possible.

But even if they are held [in custody] for a year, they will not accuse everyone they know or give a complete account of their situation. What is more, they knowingly, to their own damnation, keep to themselves many things about themselves and others and choose to confess their own situation and die rather than accuse others, thereby damnably preserving, as far as this matter is concerned, the utmost loyalty to the demon and their associates. We had an example recently in Hontmelle, otherwise known as 'Lechat'.[108] Without torture, and of his own free will and accord, he confessed what he had done, and although he was interrogated harshly,[109] to persuade him to accuse others, he was not willing to accuse anyone, even though in all likelihood he was acquainted with many [members] of the sect. Thus every day one finds that some people have difficulty in accusing others. They are very restrained when it comes to accusing other people, principally because of the promise not to bring accusations, which they made to the presiding demon during their assembly and to other associates, not only those who are members of the assembly, but people [they meet] every day in the [real] world. They are also further deflected[110] from accusing some individuals because of the great friendship they have with them, one established by kinship, or because of an act of kindness which has gone without recompense, or because they have daily contact with them, or because they have had sex with them, etc. [They are also very restrained in accusing] some people because of fear, especially when it comes to important people, in case accusing them, as the demon suggests, brings about their own death. [So] they either make themselves liable to threats from people if they accuse them, or they think (correctly) that if they accuse them, they draw these people's attention [to them] out of hope and the promise of help in escaping death. They also think and hope that, even in these circumstances, they are obliged to associate with those people in the [real] world, and hope to return to the assembly; and this is how they are afraid of the

107. Hansen (p. 99) suggests that *abbas parvi passus* should be understood as *abbas parvi sensus*, and points to a contemporary case (9 May 1460), involving Jehan Tannoye, described in the records of the Netherlands' inquisition as an 'abbé de pau de sens' which is a phrase also written in the margin of this text. The reason for the nickname is obscure.

108. Or perhaps 'Le Chat'.

109. *Questionatus aspere*. The phrase implies that torture was used at this point in the proceedings. See the author's earlier remarks on 'harsh' interrogation, supra 83–84.

110. Reading *dimoventur* for *dimonentur*.

demon and human beings. They are also devoted to that sect because it fulfils their desires, etc.

Secondly, because the demon prevents them, in the way I explained in the section immediately before this, from accusing them, lest he lose his reward, he particularly prevents them from accusing important people who are obedient to him in greater evils. Accordingly, because of these points, accusations against important people are more potent and of greater force than [those] against lesser individuals, although on the other hand the more notable and important [members of society] should be given greater consideration than those from the lowest ranks of the commons. The demon is not much bothered if Waldensians who have confessed their situation die. Indeed, he wishes, rather, that they will die quickly so that he may have their souls. But, with very great guile and malice, [and using] the power he has over them, he prevents them from accusing [anyone] except those already in prison or a few other [members] of their sect who are in a similar condition. So to solve this problem, people with practical experience of this particular situation, men of zeal and good judgement, have the power, as before, to imprison and question etc. very forcibly[111] persons of the lowest social classes as a result of only one accusation which has taken into account the circumstances of the crime; and, so they tell us, [the solution] appears to be foolproof, as recent experience in this place shows in the cases of Denisette, against whom there was a single accusation, 'the abbot', Colette Lestrevée, Jehanne d'Auvergne, Belotte Moucharde and a number of other people.

One must always bear in mind the unusual nature of this situation in which only accomplices can be witnesses or accusers, because this business is carefully concealed and extremely well hidden. One should also take great care, when Waldensians accuse themselves and others, to put everything in writing, especially all accused individuals, along with the circumstances and the evidence given by both parties regarding carnal behaviour, for the sake of agreement and concurrence [between this accusation] and others. Those doing the interrogating should not say anything which will give those being interrogated the opportunity of excusing anyone since, at the demon's prompting and because of the promise they made to him, they are inclined to excuse others and ask nothing more than to excuse them, for the reasons given above. Once they have started to confess and accuse themselves and other people, they should be heard without formal questioning as far as possible; and during interrogation, one person only should speak and ask questions while this is going on, because Waldensians under interrogation are very keen either to ramble about things other than the business in hand or to have more than one person speak with them.

While they are accusing others or themselves, few people should be present, except virtuous men of trustworthy zeal, because [Waldensians] are afraid of a crowd, either of people new to them and people they do not know or of their friends whom they would otherwise accuse. When they begin to confess their situation and to make accusations, they should be examined carefully about their

---

111. *Questionare etc. maxime.* The 'etc.' combined with *questionare* strongly suggests the use of torture.

own situation and their accusations of other people in a single sitting if possible, because otherwise, on the next occasion, it will be found that the demon (or human beings) has caused them to cry off and change their minds, unless forethought has been given to their prisons. [The reason for this is that] if the prison guard is well disposed towards the subject and a virtuous man of upright character, he can do much to bring him or them[112] to a true confession of his situation and induce him to accuse other people. If he is hostile, he can be a complete nuisance by visiting them, bringing the necessities of life over and over again (or supplying them), warning them gently [of the dangers of] confessing the truth, or diverting[113] them from telling the truth, or inducing them to deny what they earlier confessed. Be aware, Reader, that one should not hope or look for them to accuse others when they are at the point of death. What is more, at the point of death, in obedience to the demon, Waldensians unjustly excuse those whom they earlier accused, [although] these excuses are not taken seriously at all by men who are sound and reliable, because [Waldensians] have, quite often at the point of death, made a most particular promise (in accordance with the suggestion and promise I touched on earlier when dealing with all promises to a demon), to act and behave in such a way – unjustly, for example – with respect to the purposes I shall mention later, that they fall into mortal sin, disavow their situation at the point of death and deny it, saying that everything they had said [stemmed] from the violence of torture, etc.

Section 8: Accusations made by Waldensians about their accomplices should not be treated with contempt because several people say that in Waldensian assemblies, demons can take the appearance and form even of innocent people who have no personal experience or knowledge of that sect

In the first place, Waldensians who attend assemblies do not accuse demons (whom they know by name, such as the presiding demon, demon-familiars or demon-inciters to wrongdoing), who appear in human form and wait at table, or sit to be intimate with others; nor do they accuse people they see during an assembly, who are otherwise completely unknown to them and whose names they do not know. Therefore they accuse only those they know are human beings and who are known to them apart from [the fact that] they see them in a meeting. For when they accuse them, it follows they do not only know them by sight from a meeting (otherwise they would accuse everyone who attended), but also that they have seen them in the [real] world; and when they accuse them by name, they know them not only from seeing them at a meeting or in the [real] world, but also from listening to them and having a conversation with them or about them, and sometimes from having had sex with them in the [real] world or during a meeting or both, or from social intercourse and close friendship with them in the [real] world or at an assembly, or because they first took them to the sect and its meeting or were taken there by them, because instructor and pupil quite often go to and come back from a meeting at the same time.

---

112. I.e. the Waldensian under suspicion. Both 'him' and 'them' are masculine in the Latin text, although 'them' may not necessarily be gender-specific.

113. Reading *dimovendo* for *dimonendo*.

In the second place, Waldensians bring assured accusations against people they know only from a meeting, because they know their names, the towns they come from, etc., either from hearing them, or from meeting [those individuals], or from habitual association with them; and they do not accuse demons whom they know by name only because they have heard them during a meeting, or because they have met [the demons] or have had frequent association with them at a meeting where [the demons] appear in human form. Therefore it is significant that they accuse only human beings, and that they genuinely and assuredly differentiate and distinguish between humans and demons, men and male devils, and women and female devils, as I shall make clear later on.

Now, if those people who rest their case on scorning accusations made by Waldensians about other accomplices, bring forward precedents because there are plenty of precedents in books, let them deign and undertake to quote the book and the passage in which those precedents first and originally appear, so that one can see their objective and purpose in referring [to them], along with other considerations and particular circumstances; and when, by the grace of God, a response will be given to any precedent you like, sufficient and specific [enough] to satisfy anyone who demands an explanation, every person will see clearly that those specimens have no place in the situation of a Waldensian assembly in such a way that [those people] can or should depreciate or belittle accusations made by Waldensians about their accomplices. For demons, with God's permission, can look like human beings in any situation in order to deceive them, and erudite men, especially those learned in interpretation of the Scriptures, know how this is possible. Distinguished teachers study it in some detail in their books, too, and more particularly (and at length) the holy teacher St Thomas Aquinas in the first part of his *Summa*.[114]

But in the case and situation of Waldensians, the possibility that [demons] take on the appearance and likeness of complete human beings does not have precedent, as far as learned, circumspect and reliable judges are concerned – not in such a way that [people] can or should pour scorn on the accusations made by [Waldensians] about their accomplices, as what follows will show more clearly in greater detail. It is easy to see this from the confessions and trial records of Waldensians, because Waldensians clearly recognize and distinguish actual, real men from demons and female devils from women. So if such an assumption of [human] appearance were to take place there, it would be detected by the men and women standing nearby, and the person who is writing this has not seen or heard any Waldensian after interrogation who would not genuinely and clearly recognize from many indications the distinction and difference between a real woman and a female devil, and likewise between a man and a male devil.

So if those people who want to appeal to precedents they claim to have (that demons in those assemblies take on the likeness of human beings of more than one sex), are ignorant of the literature and are [thereby] the less fitted to

---

114. *Summa Theologiae*, written between 1265 and 1274, the year of St Thomas's death. In 1a.114.4, responsio 2, he notes that '[a demon] can fabricate from air a body of any shape or form so that when he assumes it, he appears visibly in it'.

speak about such matters, in addition to being afraid that in making assertions with evil intention concerning things about which they are ignorant they incur excommunication (because that is what they face when they impede the duty of the holy Inquisition and its benefit [to society]), they do none the less come within the scope, come up against and blunder into the article of faith, 'the holy Catholic Church', etc.,[115] [an article] to which they should have adhered and with which they should have agreed in all obedience, humility, fear and devoutness of faith, keeping their intellect prisoner in obedience to the Faith and acquiescing in the judgement and decision of Holy Church.

For since the Catholic Church (which is believed not to err, since she is directed by the Holy Spirit and by an infallible creed, especially in those things which affect the Faith) rightly thinks and justly and reasonably leads [others] to think that people of both sexes should be punished on account of these assemblies of Waldensians in many areas of Christendom and on account of the outrageous crimes committed during them, and proceeds against members of such assemblies who have been indicted, such people should have directed themselves to those who listen to Waldensians while they are talking, and formulate the legal proceedings [against them]. Moreover, if the kind of people who make use of precedents think they are learned, let them use their eyes and look, on the one hand at the confessions and trial records of Waldensians, let them listen to [Waldensians] as they speak and let them weigh everything in the balance of discrimination and correct judgement; and on the other hand, let them look at what they claim are precedents dealing with the possibility of taking on other appearances [described] in the books in which they first appear, with every attendant circumstance, and secondly at the treatises and books of learned men, more especially the treatise and topic 'The Discernment of Spirits':[116] and if they have any sense, they will [then] be silent and put a guard on their mouth and a door surrounding their lips.[117] But if, with a hard heart, they unreasonably endeavour to maintain their opinion, one may come to the same conclusion about them as one does about unlearned individuals in the past, and it will be easy for a man learned in the Scriptures and experienced in this matter to satisfy them fully and [provide] an explanation to anyone who demands it.

But notice, Reader, that quite often when those who claim there are precedents relating to this in the matter [we are discussing] do have treatises by the finest scholars and men of experience, they are either adherents of the sect of Waldensians or they have been suborned and induced into making those claims

---

115. A reference to the Bull *Unam Sanctam*, issued by Pope Boniface VIII on 18 November 1302.

116. *De discrecione spirituum*. There were several scholars who tried to deal with this problem of how to tell the difference between a genuine divine or angelic vision and one which stemmed from Satan or an evil spirit disguised as a saint or angel. See further N. Caciola, 2003, *Discerning Spirits: Divine and Demonic Possession in the Middle Ages* (Ithaca and London: Cornell University Press), pp. 17–8, 315–19.

117. A direct reference to Psalms 140.3 (Vulgate) = 141.3 (Authorized Version): 'Set a watch, o Lord, to my mouth and keep the door of my lips'. Translations tend to ignore the *circumstancie* which accompanies *ostium* ('door').

by their accomplices; and these accomplices have a sure demonstration of the truth which they impugn, because although on an earlier occasion out of deliberate, premeditated malice they would say that [Waldensians' experiences] were dreams and fantasies, once they have been proved wrong by the obvious truth, they take refuge (at length to their own confusion), in saying that an angel of Satan can transform himself into an angel of light. Well now, as is pretty well agreed from the trial records and confessions of Waldensians, there are male and female devils in those assemblies. But to say there are no men or women there is to come up against the incompatibility which I mentioned earlier, namely, '[our] holy Mother, the Catholic Church', etc.[118]

It is, moreover, rashly to proclaim what no one can know unless it has been revealed to him; and in addition, it is irrational and meaningless to say that only demons congregate dressed in the bodies of more than one sex without intending to deceive human beings and without humans' being present. That living, actual, real human beings of both sexes are there is clear from the trial records and confessions of Waldensians themselves; nor would anyone alive, unless he were a Waldensian and had had experience of [the assembly] or had seen Waldensians' confessions and trial records in actuality and in books, know how to make up and invent such a confession as a single unlearned Waldensian gives. Moreover, who cannot say and affirm it is true that some men and women, and demons in the form of other people, are really and personally present in those assemblies, unless he is one of their accomplices or it has been revealed to him? Nor is it plausible to believe that God would allow demons to take on the appearance of any innocent people so that [these innocents] would be punished as though they were members of the sect. For in such a case, if it were taken to be the truth, one devoutly believes that God would reveal the truth to the judges or would grant them to recognize it through inspiration, lest an innocent person be punished for belonging to the sect.[119] As well as this, in that particular situation or one which might possibly happen, by means of the confessions of Waldensians and their trial records with all their attendant circumstances, judges would sagaciously arrive with certainty at the conclusion that male and female devils were present at these meetings, not [demons] in the guise of innocent human beings, because (as I have said earlier), Waldensians who frequent such assemblies would in fact distinguish between a woman and a female devil, regardless of which woman's likeness the female devil might be assuming, and likewise in the case of a man and a male devil.

No matter how many people accused Jehanne d'Auvergne, they always said it was a male devil who sat next to her and had sex with her, and Jehanne herself confessed that during the meetings she had had only a male devil for sex. Likewise in other trial records, other Waldensians sometimes assign male and female devils to the roles of sexual partner, distinguishing between men

---

118. I.e. Pope Boniface's Bull.

119. The Latin says 'lest an innocent member *of the sect* be punished for belonging to the sect', which does not make sense in context. I have therefore omitted the first *de secta* and translated accordingly.

and male devils, and women and female devils. Notice, Reader, that accepting this as true, even if it is possible, unless there were general agreement on the subject, would be to pour scorn on the entire truth of this business and prevent every fruitful result which can follow, because one would be arguing the same in respect of certain persons – that their appearance was being imitated by demons or that their appearance (as in the case of other people) could be imitated – and thus either no one's or everyone's appearance was being imitated. Both these [arguments] are implausible, as is quite clear from what I said earlier.

One should not say, either, that at these meetings real men and women only of the lowest social class are actually present and, unless demons are imitating their appearance, none of respectable and important rank, because sometimes some of those who belong to what society and people's false thinking regard as the respectable class are less consistent in their ability to work things out, and more deceivable and gullible for some reason when it comes to that sect than those who belong to the lowest class. Nor do human reputation and public opinion, which is sometimes deceptive and mistaken, or even social behaviour which appears to be outwardly respectable and shows outward signs of devoutness, or any such things anywhere, have a place when it comes to the business of Waldensians, because they keep that business well hidden and very well concealed, and because it is highly unusual – although as far as this is concerned it should be weighed and taken into account by judges. Let it be conceded, too, that it is a truth generally believed that people of high, respectable status are possessed of much stronger and consistent powers of reasoning and are, in themselves, less inclined and given to vices. But there is something else to be taken into account which alters the contract. The demon attacks [these people] so much more [vigorously] in order to overcome them and drag them by force to the sect, and he is particularly pleased to receive them into it, as is clear from the trial of Maître Guillaume Adeline;[120] and he who is the father of arrogance refuses and scorns to receive members of the lowest class at his assembly.

You see, by means of four senses – one interior (i.e. the power to think or come to conclusions) and three exterior (i.e. sight, hearing and touch, especially in relation to embracing and sexual intercourse) – and sometimes by means of sniffing or smelling, recognition and many indications which it would take too long to go into here, Waldensians recognize and distinguish male devils from men and female devils from women, and therefore the difference between a real woman and one being imitated by a female devil, supposing such were present. The difference between a man and a male devil may be sensed the same way by the power to think or come to conclusions because, regardless of the sex he appears in, Waldensians are terrified at the sight of a demon, however much they may be used to seeing one, since he generally has a frightening appearance and an awkward way of moving his body; and by using their power to think, they infer that what they are looking at [bears them] ill will, just as a sheep flees at the sight of a wolf. [They recognize him] by sight, because when the demon forms his assumed body from condensed air or from some other substance, he leaves

120. See further Part III, no. 9 = Hansen VIa, no. 31 (pp. 467–72).

in it many signs by which he is recognized and the black colour which he always imperfectly smears over his human appearance on a body which is [either] not well defined, solid and firm or is quite often [made] with far too much material. [He may also be recognized] by the way he talks or interacts with others, from his outward behaviour and from the way he does not often eat, or sometimes from the way he pretends to eat and simulates eating (although he does not really and actually eat, just as he does not actually perform the functions of animate life the way living, real human beings do who perform all those functions and talk to one another during their assemblies). Moreover, [he may be recognized] by his arrogant behaviour and the fact that he does not talk much. Most especially and assuredly, the demon is recognized through [the sense of] sight by those who frequent the assemblies, because he has huge eyes and during those assemblies his eyes are always astonishing, frightening, grim, blazing, shining, flashing, etc.

[He can be recognized] through the sense of hearing by his voice which is not perfectly clear but harsh, as though he were speaking in a pot or a water jug or a trumpet. [He can be recognized] through the sense of touch from the composition of his body which is generally soft and cold, or composed in a different fashion from that of real, living human bodies; and [he may be recognized] especially from touching him during sexual intercourse. All of this is clear from trial records, and all of it is understood by learned judges of reliable zeal, particularly those with practical experience in this matter. A woman has little or no pleasure in the act of sex with a demon who leaves behind a substance which is extremely cold, wet, rotten and yellow, etc., and submits herself to him out of fear and obedience. With a real man during the meetings, she has equal or greater pleasure, as in the [real] world, according to what people say in their remarks [which I recorded] earlier. Sometimes [the demon can be recognized] through sniffing or smelling because the body he has assumed is that of a corpse – although this is a very rare occurrence. More often it is formed out of dense, stinking air, or the demon quickly and imperceptibly adds some stinking substance to the body thus formed. But [he can be recognized] by the faculty of comprehension because after their intimacy with the demon, Waldensians are, in the end, left feeling forsaken and miserable when they go back home, and their understanding tells them they are forsaken and miserable.

Therefore an accusation made because they have seen him is indisputable; one made from seeing and hearing him, even more so; one made from touching him (especially during sexual intercourse), and seeing and hearing him, is absolutely indisputable and very strong and carries very great weight. Likewise when the accusation is made by a pupil undergoing instruction, or an instructor teaching a pupil, and one of them accuses the other. Accusations also acquire effectiveness[121] and force from one of the parties to sexual coupling when all the details of clothing and the circumstances of place and time of the coupling [are given], especially when one of the parties to the coupling confesses. To sum the matter up: suppose all or many accomplices had been arrested; they and all their supporters would cease to speak and fight against the truth. But when anyone

---

121. Reading *robur* instead of *rubor*.

either wants to object to what he said previously, or adduce some precedent or other, let him refer to the book or passage (as I said before), and under Christ's guidance he will be given a reply to any argument or particular precedent in such a way that every person is bound to be satisfied as he or she deserves. Notice too, Reader, that if precedents dealing with demons' changing appearance or the possibility of their taking the appearance of humans, or the transformation itself, could fight for and win an opportunity to pour scorn: or (by the same reasoning), if accusations relating to obvious crimes [committed] during Waldensians' assemblies, such as theft, murder, adultery brought by witnesses who were wrong doers and accomplices [who] could not carry conviction because the wrong doers could allege that demons had taken their places because they can transform themselves, etc.[122]

Section 9: The revocation and denial of their situation and their accusation of other people, after confession and making such a confession

In true exercise of judicial authority and the best practice, after they have confessed their situation and made their accusations about others in the presence of the inquisitor and the assisting judges or commissioned notary or notaries, without having words put into their mouth, especially outwith the torture chamber (or affirmed them to be true first in the torture chamber and then outside it), if they are later visited for the purpose of another legal action a long time afterwards, and revoke, retract and deny both their situation and the accusations they made about others, [thereby] rendering themselves unworthy of the grace and mercy of the Church, especially if they do not return to their senses and re-confess everything in its entirety both anent themselves and others, they bring upon themselves the same sentence when they do not come back to a full confession as stubborn heretics who are handed over without mercy to secular justice. If they do not revert to the things I am going to say immediately afterwards in this section and the things we discussed previously in the section about the value of their accusations, the judges should not be disturbed by their denial and revocation; and in any case both the accusation or confession they make about themselves and the accusations they make about everyone else are of equal value and importance, as if they had continued to persevere in their confession and accusations of other people. If this were not the case, a firmly established, dependable verdict could not be passed on them. One could not proceed against those whom they had accused, everyone would take back what he had said and no one would be punished. So concerning oneself with such people would be a useless, unending, futile task since they would be constantly changing their confession and revoking it.

Likewise, should they take back what they have said, and retract and deny everything (for the most part at the point of death), and take the burden off others and excuse them in obedience to the demon who suggests this to them and to win his favour (as I mention later), no matter how well priests of the highest quality and discretion administer to them, they would die in a way which is not

---

122. The rest of the sentence is left hanging in the 'etc.'

in accordance with justice, and justice would have to be deferred, etc. Other people could not be brought to trial as a result of [these people's] revoking their accusations, because [the accusers] would not be speaking with a sensible frame of mind and proper exercise of their judgement. One cannot say, either, that they may be and could be justly punished regardless of their revocation and that their accusations of other people have no force. One could not proceed against those others or have those others proceed against them, because in fact the same principle applies to both, and if it is invalid for one, it is invalid for the other, too, because the principle does not apply to one with greater force than it does to the other.

It is also the case, however, that before they were taken into custody by the law, they could have decided that if they were brought to justice and made a confession, they would revoke it at once either of their own accord or because they were advised [to do so] by the demon or his accomplices, without any other person's suggesting they revoke it or for any other reason. It is more likely and more believable, however, that these revocations stem from a failure to guard [prisoners] properly, and at the suggestion or prompting of accomplices and individuals who have been accused but not yet arrested, either [making their suggestions] in person or through intermediaries, or by letter or anything else whereby everything is revealed and disclosed; [and they will do this] either because they are afraid of being accused, etc., or because they want to confuse the issue and give rise to scandal, etc., or because accusations are procured from the prison guards who are afraid for themselves or their friends, or are emotionally disturbed in some way. So one should take particular precautions when it comes to prisons, because if those who have been incarcerated were well guarded and given kindly, beneficial encouragement while they were being visited, there is no doubt that once they had started their confession they would stick to it. One should also be afraid that, in order to create confusion and scandal and prevent others from being involved, prisoners will already have promised, that when they arrive at the moment of death, they will declare that those they have accused are free from blame and say that everything they have said about themselves and others was forced [from them]. Upright judges do not have to worry about this, as I said before. It is a good idea, however, to appoint priests of ability and discretion, who generally understand this situation or business and who are well disposed and have not been led astray by accomplices, to hear their confessions and bring them and win them over to justice. Other inexperienced [priests] should not be allowed to take on their case during this time.[123]

Generally speaking, they revoke, deny or retract what they have confessed earlier for three reasons: (i) fear of death which they think will happen soon, and they hope, because of that denial, to escape or defer it; (ii) to do a favour to those who have been accused, because they think that such a denial renders accusations about others made earlier of no importance or value (although they *are* of value

---

123. This could mean that the prisoners should not be allowed fresh visitors at this particular time, but *circa eos* suggests that the *alii novi* refer to priests rather than members of the public.

if they were to persist in what they said before), in the same way that absolving others from blame should not be accepted after the first confession outwith the torture chamber because of their tendency to make excuses, and because of the corruption of simple-minded accomplices, the prompting of the demon or human beings, etc.; (iii) chiefly, don't force them to go beyond their latest confession about their involvement in such a way as to make their situation worse or aggravate their accusation of other people whom they accuse unwillingly. Allow them to think that in the end the judges will be happy to let them go back to their earlier confession without interrogating them further. Sometimes the sign of their pact, which the demon gave them, has not yet been removed from them; and if at that time, after they have revoked [their confession], they ask for a confessor, it is not a good idea to give them one, because in that situation they would be completely innocent when they made their [next judicial] confession, and that confession would be a mockery, just like the many false, derisory confessions they make. Nor, for the same reason, should one believe their oaths because they swear they are not guilty or that they have falsely accused such and such people, etc. Notice, Reader, that they should be made to go back to their former confession, first by gentle admonitions and beneficial exhortations, [and] secondly, by asking what made them confess such and such a thing – some particular detail or details from their earlier confession – or by splitting [their confession] into separate parts and helping them by asking questions about some things not included in their earlier confession, [a confession] the person speaking should say is true and praise them for telling the truth earlier, even though they did not tell [him] everything, etc.; or he can threaten them and show them the instruments of torture, if necessary. Once they have gone back [on their revocation], they should be asked why they revoked [their confession], who persuaded them to it, and then, if the judges are not going to ask them anything further, they should be arrested at once, otherwise the legal process would go on for ever.

Section 10: Prisons and prisoners
Very great foresight and legal care should be taken anent prisons, and that all guards and those people who live in the prison be loyal, honest, well disposed to the business in hand and not under suspicion, etc.; that prisoners do not associate at the same time; that accomplices from outside, or those whom [the prisoners] have accused, do not have access to the prison in person, or via inter-mediaries or letters, etc.; and that everything be kept secret, otherwise many improprieties might follow, especially if [prisoners'] accusations of other people were to be revealed. Conspiracy, among other things, and an attempt to cause harm to judges or those who concern themselves with the situation could be a consequence. Note likewise, Reader, that if those detained in prisons after being properly accused were not given encouragement, daily news and hope while people were communicating with them in prison, or if they were shown a gloomy prison where they would have to live under rigorous conditions, or if they were transferred to another town, perhaps they would confess their situation; and let it be taken for granted that if they never confess the situation of which they have been legally accused, they should not go away unpunished, etc.

Section 11: Any priests may minister to them in the case of their denial and retraction, especially at the point of death

One should not be surprised if Waldensians at the point of death deny their situation, calling for divine judgement on their judges, saying they confessed because of violence, and are dying for no reason, etc., calling upon the sweet name of Jesus, and invoking the saints, etc., and [saying] they swear upon their souls they have never been Waldensians; and in this way they are willing to die while making excuses for other people.

When there are important teachers[124] in the sect, they pronounce the following words, 'But Jesus, passing through the midst of them',[125] because, as is pretty well known by those with experience [in these matters], and as has been written in [learned] treatises, if Waldensians lie ill in their bed for many months or days (not because they have been detained by the law): and if, as it were miraculously, they are touched by God and of their own volition make a full confession at the beginning of their illness [anent] this sect and its reality, along with their acts of harmful magic:[126] yet because the demon lies in ambush, particularly at the end of life (that is, to devour their souls at the end and the point of death), at the very moment of death, when a priest has been summoned, they take back, at the demon's prompting, what they confessed earlier about the reality and actuality of the sect, the result of which is that they are liars and their confession is not complete. They will say they dreamed it and that what they confessed before is not true. One often finds the same thing among those condemned to perpetual imprisonment. While they are dying in prison they revoke everything when they are in that state, just as Waldensians quite often do at the point of death, as I said earlier. [They do so] first in contempt of the fact that they are dying, and sometimes perhaps [because] they have been given hope of the Church's grace and mercy during their ordeal (from which they begin to hope they are not actually dying); [they do so] secondly because the demon works hard on their imagination and hence upon their rational faculty, so that they deduce and tell themselves – although in this they are deceived – that if they deny everything, they will not die but will be taken back to their town by decision of the secular court. Thus they are made liars, perjurers and excommunicates and commit a mortal sin. Justice, however, does not go in for pretence, and they die in that condition to their peril – and with this besides, that in general they did not tell the judges everything they were asked before about themselves and others, but knowingly hid much, and [so] perhaps did not make a full confession in the law court of their heart. If on occasion they show contrition by weeping or

124. *Rabini*, literally 'Rabbis', which is consistent with the occasional use of 'synagogue' to describe 'Waldensian' meetings.

125. Luke 4.30. Jesus has begun to preach in Galilee after His temptation in the desert, and members of the synagogue are so angered by what He says that they take Him out of the city to the top of a hill, intending to throw Him down to His death. 'But He, passing through the midst of them, went His way'.

126. *Maleficiis*, which could simply mean 'their wicked deeds'. The whole thrust of the *Recollectio*, however, suggests that the Waldensians are witches and that their crimes are a mixture of wrongdoing and hostile magic.

other outward signs, they do so only because they are afraid of physical death (generally speaking), and so that they can escape it, or on account of a notion of worldly honour.

Thirdly, when this business is new to a population and it is thought [the Waldensians] have a large number of accomplices, the demon suggests they deny their situation. His idea is to rouse the populace, assisted by the accomplices, against the judges and public officials they think have condemned people who are innocent, [most inflammatory] being the fine words of the dying who choose to die at last in that denial. [They do this], too, at that moment so that legal proceedings will not be started against other accomplices; so that those held in prison may be set free, justice default, and those standing on the sidelines believe that [the contents of Waldensians' confessions] are dreams and fantasies; and so that the demon does not lose others or another prize, but keep them still obedient to him to carry out wicked deeds. It is also relevant that they legitimately abandon Waldensians this way at the point of death, [for Waldensians] have especially merited this in life, since they unjustly abandon God for long periods of it. God is just, and such a life drags them along to such a death, particularly because during their reception into that sect and assemblage, they gave their soul to a demon to have when they died. Moreover, although they can be worn down and confess the gift of their soul and are not in a situation in which it is impossible for them to be penitent, they do not generally confess this particular point. Nor do Waldensians confess or become worn down, but die impenitent, stubborn and obdurate without making a full confession – and they die in prison either at the hands of the law or by any way they can. The signs of their contrition, you see, are very frequently sham, [made] so that they can escape temporal death or embarrassment to their sense of worldly honour, etc. One must likewise bear in mind that when they are near death, a demon appears visibly to them and, by terrifying them and dropping hints, induces them to make nothing of and deny what they confessed earlier, so that they say they were forced to say it in order to excuse themselves and other accomplices.

Section 12: When sentence was first carried out in this place, the Waldensians, as is clear from the trial records, were legitimately abandoned[127] to secular justice
(i) They were abandoned as an example (by which I mean so that the people might be given an example and be favourably edified thereby); (ii) because of the novelty [of the situation] which was first recognized in this place; and (iii) because of the inherent outrageous nature of the situation and the large number of accomplices. Now, while it may be true that the Church should be merciful and clement and should not close her bosom the first time someone returns to her, this holds good when someone returns to the Church personally, of his or her own free will and accord and in an honest fashion which can be established from outward signs. Under those circumstances, mercy should be imparted, especially if the person who returns has not been a murderer, harmed crops or

---

127. *Relicti aut relicte*, which makes it clear that both men and women were involved.

carried out acts of harmful magic of this nature [*eiusmodi maleficia*] and has not been handed over to the Church by a secular court, carrying the burden of [having performed] acts of harmful magic. But when one plausibly believes that cases are putting themselves forward a second time as more deserving of grace and mercy, or [are doing so] as a way of propitiating their many accomplices, on that occasion the Church can defer imparting [mercy] and undertake to offer grace or open the bowels of her mercy on other occasions, and not give grace in the first instance or at the first execution. Indeed, when someone returns to the Church under compulsion and dishonesty and appears to be impenitent and does not show genuine signs of contrition, only [signs] which are untrue and feigned; [when] he has belonged to the sect for a long time; when, after being asked, he does not tell everything he knows about it and the judges do not believe he has told the truth about himself and others; and [when] he has given instruction to many people and brought them into the sect, the Church's mercy is rightly denied to such a person, even on the first occasion.

This was the situation regarding all six to be executed first. After [they had given] many other signs of being impenitent, recognized by the judges, in the end, in confirmation of their impenitence and the signs of it [which they had given], most of them denied their situation at the point of death. Indeed, two women of their number had acknowledged their situation in the secular court and had been handed over to the ecclesiastical court, charged, in addition to being members of the sect of Waldensian idolaters, with having committed a sin against Nature by abusing [themselves] with demons in human form and various brute animal shapes; performing acts of sorcery and witchcraft [*sortilegia et fascinaciones*] by means of powders given to them by demons, and certain other compounds. All this they acknowledged in the ecclesiastical court, saying also that because of what the sect of Waldensians was like, they used to have a demon-familiar and an overt pact[128] with him. The other four women or men[129] used to join these two in all the forementioned crimes and, in addition, had committed many acts of harmful magic and sacrilege by giving consecrated Hosts to toads, caused loss of crops and introduced several people to this damned sect of Waldensians, [not][130] without many perjuries, etc. One of them, Denisetta, had committed infanticide and 'the abbot of little sense' several murders. The sentence, trial records, etc. show that all the foregoing are clearly true.

Section 13: A brief exhortation to judges
The sect of Waldensians, which is abhorrent to the general public and is growing[131] excessively at this time, by the action of the enemy of the human

---

128. *Pactum expressum*. '*Expressus*' may also mean 'forced out, squeezed, extorted'.

129. 'Or' reads a little oddly. It seems to suggest that the author of the *Recollectio*, or his source, was not sure of his facts.

130. The sense seems to require *non absque* rather than just the *absque* of Hansen's text.

131. *Succrescente*, 'growing up from below', as though it were a plant. Cf. Columella, 'The soil needs to be worked frequently until the vines have grown enough to shade it and do not allow weeds to grow under them', *De re rustica* 4.14.2.

race, was concealed as though it did not exist, hidden in earlier years throughout
the country byways and secret places of the woods in this region. God must be
implored by the earnest prayers of the faithful to rise and scatter His enemies
– 'Let those who hate Him flee before His face'[132] – so that the writers on and
judges of such important matters, under the auspices of Christ whose cause is
here involved and assisted by the prayers of those same faithful, may agree as
one and work with their Creator in reaching the heart [of the matter], so that by
their work at this season God may be exalted and His highest honour restored
to Him whose [position] has been usurped from ancient times arrogantly and
unfairly in his eagerness for advancement in glory by the savage prince of
darkness. Therefore let it now come into the mind of judges how insubstantial,
how superficial and fleeting is this mortal life, and how transitory is every
source of pleasure in [this] world. Let these mortal men consider carefully that
it is becoming, fine, praiseworthy and meritorious to join in single combat and
struggle against the demon for the sake of Christ's faith and God, and how
divine and almost saintly it is to render honour to the true and living God when
He shows Himself most powerful by means of such assured building material
of virtue, the building matter of eternal happiness and salvation, and when, in
addition, the harvest which demands many workers, is plentiful.[133] Let them
ponder anxiously within themselves for days and years that if, influenced by
worldly fear or human partiality or any kind of baleful pretext, they have shut
their eyes and pretended not to notice such great, such unheard of crimes against
God and Christ and have failed to punish them and put things right, now when
there is need for action in such great matters, with what great confusion of their
souls they will appear before Christ, their strict, impartial judge on that fearful
Day of Judgement, and will receive eternal damnation with the Devil and his
angels in return for their dissimulation and neglect. But if, on the other hand,
they have acted honourably, virtuously, eagerly and earnestly with God before
their eyes, there is no doubt that, transported at length to the dwelling place
of Heaven by God Himself in return for such divine work, they will have the
greatest joys for ever and ever. Amen.

*[Hansen next includes two extracts, the second in French, from a short work by
Jean Tinctor (1405/1410–1469), a canon of Tournai, dating to the same year as
the* Recollectio *and obviously stimulated, as was the* Recollectio, *by the trials and
executions of various men and women in Arras that year on charges of heresy
and witchcraft. In c.1460, too, there appeared a brief account of Waldensianism
– 'La Vauderie de Lyonnais en bref' – and this also Hansen includes, although it
is very similar to the* Recollectio.*]*

---

132. Psalms 67.1 (Vulgate) = 68.1 (AV). The Vulgate text reads *oderunt* and I have
emended Hansen's *oderant* accordingly.

133. Reminiscent of Matthew 9.37–8 (repeated in Luke 10.2), 'The harvest indeed is
plentiful, but the workers few. Therefore ask the Lord of the harvest to send workers to His
harvest'.

12. Demons use illusion to fool witches into thinking their magical feats are real, Giordano da Bergamo, *c.*1460/1470

Hansen II, no. 35 (pp. 195–200)

[*Giordano da Bergamo was a Dominican and a Master of Theology, and this is more or less all we know about him. The title of his little treatise is* Quaestio de strigis ('A Question about Witches').]

You asked me, venerable Agostino Spica of Cortona, to make some concise remarks about witches [*strigarum*] and expose, in Dominican fashion, what is beside the point and irrelevant. So although I was very busy at the time, I am very much affected by your earnest request and wish to satisfy it.

It occurred to me that the four following things should be said about these witches, namely, in order: (i) what we are to understand by 'witches' [*strigas* or *strigones*][134]; (ii) whether, as the common people believe, such individuals can be changed into cats or any other kind of animal; (iii) given that this is not possible, one will have to see how these witches [*striges*] do what they do by means of a demon's[135] creating an illusion or by his actually doing the work; (iv) finally, if we can have any kind of credence in this sort of thing without committing a sin. Once these points have been explained, I think your request will be satisfied.

Point 1: Almost everyone understands *strigas* or *strigones* to mean men or women who run around houses or range over long distances at night by means of the power of a demon. They are also said to cast the evil eye [*fascinare*] on small children ... .[136] Women of this kind are usually called 'evil doing women', from the evil things they do, [while] others call them 'plant women', from the similar outcomes they produce. {In the margin another hand has written}: 'women who cast the evil eye', because they cast the evil eye on children; in French, '*fastinères*' or '*festurières*'; 'little box women', after the boxes in which they put their ointments; 'stick women', because by the power of a demon they are transported by a stick.[137]

Point 2: In connection with the second [point], one should take careful note that there was a popular idea among the ancients that the human soul can cross over from the human body into any other body of any animal ... and many modern people have started to have ideas which strongly agree with the notion that a man or a woman can be changed into a cat or a wolf and so forth by the power of a demon. Many arguments, reasons or illustrative anecdotes can be adduced in support of their position ... . But that this position is impossible, I shall demonstrate with many reasoned arguments and authoritative statements from learned men and the saints ... . [This he proceeds to do from a variety of Greek, Arabic, Patristic and Conciliar sources]. From these it is clear that not only is it impossible for a witch [*strigam*] to be changed into a cat by the power

---

134. These are probably meant to indicate female and male witches respectively. Throughout his essay, Giordano tends to use *strigae*, the feminine form, most of the time.

135. Reading *demonis* instead of *demones*.

136. This and the later omissions occur in Hansen's text.

137. The Latin/Italian terms are *maliarde, herbarie, fascinatrices, pixidarie* and *bacularie*.

of a demon, but also that it is heretical to have a stubborn belief [that such a thing can happen].

Point 3: You have to see how the demon operates in the case of this kind of witch (with the permission of divine justice), because people are sinful and faithless, and how he fools witches by showing them something which does not exist. In support of this, note first that the demon's power is great … . [Citation of Job 41 which describes Leviathan]. Note secondly, that although they cannot, by the power of a demon, immediately and directly draw forth any form from its potentiality in matter, because matter does not obey an angel's nod of command – as St Augustine says in book 18 of The City of God[138] – nevertheless, when it comes to moving someone or something from one place to another, [the demon] can produce many different outcomes. For he can shift the air, water, fire and earth, not by transferring one entire element out of its place, but parts of it, as I have explained in 'Questions about Incantations'.[139] So a demon can produce those outcomes in things which are open to being changed for the worse, [outcomes] which are produced as a result of the disturbance of parts of the elements or from the change of an element or a compound.[140] This is why I say the demon can fool the witches in three ways and make use of them for his own purpose. These ways are (i) deceitful illusion (ii) shifting things round while [the witches] are asleep and dreaming (iii) moving things from one place to another.

(i) He deceives with deceitful illusion when in visible form in front of the eyes he displays some shape, in colour;[141] but although something *does* appear to [the eyes], it does not actually exist. For example, he can put together the shape and colour of something which looks like a cat or a monkey or a horse or something of that kind, and does so in two ways. (a) The demon removes air and vapours by taking a cloud and shaping it into a body which resembles some animal. Then he puts it on and moves with localized movement appropriate to such a creature; and when he appears like this, it does not seem to be a deceitful illusion in the eyes of those who see it, because they really and truly see something which has colour. Their awareness of what that thing actually is, however, is deceived by what it does, because while one's capacity to perceive through the senses is not deceived by the particular object [one is looking at], it can be deceived about an object because of what that object does, as Aristotle says in 'The Soul', book 2.[142]

---

138. *De civitate Dei* 18.18: 'Certainly demons do not create actual beings … . They change things which have been created by the true God, but only as far as their appearance is concerned, with the result that they seem to be what they are not'. A reference to a demon's being an 'angelic created being' accounts for Giordano's mention of an angel's nod of command.

139. This does not appear to have survived.

140. The Latin is odd at this point. I have read *qui* for *que*, and taken *nati sunt* to refer back to *effectus*. Hansen himself added an exclamation mark to *consequi*.

141. The mention of colour is important, since this gives the object seen a stronger appearance of reality because, according to Aristotle's definition, in a work Giordano knows and cites, 'seeing' implies seeing colour and seeing in colour, *De anima* 3.2.

142. *De anima* 2.7: 'The thing seen is colour … . Every colour can produce movement in the "transparent" in a state of activity'.

It is most often in this way that a demon takes on the shape of a cat and goes for a walk along the rooftops, enters houses and bedrooms and casts the evil eye on children [*pueros infascinat*] and kills them, because this is what the sins of their forebears compel him to do.

(b) Another method [of deceiving by illusion] is when he appears [in animal form] because of some humour or layout of the eye or some inherent quality in the eye resulting from [that layout], which makes someone think he or she is seeing flies.

When this happens as a result of the activity of a demon, it is correctly called 'deceitful illusion', and he fools these witches by both methods to such an extent that he has sex with them at any time [he wants]. For demons, in the bodies they have assumed, become incubi when [they have sex] with women and succubi [when they have sex] with men, as St Augustine specifically says when he discusses the act of procreation, and as the saintly Doctor says in Part 1 [of the *Summa Theologiae*].[143] Consequently, witches say and constantly maintain that a demon's penis or the semen from it is cold.

I have also been told by Lord Ermolao [Barbaro], the Bishop of Verona, a man of the most excellent character, that he had in his service a man who had killed his father, and that for nearly five years a demon in the assumed body of a woman (or in a body shaped like a woman), would appear to him at certain times without fail, do him a great many services, and have sex with him. Another very old, trustworthy man from the fortress called Peschiera, which is at the far end of Lake Benaco or 'Garda', once told me that a demon wearing the body of a very pretty girl appeared to a hermit who was living near a military[144] fortress, and made him have sex with her. When they had finished, she got up – a woman, but a demon – and immediately disappeared from his sight while he, astonished, stayed where he was. Because the demon had used his power to draw off a very great abundance of semen, the hermit was completely drained and died a month later. My informant and several other people showed me the place, etc., and one should have no doubt that a demon can do this. I was also told by an aged, venerable monk that a particularly brutish woman (whom I know), continually suffered sexual assault by a demon.

This is the first illusion whereby a demon is accustomed to fool witches.

(ii) Secondly, he fools them by disturbing them while they sleep and dream. As Aristotle says in his book, 'Sleeping and Waking', because the parts of the body, such as the liver, which look after the digestion in particular, become upset, the

---

143. Hansen takes *super generatione* to refer to a lost treatise by St Augustine, but I think there may be confusion here, arising from Jordanes. The reference to St Thomas Aquinas's *Summa* is to Part 1, question 53, article 3 where he discusses angels and assumed bodies. His reference to incubi occurs in a quotation from St Augustine's *De civitate Dei* 15.8 where he says that Roman gods associated with forests and uncultivated lands, 'commonly called incubi', have, according to many people, approached women and had sex with them. St Augustine also discusses the use of semen by demons to father children (*De Trinitate* 3.23), in a passage referred to by Aquinas, so Giordanos's mention of his talk of demons and the act of procreation may stem from here.

144. Reading *militare* for *miliare*.

humours ascend to the brain and the result is various, different likenesses of things in the imagination, [likenesses] which are so distinct and definite that the dreamer thinks he or she is awake and that these things really do exist.[145] This has very often happened to me. Indeed, on many occasions, the combination of humours [*complexio*] in the brain can take place so as to allow the heavenly constellations to form such figures and likenesses in the brain or the imagination in such a way that many things are revealed to the dreamer. [References to Job 4 and St Augustine, *De civitate Dei* 18.][146] In this fashion, by the power of a demon, the humours can be moved to a witch's imagination and there form many likenesses and dream images, particularly of places, bodies and so forth, to the extent that the witches think at one point they are in a palace and at another [they are] under a walnut – (which, since it is very moist, is very much like our brain, as [Aristotle], 'The Soul', chapter makes clear[147] – at another, in woods, at another, on level ground, at another, in mountains with a large number of women and men. Manifestations of food, conversations, things seen and so forth also take place; and these fantasies, which happen through the power of a demon, are so definite and unwavering in the brain of female and male witches [*strige et strigonis*] that when they wake up, they maintain to the point of death that [these things] are real.

[The demon] also uses a similar method to persuade them that they are really and truly turned into cats or birds or something of the kind, this being a common illusion which the demon generally operates in the witches' brain [*in cerebro strigarum*], as is made clear in the Council of Aquileia I mentioned earlier, and exemplified in the legend of St Andrew, and book 18 of 'The City of God'. (Look it up to see what it says there.)[148] By means of this illusion, too, witches imagine they move clouds, rouse winds, produce showers of rain and hail and manufacture great storms. But this is false, and [these things] are done by a demon (divine justice permitting), as Job 1 makes clear when he talks about a fire coming down from the airy sky, which touched Job's sheep and reduced them to ashes, and a very great wind which was stirred up, rushed very quickly

---

145. Aristotle does not actually say any of this. In section 2 of his essay, he notes that 'some people move themselves about while they are asleep and do many of the things they do when they are awake, and these are accompanied by a mental image [*phantasma*] and a sense that they can be felt'. In section 3, he mentions evaporation from the nutrients which are ingested during a meal. This evaporation is hot and therefore rises, but when it cools, it falls back down again. These two passages are the closest Aristotle comes to Jordanes's interpretation.

146. Job 4.12–13: 'A secret word was said to me and, like a thief, my ear received the rivulets of its whisper'. This is followed in vv. 13–16 by Job's account of his terror at the sight of a spirit whose image was before his eyes and whose voice was in his ears. St Augustine, *De civitate Dei* 18.34 quotes Daniel 7.13: 'I saw in a vision by night', etc.

147. Giordano is mistaken in his reference. Aristotle does discuss the brain, however, in *De partibus animalium* 2.7: 'The brain is compounded of [the elements] water and earth'; and 2.14: 'The human brain is the biggest and most fluid of all brains'.

148. Jacopo da Voragine records that the Devil once appeared to St Andrew in the form of an extremely beautiful woman, *Legenda Aurea* 2. St Augustine, *De civitate Dei* 18.18. The chapter is headed with a summary of its contents. 'What one should believe about transformations which seem to happen to people as the result of a trick by demons'.

over the house or palace belonging to his sons who were having dinner there at the time, and killed them.[149]

(iii) Thirdly, the demon fools these witches either by using them to act as his servants or, by changing things from one place to another, to commit crimes and the most stinking iniquities against the honour of God. The demon can also, as I said before, transfer bodies from place to place, and the greater the power and effectiveness used in moving them, the faster they move, according to what the Philosopher says in books 7 and 8 of 'Things in Nature'.[150] Consequently, on one occasion he carries witches through various places, on another, along the rooftops; on another he brings them[151] into [the houses] via unopened lattices or gateways, but at such speed, the witches seem to enter by closed doors – which is not true – and once inside, they cast the evil eye on the children, suck their blood, inflict wounds on them and then leave. He also brings them[152] to places in which they worship and venerate the demon in particular ways and where they do many disgusting things in contempt of the Church and the Christian faith. There is no doubt this can happen by the power of a demon, because one reads that the most holy Ambrose was transported from Milan to Rome and back again in three hours at his command and insistence in order to demonstrate in this way the power of saints over what a demon can do. For, according to what St Augustine says, [people] can make use of evils in a good cause.[153]

Nevertheless, the common folk generally believe, and witches themselves maintain, that on certain days and nights, they smear a stick with a particular ointment, mount it and are immediately carried away to places designated by the demon; or they anoint themselves right next to their backsides, and in designated places where hairs grow, and sometimes carry similar ointments along with certain amulets [hidden] under their hair – all superstitions which contribute nothing to their being transported. This is why I have sometimes seen inquisitors shave the hairy parts of the whole body of arrested witches. It is something I have never liked. They cannot be transported by this kind of ointment or by

149. Job 1.16 and 19: 'A second man came and said, The fire of God has fallen from the sky, touched your sheep, and destroyed them and your children ... . Suddenly a very strong wind rushed in from the desert, struck the four corners of the house, overthrew them, and fell upon your children. They are dead'.

150. Reading *relatum* for *reatum*. The 'Philosopher' is Aristotle. With so vague a reference, it is difficult to pin down what Giordano had in mind. Perhaps the closest to what he says here actually occurs at the beginning of *Physica* 6.2 where Aristotle discusses speed of movement, lesser or greater, in relation to time. But Aristotle also talks about local movement (7.4) and things which move of themselves or are moved by an external agent (8.4).

151. *Illas*, specifically feminine.

152. *Eas*, again specifically feminine.

153. Bartolomeo Spina tells a variant upon the Ambrose story in which the saint once fell asleep for three hours while he was saying Mass, and when he woke up he told people he had been in Tours, conducting the funeral of St Martin. See W. Stephens, 2002, *Demon Lovers* (Chicago and London: University of Chicago Press), pp. 171 and 393, note 59. The actual source of these variants is not known. St Augustine, *Retractationes* 2.22: 'Just as it is wicked to use good things in an evil way, so it is good to use evil things in a good way'.

sticks. It is all done by the power of the demon who is transporting them. But I should make it known that it has been found that torture has no effect on some people as long as they are wearing certain amulets or some other superstitious object on some part of their body – for example, under the nails, in the mouth, in the ear, under the hair, under the arms and so forth. It works entirely by the power of a demon with whom an open or tacit pact is made by means of this kind of superstitious thing; and all arguments to the contrary can be dismissed by everything I have just been saying. [References to Classical and Biblical instances of shape changing.]

Point 4: What the faithful ought to think about the foresaid witches can be suggested very briefly. As a guide to this, let me say to you that since the object of our faith is Truth, in no way can something which is false belong to the faith ... .[154] Therefore when it comes to witches, one can believe only what is true about them; and because some people think that witches *can* be changed into cats by the power of a demon and travel to various places over long distances by means of ointments or sticks: and that by the power of words or small signs, witches can produce hailstorms, showers of rain and so forth – which they can't – the faith of those people is in peril, and they are in danger of being cast away, as it says in the Council of Aquileia. Several other people think witches cannot do anything by the power of a demon in reality, but only in appearance or in their imagination or by dreaming they do. Those people who do not recognize how much power a demon has to carry out such things (divine justice permitting), should be considered ignorant; and although in the foresaid Council, question 26, chapter 5, 'Episcopi', it is considered that a demon carries out his intention by means of illusion [operating] in the imaginative faculty and through various manifestations, [the canon] denies that demons can genuinely use witches to do many things, and vice versa, that witches do many things through their [own] malice with the help of a demon's power, as I explained earlier on. So the faithful should rid their hearts of certain ideas about witches, but hold firmly to several [others].

So, venerable Agostino Spica, this is what occurs [to me] should be said about witches. I could have continued both more succinctly and at much greater length, but in my opinion the things I have touched on are sufficient to deal with what I proposed to do in the way I thought of doing it. In return for this, you may pay me in prayers. Goodbye. I have finished.

[*Hansen II no. 36. Girolamo Visconti was Professor of Logic in Mlan and Inquisitor of Lombardy from 1465. In about 1460 he wrote* Lamiarum sive striarum opusculum ('A little work dealing with women who devour children or women who suck people's blood'), *as an answer, he says, to the many inquiries he received from those who did not know whether to believe in the veracity of witchcraft or not. His view is that much of it is diabolical illusion, but that those who subscribe to it, or claim to take part in witches' assemblies and practices, should be regarded as heretics.*]

154. Hansen's omission.

(Hansen, p. 206) 'People should be aware that not only women go to the assembly[155] but also men, but because many are women, one talks about them more. Members of the lower classes are stained by this disgrace, but so are nobles, and [all of them] have demons assigned to them, with whom they have sex. These [demons] frequently appear to them within and outwith the house when they are wide awake (as these people tell us)'.

[Hansen II no. 37. Michael Behaim (c.1416–c.1470) was a weaver and a professional singer. He wrote two long-verse chronicles and several poems, of which Hansen includes one dealing with heretics and practitioners of magic. The subject matter is entirely predictable – changing the weather, flying long distances through the air, the use of magical ointment and so forth.]

[Hansen II no. 38 is taken from the Flagellum Maleficorum *('A Scourge for Workers of Harmful Magic'), c.1462, of Pierre Mamor who was Rector of the University of Poitiers. France, he said, had been devastated for a long time by English invasions, and these warlike people in their deadly fashion, taught many of the French magical chants, conjuring tricks, incantations and how to work harmful magic, none of which the French knew anything about before. Apart from this historical insight, Mamor says little which is new.]*

[Hansen II no. 40 is taken from Tractatus de haereticis *(c.1468) by Ambrosio de Vignate, Professor of Canon and Civil Law in the universities of Padua, Bologna and Turin. This treatise grew out of his lectures and contains a number of questions: for example (1) Which type of faithlessness is worst? (2) Who are heretics? (3) [Who are] blasphemers? (4) Is it illicit to hang God's words round one's neck [as an amulet]? (5) Is divination by throwing lots illicit? (6) Is one permitted to practise divination? (7) Is divination done by invoking demons licit?[156] (8) Is divination done by astrology illicit? (9) Is divination done by dreams illicit? (10) Is divination done by looking at natural signs and by other similar observations of external things illicit? (11) Are fortune tellers [sortilegi] and diviners subject to the authority of the Inquisition? (12) Women who devour children [lamiis], witches [strigibus][157] and other criminals.*

On witches and the accusations against them, especially those involving the Sabbat, he has this to say:]

I have quite often tried this [kind of] case, actually, and among the rest which came before me was this one. A man accused of belonging to a sect of 'masked people'[158] or 'workers of harmful magic' confessed that he did and accused many other men and women of belonging to the same sect, gadding about at

155. *Ad ludum. Ludus* means 'game' or 'school', and it is worth remembering that the presiding demon is often called *magister*, 'instructor', as are those in important positions in the 'sect'.

156. This should probably read 'illicit', as in the other questions.

157. Or possibly 'vampiric women'.

158. *Masca* was a term sometimes used of witches, and there are several examples of witnesses' telling a court that people wearing masks to hide their identity could be seen at witches' assemblies.

night and racing around where three roads meet, or four, or round junctions, and of doing many wicked things. In response to this man's deposition, the inquisitor of heretical wickedness arrested and imprisoned a number of women, some of whom confessed of their own accord to these and similar things, while others confessed under torture. I thought there were two main points to be investigated in connection with this case: (1) Were the things confessed possible, likely and believable or not? (2) Can it be said that the man's confession about himself and the confession of one of the women, or two of them, or three, or four, which was saying similar things is sufficient to warrant sending [the women] to torture?

[His conclusions anent the first, after he has weighed evidence from Biblical, Patristic, Classical and modern sources is that (p. 223), 'A great deal of what these women confess about such things, such as being changed into mice, is impossible, but many others seem to be consistent with the facts'. Anent the second point, he concludes that if people confess impossibilities or accuse others of impossibilities, the testimony is not sufficient, of itself, to furnish proof of guilt.]

13. What workers of magic do, Jean Vincent, c.1475

Hansen II, no. 41 (pp. 227–31)

[Jean Vincent, Prior of Les Moustiers en Lai in La Vendée, wrote 'A Book against the Magical Arts and those who say these Arts are Ineffective'. He is one of the earliest writers to use the term 'Sabbat' to describe witches' assemblies. This was not the usual word for them during the fifteenth century which preferred to call such meetings 'synagogues' or 'sects'.]

(i) Chap. 4, folio 15: There are workers of harmful magic [*malefici*] who imprison demon-familiars by enclosing them in rings, consult them about future events and achieve whatever they do by means of their advice, although [the demons] deceive them in the end. Indeed, I remember the type of people who used to follow the advice of these demons they had enclosed in rings. Although they were going to be important in the secular world, raised high by wealth and honours and made the confidants of princes, yet in the end they died a very wretched death.

(ii) Chap. 7, folio 19: I think the word *maleficium* has been derived from the particular and very powerful ability to do evil, and it is because of this that the common people call [witches] 'workers of harmful magic', on account of the large number of criminal acts they commit. For while it is permissible to vent one's rage on the rest of the practices used by magicians [*magorum*] by inflicting so great a mischief of revenge on their bodies, only to the person without sin has it been granted, not to compel, but to incline a person's free will to the mischief of sin … . Anyway, other [acts of harmful magic] were appointed to sow hatred between a husband and wife – something workers of harmful magic [*malefici*] do by removing brands[159] from the fire and turning them round so that the part which is scorched lies outwith the fire and the part which has not been burned is turned towards the fire. I have seen an elderly woman who was detained in the prison of the reverend father in Christ and my lord, Nicolas, Bishop of Luçon, on a charge of divination [*sortilegii*][160], and she said more than once that she had aroused hatred between a man and his wife in just such a way, the result being that they were completely unwilling to look at each other … .

But one must take steps to resolve the present question – in what way can these kinds of acts of harmful magic be undone? – since the law always presumes that certain other things which have lasted for, let us say, three years, are considered to be secular [matters]. So I think the reply should be that an act of harmful magic caused by a worker of harmful magic using the power of a superior demon because he has a pact with a demon of inferior power, cannot be undone because the strength of the inferior demon is less than that of the superior demon. On the other hand, I don't dispute it can happen … [but one must not use one piece of harmful magic to undo another, because one must not ask help in any way of workers of harmful magic.]

(iii) Chap. 8, folio 23: A spiritual cause of dreams comes from the working of demons who display extraordinary things to the imagination of those who are asleep, and from these some [demons] reveal some future [events] to those who have illicit pacts with them … .

But workers of magic [*magici*] can not only send someone to sleep, they can also keep him stupefied[161] for a long time. I have read about a female worker of harmful magic who, while being taken to the final punishment of being burned, had a dead person's hand hanging round her neck, and with this she kept people asleep by making a reverse sign of the cross with it. It is not surprising that such things can happen by means of a demon's device, because physicians, too, do something similar [when] they give a drink of mandragora bark mixed in wine to those whose leg or arm they intend to cut open. This drink puts [patients] into such a deep sleep that they don't notice the pain of the incision at all … .

Workers of harmful magic who say they are transported to the Sabbats of demons keep on saying they have gone to a demon's Sabbats on the very night their close friends and family have seen them stupefied uninterruptedly in their beds. There, [they say], they have worshipped a demon, discharged lightning, stirred up hailstorms, completely destroyed vines and roasted alive small children whom they had taken from their mothers' sides. Now, the demon, who sees the results of what he causes (for example, children's illnesses, which vines are threatened with destruction, future hailstorms), sometimes suggests these to workers of harmful magic while they are asleep; and he deludes them in such a way that they think they are [actually] at his assemblies and that there they really do roast children taken from their mothers, discharge lightning, blast people

---

159. Reading *torres* for *torces*.

160. Or 'sorcery'.

161. *Soporatum*. Vincent uses this verb quite frequently in this passage to indicate the depth of sleep involved.

with their lightning bolt and destroy vines. When, later on, they see that these things have happened, or are told they have happened, they believe they have done it, whereas it is possible that each of these things has happened naturally. But if they confess they have performed these things and instruments of magic are found in their homes – curses pinned [to a wall], images, powders, cups or any other objects with which they say they have performed these things – and if there are witnesses who depose [such things] in evidence, the truth of the matter is that it actually has taken place, and soon there will be general talk that they have perpetrated these evil deeds, and they are accused and said to be guilty of performing acts of harmful magic, and then they must be made liable to legal penalties.

In order to counter troublesome dreams which oppress the hearts of mortals and are brought by the malice of demons, when someone lies down to sleep, he should protect himself with devout prayers, regardless of the fact that there are those who say things like this happen naturally. [References to Avicenna and Pliny the Elder, both of whom give natural explanations for dreaming.] Although Avicenna, along with physicians, speaks the truth, nevertheless Guillaume de Paris[162] maintains that so oppressive a dream has been sent by an incubus-demon[163] pressing upon a person's heart. Therefore, when a person is composing himself to sleep, he must sprinkle the room and bed with holy water, devoutly protect himself with the sign of the cross, fortify himself with prayers, and commend himself to his defender, his good angel, so that when he [she?] is oppressed by an incubus-demon, he may not be struck suddenly with the javelin of death. He must also meditate often on the articles of the Faith, the Lord's prayer, and the angel's greeting to Blessed Mary, devoutly utter the name of Jesus and, before he goes to sleep, sincerely recite the Church's hymns, 'Before the end of light', 'You who are light and day', and 'Jesus, Saviour of the world'.[164]

(iv) Chap. 10, folio 31: In connection with two effective types of magical practice, I must come now to things in Nature which workers of magic [*magici*] employ to perform their acts of harmful magic, namely, a poisonous substance [*veneficio*] and incantation ... . 'Poisonous magic' [*veneficium*] is derived from *venenum*, 'poison', and incantation employs only the spoken word.

Workers of poisonous magic [*venefici*], therefore, use poisonous substances together with certain drinks and ointments which throw people's minds into confusion, change their bodies and mostly kill people. They say they are transported at night to demons' far distant Sabbats by the power of these poisonous substances. The correct deduction, however, [is that] not one of these should be attributed to any natural power belonging to such poisonous substances, but

162. Guillaume d'Auvergne (1180/90–1249), Bishop of Paris from 1228.

163. Although the references to 'person' are consistently masculine because of the use of the word *homo*, 'man', this mention of incubus suggests that the recipient of the dream is a woman. Otherwise the term would be succubus.

164. Hymns from the office of Compline. In the second, Hansen gives *reple qui lux es et dies* as the initial line. The usual version begins 'Christe'.

rather to the deceitful cleverness of a demon who, as a result of a pact expressly made with the principal inventors of this damned practice, stands by with this kind of ointment to smear on [a person's body] or drinks for him or her to consume. The demon himself, by applying active to passive [characteristics], performs those things which people believe take place through the power of the foresaid [substances]. He is the principal effective cause, whereas poisons of this kind are the extraneous cause via workers of harmful magic, and without this [principal] cause these things would not happen. Those who use such things in the manner of the first workers of harmful magic are proved to have, not an express but a tacit pact with a demon.

But I have no doubt that there are remarkable powers in herbs, stones and waters which demons can take in order to produce unusual effects upon human beings. They also hand over powders or drinks made from these [substances] to workers of harmful magic who have a pact with them. But because workers of harmful magic take pride in suspending, postponing or accelerating at will the effect of their drinks or powders, it is clear that, as far as these things are concerned, it is the pact with the demon more than the active power rooted in the natural substance which makes things happen. [References to aphrodisiacs in Pliny and Ovid.]

Incantation relies on spoken words alone, and since these have no natural power to produce those effects to which enchanters [*incantatores*] direct their spells [*carmina*],[165] one's conclusion is that their efficacy depends on a spell-demon who made a pact with the first enchanters and contracted them to these things. But those learned in this practice do indeed draw out wine from wood with a hole in it, which they have seen in cellars far away from where they are, cure horses suffering from a nail in their foot and treat the wounds of the injured even if those people are dying; and they are unwilling to employ surgeons to give those people treatment, knowing that spells work better than medicine in these situations. With a spell they stem blood flowing from the body, call dogs to them and make them follow, get rid of jackdaws, doves, mice, rabbits and crows from the places they have been living in and transfer them elsewhere, and change ripened corn from one field to another. Hence Vergil in *Eclogues*: 'I have seen [Moeris] enchant sown crops to somewhere else'. People kill, too, by incantation alone, without any drink of poison. Hence Lucan 6: 'Even when it has not been defiled by a drink of poison, the mind dies after it has been enchanted away'.[166] [Reference to Justinian's Code.]

(v) Chap. 12, folio 33: As I recall, an elderly female fortune teller [*sortilega*][167] called Chandelle, from Chaillé in the diocese of Luçon, conceived a hatred for

---

165. *Carmen* refers to a ritual utterance, usually sung or chanted, and hence to a song or poem. By 'spell', therefore, we are to understand a quasi-religious, often metrical vocal performance, half-spoken, half-chanted.

166. Vergil: *Eclogues* 8.99. Lucan: *De bello civili* 6.457–8. Vincent gives a garbled version of Lucan's verses.

167. The chapter has been discussing various forms of divination, hence it seems appropriate to translate *sortilega* here as 'fortune-teller'. The anecdote deals with an act of harmful magic, but there is no reason to suppose that a fortune-teller was not capable of such. Various

the local prior. She constructed a doll [*votum*] or image and had it baptized, under the name of the said prior, by a priest from (Tableyo). She dressed it in a piece of black cloth, dusted its shins with powders a demon had given her and buried it under the threshold of the prior's door. Immediately, the prior was seized by a serious illness, took to his bed and suffered such a great humoral flux in his shins that the discharge kept on flowing down in rivulets from his open ulcers. He remained in this state of weakness for a long time, and neither physicians' remedies nor those of surgeons were able to bring him relief. One day this Chandelle was looking after her animals out at pasture when a demon appeared in the likeness of a black man wearing, she thought, short clothes; and when she complained, [asking him] why he did not destroy the said prior who was his enemy, he replied that he had taken his revenge on [the prior] that very hour. Having said this, the demon went to the prior's house and, with a mighty blast, carried off that part of the building in which the prior was lying ill in bed, and the iron window frame, to a stream quite a distance away.

I thought that these things, taken from the foresaid prior's deposition (which I committed to writing in accordance with the instruction of the reverend father in Christ, my lord, the Bishop of Luçon), and from Chandelle's confession and the statements of other witnesses, should be written down so that at least those people who allege that magical practices have no effect may come to their senses and realize how much damage, with God's permission, a demon may do to human beings. From whose cunning may our Lord Jesus Christ, son of the Virgin Mary, through His most holy mercy, keep us safe: who with the Father and the Holy Spirit lives and reigns, one God, for ever and ever, Amen.

[*Hansen II no. 42 comes from the* Chronicle of Matthias Widmann *from Kemnat. Widmann was chaplain to the Elector Friedrich of the Palatinate, and a mention (Hansen, p. 235) of two women who were burned in Tilburg in 1475 helps to date the work. Its content is very similar to that of the* Errores Gazariorum.]

[*Hansen II no. 43 is taken from Bernard Basin,* Tractatus de artibus magicis ac magorum maleficiis ('Treatise on magical practices and on the acts of harmful magic done by magicians'), 1482. *It seems to have been based on a speech Basin delivered in Rome before a cardinal and other learned men. He comments on the canon* Episcopi *conventionally enough, but also refers to one or two practices not often noted elsewhere (p. 238):*]

What about certain elderly women who say that in a trace state [*raptu*] they see the souls in Purgatory and much else, such as things stolen and goods lost, and when their feet are scorched do not feel the fire? The answer must be that a demon brings fantasies into their imaginative faculties to such an extent that they feel nothing outwith themselves. An example is those who have the falling sickness. They, too, do not feel burning while their illness is upon them because while they are burdened by their interior sufferings, they do not feel the fire on the outside.

magical practices, including healing and foretelling the future, very often blend with harmful practices in the same individual.

[Hansen II no. 47 comes from Ulrich Molitor who in 1489 published a dialogue, De laniis et phitonicis mulieribus *('Butchers and Women who see the Future'), purporting to be between himself, Sigismund, Archduke of Austria, and Conrad Schatz, chief magistrate of Konstanz.*[168] *Molitor was Professor of Canon and Civil Law in the University of Konstanz. His dialogue discusses various aspects of the usual assertions about the extent of demons' powers and witches' reliance on them, shape changing, illusion and reality, divination and the extent to which belief in the Devil's fantasies constitutes apostasy and heresy. In spite of the dialogue's sceptical tone, Molitor concludes that when witches fall into apostasy, they should be executed. Hansen provides very little from this work, but does reproduce the woodcuts which are a major feature of it.]*

[Hansen II no. 48 is an extract from an anonymous Repertorium perutile de pravitate hereticorum *('A very useful summary of heretics' wickedness'), 1494. The principal task of an inquisitor, it says, is to see whether accusations against someone involve heresy or not. If anyone resolutely refuses to confess after appropriate witnesses have shown he is a heretic and remains obdurate, he should not be accorded the mercy of perpetual imprisonment, but burned. It is noteworthy that the author refers to aspects of such individuals' behaviour as 'Judaizing', which suggests that his opinions have been influenced by experience in the Iberian peninsula. This impression is strengthened by his use of* xorguinae, *a word of Spanish derivation, to refer to witches. (Hansen, p. 250): 'Are such people as* xorguinae *to be encountered, and if one does encounter them, can inquisitors proceed against them?'*

Referring to the canon Episcopi, *the author concludes that if the kind of women referred to therein persevere in their faithlessness and continue to sacrifice to demons, they must (if they have been baptized) be heretics. They are, however, deluded in their beliefs. (Hansen, p. 251): 'No one should be stupid enough to believe that [flying through the air and shape changing] which take place only in sleep and in spirit, take place physically, otherwise he or she has less faith than heathens, and is worse than they are, and can be proceeded against as a heretic'.]*

[Hansen II no. 48a is taken from a lawyer's handbook (1495) by Willem van der Taverijn from Brabant. He offers definitions – the Latin sortilegium, *for example, he says, refers to magic or foretelling the future – and lists the kind of things witches do: weather magic, flying with the help of an ointment, harmful magic, necromancy, incantation, invocation, sacrificing to the Devil and various types of divination such as those using fire or water and those reading palms or interpreting marks made in sand or soil.]*

[Hansen II no. 50 comes from De maleficiis *('Acts of Harmful Magic'), 1500, by Cardinal Thomas Cajetan, otherwise Tommaso de Vio (1469–1534), He asks the question, 'Is it permissible to undo an act of harmful magic with the help of*

---

168. The word 'butchers' (*laniis*) is sometimes printed as *lamiis* ('women who devour children'). St Isidore of Seville suggested that the two words were etymologically connected, *Etymologiae* 8.11.102.

a worker of harmful magic who is prepared to use [the magic] for this purpose?'
and answers no, even though some people have argued the opposite (p. 255):]

There are two ways an act of harmful magic can be undone by [other] acts
of harmful magic. First, by straightforward breaking up or destruction of the
instrument of harmful magic made earlier on – for example, by breaking up a
band of hairs with a wooden ring. This is undoubtedly licit. It is not the work of
a worker of harmful magic qua *maleficus*,[169] but of someone who recognizes the
hindrance to his good neighbour and does not involve the invocation of demons.
It is simply the destruction of a sign which the Devil had decided should preserve
the evil to other men as long as it was in existence. Secondly, [an act of harmful
magic can be undone] by invoking demons or by using another act of harmful
magic. This is undoubtedly a mortal sin and is the work of a worker of harmful
magic qua *maleficus*; and because such a work stems, not from the will of the
worker of harmful magic, but from something demanded of him [by someone
else], he yokes himself to the ugliness of a sin. Therefore, not only those who
do this, but also those who ask it and consent to it subject themselves to sin. So
although it is permissible, provided one takes due precautions, to go to a worker
of harmful magic [to ask him] to destroy something which has been made as an
instrument of harmful magic, simply by breaking it up, it is not permissible to
go to him, asking him to destroy it by means of another act of harmful magic or
by invocation of demons.

[Hansen II no. 51 is an extract from Dialogus in magicarum artium destruc-
tionem *('A dialogue on the destruction of magical practices'), c.1500, by
Symphorien Champier. Champier (1472–c.1540) was a physician who cast a
medical eye over his subject matter. He subscribes to the notion that demons
create illusions and make people see things which are not there in reality. In
consequence, he says, judges should consider this view very carefully when they
are endeavouring to track down the truth.]*

[Hansen II, no. 51 comes from Opusculum de sagis maleficis *('A little work
dealing with wise women who work harmful magic'), 1505, by Martin Plantsch,
a priest at Tübingen. It is based on a sermon he preached that year at the burning
of a female worker of harmful magic and is entirely conventional in its tone and
message.]*

14. Impotence magic at the Spanish Court, anonymous, c.1505

Hansen II, no. 53 (p. 262)

*[This reminiscence dates to the year of Queen Isabella's death or just after it.
Diego de Deza was a member of the Inquisition in Spain and later became its
head.]*

The Condessa de Haro, [wife] of the most illustrious Bernardino de Velasco,

---

169. Referred to as masculine throughout this text.

Condestable and Duque de Frias, who right up to the present day not unmer-
itedly has a leading place among the magnates of the kingdom, told the Queen
that her granddaughter, who was married to a nobleman, had suffered an
impediment, perhaps because of the treacherous practice of demons – [a practice]
called *ligadura* in Spanish – the result of an act of harmful magic by one of the
foresaid noble's brothers. She begged for an appropriate remedy. The Queen then
ordered us to be summoned.

We said that perhaps there was an impediment because they had been
[magically] bound. The Queen said, 'Catholics should not allege or believe
that at all. It's a mistaken notion of the common people'.... . At once she issued
instructions that Diego de Deza, Master of Sacred Theology and a member of the
Dominican Order, be sent for'.... .

Then the most devoted Queen spoke to him as follows. 'Bishop, I have been
told that in the sacrament of marriage, an illusion of the Devil or the working of
a demon is able to have an effect upon so holy a matter – not that I believe this
at all, because marriage is a spiritual thing'.

The Archbishop replied as follows. 'Most excellent Lady, this is how it is. It is
quite certain – and this has been demonstrated by holy Doctors [of the Church]
– it is perfectly clear that such things can take place because of activity by the
Devil, and that they have affected many people', and he adduced St Thomas
[Aquinas] and other Doctors of the Church in support of this.

The Most Christian Queen heard his reply and said, 'I hear you, Bishop, but
I ask, isn't it contrary to the Catholic faith to believe this?'

Then he replied that it was not an article of faith, but the Doctors [of the
Church] believed this and seriously maintained it.

Finally the Catholic Queen said, 'I agree with Holy Church. But if it is not
contrary to the Faith, and even though Doctors [of the Church] confirm it, I shall
assuredly not believe that a demon can exercise any power over those joined
together in matrimony and, as people say, 'bind' them. These things owe more to
people's quarrelling with each other than to the power of demons'.

Afterword

The Queen's scepticism and the Archbishop's acceptance of the reality of
demons' magical powers may be taken as an appropriate point at which to
leave Hansen's extracts from learned authors. His remaining examples, which
cover the next 35 years or so, simply reiterate the arguments for one side or the
other, which have already been well rehearsed. Samuel de Cassini, Martín de
Arles and Giovanni Ponzinibio, for example, maintain that the Sabbat, flying
and all the rest of it is a fable or an illusion; Vincenzo Dado, Bernardo di Como,
Johann Trithemius, Silvester Prierias, Gianfrancesco Pico della Mirandola and
Bartolommeo de Spina uphold its reality. Geiler von Kaisersberg has it both ways
and says the journey to the Sabbat may be a reality or an illusion, and Paolo
Grillando tells us he began as a sceptic but has since changed his mind, while
Francesco de Vitoria is inclined to scepticism: 'I have not come across anyone

worthy of belief', he says, 'who would positively maintain he had seen anything magical or verify it as such' (Hansen, p. 355). The canon *Episcopi* continues to act beyond the beginning of the sixteenth century as a key reference point for both sides of the argument.

Every so often, however, a writer will tell us a new, or relatively new, piece of information, or a personal anecdote.

Bernardo di Como, Dominican inquisitor
Tractatus de strigiis ('A Treatise on Witches'), c.1508. Hansen II, no. 57 (p. 280)

An appalling sect of men, and especially of women, rose in damnable fashion some years ago in parts of Italy, the Devil sowing [the seeds] of all the wickedness. Some people call these individuals 'masked women'. In Lombardy, we call them *strigiae* (from the word *stix*, a word meaning 'Hell' or 'the marsh of Hell'). [The word may be derived] from Greek *stigētos* ('distress' in Latin), because by means of their acts of harmful magic, they make a very large number of people distressed.[170]

Martin de Arles y Androsilla, Archdeacon of Aibar in Navarre
Tractatus de superstitionibus contra maleficia seu sortilegia quae hodie vigent in orbe terrarum ('A treatise on superstitions and against acts of harmful magic or fortune telling, which flourish in the world today'), c.1515. Hansen II, no. 64 (p. 608)

First [let me deal with] the false opinion of those who believe that witches and fortune tellers who, for the most part, flourish in the Basque region north of the Pyrenees and are known as *broxae* in the local tongue, can be transported from place to place in a real change of location.

Andreas Alciati, a lawyer, gives a legal opinion
c.1515. Hansen II, no. 65 (pp. 310–11)

As soon as I got back home after receiving my doctorate, the first legal opinion I had to give happened as follows.

An inquisitor 'of heretical wickedness', as it is called, had come to the subalpine valleys in order to investigate female heretics whom the ancients called 'child devourers' [*lamias*] and we call 'witches' [*striges*]. He had already burned a large number – more than a hundred, actually – and was presenting Vulcan with more and more fresh burnt offerings (not a few of whom seemed to be in need of purging with hellebore rather than with fire), until the peasants seized their weapons and began to put a stop to that violence and take the business to the bishop for him to pass judgement. The documents were sent to me, and the bishop asked if I would give him my considered opinion in this matter.

---

170. Neither etymology is correct. *Strigiae* is cognate with *strix* = 'owl' or 'vampire', and *stygētos* means 'hated' or 'hateful', from *stygeō* = 'I detest'.

There was more than one kind of witch involved. Some had spat on the cross; some had denied the divinity of Christ; and these women, in person and wide awake, had killed small children with acts of poisonous magic [*veneficiis*] and incantations [*devotionibus*].[171] I replied that in the case of these women, the magistrate should do his duty.

Some had issued threats against mothers during the day, and at night had crept into these women's houses, even though the doors were barred and bolted, [come] to their children[172] and cast the evil eye on them; and the common agreement was that they had died of a sudden illness which the physicians did not recognize. I made the same reply as before, because even if we grant they had not come in person, it is possible for them to have given instructions to malevolent ghosts over whom they had control [*lemuribus suis*], and in this case the wrongdoing did not take place in dreams.

Some had no accusation brought against them other than that of dancing under a tree in the Val Tellina[173] and going to the Sabbat [*ludum*], an accusation they denied, although some of their associates testified [to its truth]. The magistrate was saying these women should undergo torture because it has been decided in favour of the Faith that the evidence of accomplices who were privy to what was going on is admissible [in court]. I replied that this was true with respect to those who had seen things while they were awake, but not with respect to those who were asleep and dreaming. Doubt, therefore, hinged upon this point: did they go to the Sabbat in person or (in what is undoubtedly a false idea), did they take for real something they had seen while they were asleep?

Modern theologians seem to maintain, and maintain forcibly, that these women go there in person, and do so with the aid of the Devil who carries them – for in the Gospel one reads he could even do such a thing as to put Christ Himself on the topmost point of the Temple – and although some of their husbands, men of great faith, maintained that at the very time the women were said to have been at the Sabbat [*ludo*], it turned out on close investigation [their wives] had been in bed with them, it was answered they were not [real] women and that an evil demon had taken on the shape of their wife and fooled the husband. But my reply was, why don't you assume, rather, that the evil demon had been with his demons and the wife with her husband? Why will you invent a real body in a fictitious game, and a fantasy [body] in a real bed? Why in this situation is there a need to increase the number of miracles to such an extent, to behave not so much as theologians, more like *un homme verbeux*,[174] and to choose the more severe role when it comes to punishments? According to these documents, it was established that on one occasion during that theatrical performance, some silly

171. Since this is a Christian context, these *devotiones* are likely to have incorporated Christian names, motifs or invocations, as magical attempts to cure often did.

172. *Filios*. This could simply mean 'sons', but it seems unlikely that the witches would have ignored the daughters, and *filius* in the plural commonly indicates both male and female children.

173. A valley in Lombardy, near the border with Switzerland.

174. Alciati here invents a Greek word, *tetratologos*, 'someone using four words'. I have given the sense and imitated his use of a foreign language.

little woman invoked the name of Jesus and the whole show – all the dancing women, along with their lovers – suddenly disappeared. Who could have made this happen if the bodies had been real?

Arnaldo Albertini (1480–1544), became Inquisitor General of Sicily in 1534

De agnoscendis assertionibus Catholicis et haereticis ('The claims of Catholics and heretics, which need to be acknowledged'), c.1540. Hansen II, no. 75 (pp. 349–50)

[What witches are alleged to do, they do in body and in reality]. During the last few days, these things have actually happened in the inquisitional district of Navarre; for some women, infected by these acts of harmful magic, have been seen to go out of their houses at night via the upper-storey windows without any assistance, as far as onlookers could tell; and after they had been arrested, they confessed that they were taken by a demon through different parts of the country, as I have been told by honest, trustworthy individuals, and as is contained in the trials and confessions of those women during the sitting of the said inquisition. It cannot reasonably be denied that these things were really and physically done, any more than anyone could deny that I am putting pen to paper at this very moment, [saying] that I am deluded and merely seem, to myself or others, to be writing. So I think this is true and a more reliable opinion [than the opposite], although when I was summoned to a meeting of the inquisition in Saragossa in 1521 by order of Pope Adrian [VI] to investigate two legal processes which had been drawn up against two female witches [*mulieres bruxias*], I held the opposite view and thought it true at that time. But now, as I make further inquiries, I come to the conclusion that these things can happen, sometimes actually and physically, sometimes in the imagination, the mind or the fantasy; and the basis for this must be the witnesses and the confessions of the said women, their accomplices and cronies.

From this conclusion, which is dependable, I infer more. The first is that if this kind of woman, especially those who are elderly, says she has cast the evil eye [*fascinasse*] on any children, she should be believed, since casting the evil eye this way is possible in two ways. First, when someone is hurt by a malevolent glance, particularly [when it comes] from elderly women who bewitch [*fascinant*] children with a burning look and an envious glance which causes [the children] to fall ill and vomit up their food, [*authorities cited in support*]. So when a soul has been violently driven towards malice, as happens especially in elderly women, her poisonous, injurious glance is formed in the way [scholarly authorities] describe, particularly in relation to children who have a fragile body which easily receives an impression stamped upon it. It is also possible that, with God's permission or for some other reason, the malignity of demons, with whom elderly sorceresses [*vetulae sortilege*] have some treaty, works with them to this end. Secondly, casting the evil eye is done to play with the sense [of sight] (its usual practice with the aid of magic) – for example, when a person looks like a lion to other people, or seems to have horns, and so forth. This can be done by demons, who have the power to move images in the head and bring them back to the roots of the senses by changing the senses themselves.

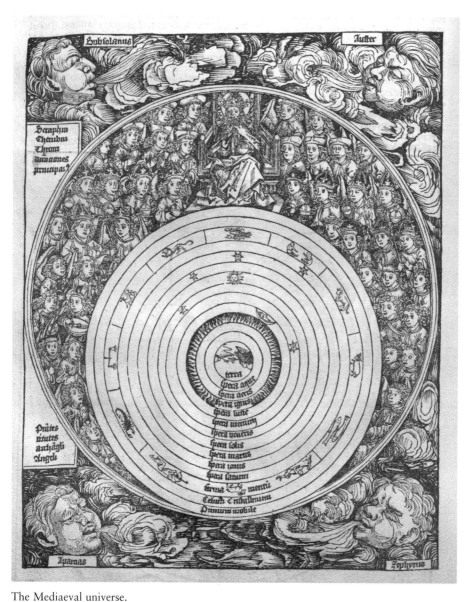

The Mediaeval universe.
From Hartmann Schedel, *Historia aetatum mundi et civitatum descriptio*, Nuremberg 1490

Map showing Pays de Vaud, Bern, Lausanne, Simmental, Valais and Haute Savoie.

The strappado, with weight attached.
Nineteenth-century engraving

Witches' activities.
From Ulrich Molitor, *De laniis et phitonicis mulieribus*, 1489

Conjuration to get rid of a diabolic snake.
Schwarzenberg, 1525

The Devil causes plague in a town.
German woodcut, early sixteenth century

Part III

Trials of Witches and Other Workers of Magic (a) Conducted by inquisitors, 1245–1540

1. *Women from the south of France offer magical cures, 1245*

Hansen VIa, no. 1 (p. 446)

3 July

Item: Alisson, a female diviner, said that on several occasions she told sick people to send her a belt, an item of underwear, a veil or shoes, and when she had these belts, items of underwear or shoes, she would cast a spell on a crystal and afterwards say, 'Make such and such a plaster from herbs'. She used to say all this in order to get small sums of money [*denarios*].

Item: She said that on many occasions she cast lead[1] for the sick in return for money. She also [said] she did not believe the lead had any power.

Item: She said that on many occasions Na Garejuda de Valerio cast a spell on lead and gave people to understand that this enchanted lead would cure their illnesses.

Item: She said she had never seen a heretic unless he was under arrest, and that she did not believe in or listen to their sermons, or give them anything.

2. *Magic and the dead in Montaillou, 1321*

Hansen VIa, no. 3 (pp. 446–7)

[Part of the testimony of Alazais, wife of the late Pons Azéma, from Montaillou, a witness in the case of Pierre Clergues, parish priest of Montaillou.]

Item: She said that when Pons Clergues, father of the present rector of Montaillou, died, Mengarde, his wife, said to her and to Brune, wife of the late Guillaume Pourcel, the two of them should cut off some of the fringe of hair around the dead man's forehead and some of his fingernails and toenails, so that the family home might continue to be attended by good fortune. This, she said, she and Brune did, once they had closed the door to the house in which the dead body was lying. They gave the hair and nail clippings to Guillemette, the house servant, and she [Alazais] believes that Guillemette gave them to Mengarde.

Asked if she pronounced any exorcisms while they were cutting the hair and nails from the body, she said no.

Asked about who was present [at that time], she said herself, Brune and Guillemette, the servant.

Asked whether they had done these things before or after the body had been washed, she replied that in that region the bodies of the dead are not washed. Water is simply sprinkled on their faces. [She and Guillemette] did what they had done after this sprinkling.

---

1.   I.e. a leaden image, reading *fecit* for *iescit*. Images were made from a variety of substances, including lead, and, in the case of the sick, used as sources of divination to find out what was causing the illness.

Asked if she knew how Mengarde had learned to do this kind of thing, she replied that when Pons had died, Brune, the wife of the late Venerable Vitale from Montaillou, said to Mengarde in [Alazais's] hearing, 'Madame, I have heard that if some of the dead man's hair, fingernails and toenails are removed after his death, he will not take the house's star or good fortune with him when he leaves'. Then Mengarde told Alazais and Brune that they would do it.

3. *Clerical magic in Toulouse, 1323*

Hansen VIa, no. 4 (pp. 447–9)

[The passage begins with a note from an official from Toulouse, saying that he has actually seen, read and handled the documents containing confessions made by Pierre Sparner and Pierre Engilbert (both of whom were clerics), as recorded by the secretary of the criminal court of the Archbishop of Toulouse. These confessions, written down in the court book, had been summarized and put into official language by Pierre le Cellérier public notary of Toulouse, and it is this version which the unnamed official now reproduces.]

27 June

Pierre Raimond Sparner, cleric, sworn and examined about the manufacture of the images which were found by the secular court in his house in Toulouse, said and confessed that one day this year (he said he could not remember which day it was), when he came from the Roman Curia, the Prior of Saint Sulpice, who was staying in his house, was in a room upstairs, talking secretly with Pierre Engilbert, Maître Pierre Fabre and his squire who was formerly known as 'Bertrand'. After they had been talking secretly like this for a while, they finished their conversation or discussion and came downstairs together, and [Sparner] asked the prior what kind of a discussion they had been having in such a secret manner. The prior replied and said, 'That's none of your business, because you're such a gossip, you can't keep anything a secret. Still, if you're willing to be trustworthy and keep it a secret, I'll be happy to tell you'.

Then [Sparner] promised he would tell no one and keep whatever he was told a secret, and the prior showed him a piece of parchment on which a picture in the form of a human being had been drawn. 'I was talking to Pierre Engilbert', [he said], '[asking him] to find me a man who would secretly carve me a stone mould in the likeness of this picture. The lead image we shall make in that mould will speak (so Pierre said), and once a month only it will tell us the truth in answer to questions put to it. For example, it will tell us the truth about Alquinna with whom we are having a lot of trouble. Likewise, it will tell us the truth about whether the daughters of le vicomte Bruniquelle have had "protectors", because the vicomte believes they have, and he's asked me, with some urgency, to find out the truth for him in any way I can'.

Item: [Sparner] said that Pierre Engilbert had had a mould made for Pierre Calhavelle. Three test figures were made out of lead in this, and the prior then put them in a chest, the key to which had been given to him by [Sparner's] mother. Pierre Engilbert, a cleric from Toulouse, sworn to tell the truth and examined about the foregoing, said more or less the same as Pierre Raimond [Sparner], and that he had had the mould made at the entreaties of the said prior, Pierre Calhavelle, and that Pierre Fabre said, in his hearing and that of the prior, that he knew how to make images made in that mould speak, provided they were made under the proper constellation and that those images would speak to them and reveal [the whereabouts] of treasure which had been hidden in that area.

He also said that in his presence and that of Pierre Fabre, the prior made three test images from lead in that mould, but they had not worked for them at all because they had no vitality, not having been made under the proper constellation.

He also said that the figure of a scorpion had been drawn above the image, and on the back, letters which could not easily be read. Nevertheless (he said), he thought the writing said, 'King Solomon'.

[The official now records that the confessions were made in the presence of the Archbishop's procurator, Pons Malefosse the Archbishop's treasurer, Bertrand Deyde registrar and Etienne Brossard notary of the Archbishop's criminal court. Brossard then recorded the confessions in the court book and registered them, Pierre le Cellérier summarized them and put them into official language, and the official from Toulouse appended the seal of the Archbishop's court as a warrant of their authenticity.]²

4. A notary practises magic and summons demons, 1410

Hansen VIa, no. 13 (pp. 454–5)

Notebook containing the Inquisitor's proceedings against Maître Geraud Cassendi, a notary from Bogoyran, accused of invoking demons and doing other acts of harmful magic [*maléfices*]. Witnesses saw him take some gold threads from a statue of the Blessed Virgin and put them in his shirt. They also saw him reading from a book and invoking demons, and a number of demons appeared in front of him. The man giving evidence was terrified and threw one of his shoes at them, saying, 'Go away!' and the demons went away at once.³ Then he gave evidence that once, in the wood of Bogoyran, Cassendi invoked demons seven times. [Cassendi] was accused of debauching his wife and daughters through the practice of magic and the invocation of demons.

---

2.   Sections 6 and 7 in Hansen are taken from volume 3 of Lamothe-Langon's *History of the Inquisition in France*, which has been shown to contain forgeries, of which no. 7 is certainly one. See further Cohn, *Europe's Inner Demons*, pp. 127–46.

3.   This last part of the sentence is in Latin.

5. The Devil appears in the form of a goat, 1432

Hansen VIa, no. 20 (pp. 456–7)

12 and 14 June

Agnese, wife of Giacomo Arizonelli from Astanca (Lotancha, in the neighbourhood of Quinto), found herself in 'the place of torture' in Faido,[4] having
been denounced by Brother Giovanni di Abbiategrasso, a Dominican, vicar of
the most reverend father in Christ, Don Marco de' Capitani from Vicomercato,
'Professor of Sacred Theology and Inquisitor of heretical wickedness in
Lombardy'. Interrogated by another brother, Vincenzo, whether she knew she
had done 'something contrary to the Catholic faith', the oath was administered
and she protested 'she knew nothing and had done nothing contrary to the
Catholic faith'. Witnesses to her deposition were Andriolo de Zoi, priest and
ecclesiastical vicar of Leventina, and others, and Giovanni d'Asti, chancellor of
the foresaid inquisitor.

Two days later, interrogated for a second time, 'so that she may tell the truth,
for the salvation of her soul, about what she had done contrary to the Catholic
faith', the first confession was extracted from her, namely, that ten years previously she took herself off 'to the bridge of Lotancha at about midday and there
invoked a devil called Lucifer. She called on Lucifer to come to her, and then the
Devil came in the form of a goat [*becco*], and she asked him for food for her
own consumption'. The Devil laid out 'a lot of bread and cheese' on the grass
for her. 'She took them and carried them home and would have some to eat
whenever she wanted'. In return for this bread and cheese, the accused gave the
Devil nothing less than a third of her valley's hay which had been cut and was
lying in the open meadows.

When the Devil was invoked for a second time, he appeared to her as usual
on the bridge of Altanca, once again in the form of a goat, 'and put bread and
cheese on top of a piece of turf on the ground, so that she could eat some'. In
return, the accused, Agnese, gave him 'a wood, some arable land and hostelries'[5]
situated outwith Altanca, and Lucifer made this wood and these hostelries burn,
to destroy them completely.

Interrogated once again [and asked] whether she used to talk to the Devil,
she answered no, she merely summoned him aloud. She sent for a woman like
herself from Formazza [to act] as her accomplice at a time when nothing else was
happening, but no other person apart from her had had contact with the Devil.

Agnese swore on the sacred Scriptures she had done this, [swearing to it] in
the presence of the above-mentioned inquisitor, his servant Fatio di Aliate, the
chancellor Giovanni d'Asti and the witnesses Alberto Verdoja di Prato, Zane
Furni de Bedoredo and the ecclesiastical vicar of Leventina, the priest Andriolo
de Zoi.

---

4. The phrases in inverted commas appear in Latin in the original.
5. Reading *gannea* for *gana*.

6. A priest charged with invoking demons and divining the future with their help in Carcassonne, 1435

Hansen VIa, no. 23 (pp. 457–8)

[The trial of] Etienne de Vals, a priest, canon of Montréal, accused of invoking demons, being acquainted with the practice of necromancy, learning different ways to invoke demons, consulting them, listening to their replies, accepting their advice, knowing about the future.

7. A pseudo Jeanne d'Arc, c.1435

Hansen VIa, no. 24 (pp. 458–9)

[This passage comes from the Formicarius *of Johannes Nider, a Dominican theologian who made an impact at the Council of Basel (1431–1449) and was a source of information for Heinrich Institoris's* Malleus Maleficarum. *Nider discusses witchcraft in book 5 which is written in the form of a dialogue, and provides illustrative anecdotes drawn from a variety of sources. This one reminds us that what we should call 'conjuring tricks' or 'illusional magic' were practised during the Middle Ages, and the young woman concerned here was clearly adept at this kind of activity.]*

We have today a distinguished Professor of Sacred Theology, Brother Heinrich Kalteisen, inquisitor of heretical wickedness. Last year, he told me, while he was engaged in his inquisitorial duty in the city of Köln, he noticed there was a young woman in the neighbourhood of Köln, who went around in men's clothing all the time. She used to carry weapons and [wear] her clothes loose, as though she were a mercenary soldier in the pay of a nobleman. She would dance with men, and drink and eat with them, to such an extent that it seemed she far exceeded the bounds of the feminine sex – a sex to which she did not deny she belonged. Now, because at that time (as, alas, today), two people were making trouble by passionately disputing the see of the church in Trier, she boasted she could and would enthrone one of the parties, just as the virgin Jeanne (about whom I shall speak in a moment), had done a little earlier for the French King Charles by securing him in his kingship; or (more precisely), she asserted she was this same Jeanne, resurrected by God.

So one day she entered Köln with the younger Graf von Virneburg who was one of her patrons and supporters, and there did extraordinary things while nobles were looking on, things which appeared to be done by means of magic. After a while she was investigated by the foresaid inquisitor who made diligent inquiry and publicly summoned her to appear in court. It was said she had torn up a napkin and suddenly put it together again in front of everyone's eyes. She had thrown a glass at a wall where it broke in pieces, and she had made it as good as new in an instant. She had also shown off with many similar frivolities. But the unfortunate woman refused to comply with the commands of the

Church. She went to the Graf for protection, and he secretly took her away from Köln so that she would not be arrested. But she did not escape the inquisitor's hands or the fetter of excommunication, [for] at length, hemmed in as she was, she left Germany and crossed the border into France where she married a soldier to avoid being harried by ecclesiastical interdict and death by the sword. Then a priest (one would do better to call him a brothel keeper), flattered this female worker of magic [*magam*] with words of love, and in the end she went off with him, like a thief, and entered the city of Metz where she lived with him as his concubine and demonstrated to everyone what kind of arrogance had brought her there.

8. *Invoking Beelzebub and taking him as a teacher of harmful magic, 1438*

Hansen VIa, no. 25 (pp. 459–660)

[The first of two documents is a judgement, dated 15 March 1438, delivered by Jean de Scalone, an officer of the Archbishop of Vienne, and Antoine Andrée, vicar of the local inquisitor, against Pierre Vallin from the parish of Sainte Blandine in La Tour-du-Pin, and summarizes Vallin's offences. The second document, which is translated here, gives much more detail of these offences and the legal process involved in his case.]

Against Pierre Vallin, alias 'Perrer', from [the parish] of Sainte Blandine in the district of La Tour-du-Pin, a retainer of the illustrious and powerful lady, Helinorgia de Golea, Lady of Tournon and of the domain of the said Tour-du-Pin, a man subject to this lady's jurisdiction.

In the year of our Lord 1438, 16 March, the procurator fiscal, for the sake of the legal right and interest of this lady, gives and hands over the articles written below. Since public opinion is repeating and referring to the evidence contained in a written factual statement – that this Pierre has been accused [of committing] and has committed and perpetrated the following outrageous offences, excesses and crimes – the procurator is asking the said accused, Pierre, to reply to the points contained in [these articles] and to answer them and their conclusions in a court of law.

First: The said accused, Pierre, having been thoroughly instructed in the devilish practice [of magic], unmindful of his salvation, and not having God before his eyes but turning aside from the Catholic faith and chasing after heretical wickedness, committed and perpetrated as many acts of sorcery [*sortilegia*] as he could, and thereby, having invoked a demon from Hell, took him as his teacher, invoked him and, during the course of his activities, called this demon from Hell 'Beelzebub.'

Item: This same accused was obedient to this demon he called Beelzebub for a period of 63 years and more, paid homage to him on bended knee by kissing the thumb of his left hand, and giving him, in sign of homage, a liard [*small coin*] as a registration fee.

Item: Every year after that, he took the hellish demon Beelzebub as his teacher by denying our omnipotent Creator and then handing over and granting his body and his soul to this teacher of his, the hellish Beelzebub.

Item: At this demon's demand, he made a cross on the ground, spat on it three times, then, at the urging of his teacher Beelzebub, stamped or trampled on it and smashed it as a sign of contempt and opprobrium for our Creator whom [Pierre's] instructor Beelzebub used to call 'the prophet'.

Item: Moreover, the accused gave his daughter Françoise, then aged six months, to this devil, his teacher, and Beelzebub, his teacher, killed her; and thereafter [Pierre] committed and perpetrated many acts of sorcery by following his teacher's instructions on what he should do and when he should do it.

Item: (An important point). At the Devil, his teacher's, instruction, the accused whipped or struck a spring, and from this spring, by means of and because of this devilish magic [*arte dyabolica*], unnatural storms came out and spread abroad, causing and inflicting a great deal of damage to the land and its produce by order of [Pierre's] teacher Beelzebub, the hellish demon, as has been said.

Item: Persisting in his various successive acts of harm[6] and faithlessness contrary to the law of God, he resorted to the help of his teacher and demon, and attached himself to the hell of this same demon-teacher Beelzebub by riding, in reality, with the help of this devil's stick, to certain 'synagogues'[7] at night and in various places and there ate certain small children along with his own urine.[8]

Item: He also had sex with his demon-teacher Beelzebub who manifested himself to him in the form of a 20-year-old woman, appearing to him on a series of specific occasions.

Item: With his teacher's help, on many occasions he did and committed [undesirable] acts of heretical wickedness contrary to the Catholic faith; and, for example, what he did and the inquisitor's proof that he had done so is contained in the sentence subsequently [given] against him by the ecclesiastical court – [pronounced], as one might expect, by the official from the Roman court and the inquisitor's substitute – and [his actions] deserve punitive treatment and punishment.

Item: This Pierre Vallin, alias 'Perrer', was accused eight years ago of acts of sorcery [*sortilegiis*] and specific things [following] therefrom and, after being found guilty with respect to these points which were found against him at that time, by the Lady of Tournon's court, he was sentenced on the last day of August 1431. He was sentenced judicially and definitively by the judge of La Tour-du-Pin (or his depute) to [pay] a certain sum of money, and he was forbidden, under pain of being burned, to use or venture to use the said practice [of magic] and acts of sorcery;[9] otherwise proceedings will be taken against him and he will be punished by being burned. To these conditions he consented and submitted of his own free will.

---

6.   Reading *maleficiis* for *maliciis*.
7.   I.e. assemblies of witches.
8.   *Cum sua comictiva*, from *commingo = commeio*, 'I defile with urine'.
9.   Or 'fortune-telling', since magic (*arte*) is clearly distinguished from *sortilegiis*.

Item: This Pierre has used the said wicked practice and acts of sorcery since then on many occasions and continues to use them daily, openly and publicly, as everybody knows.

Item: All the foregoing is true, well known, and perfectly clear, and there is public talk and gossip about all of it. Consequently, the procurator fiscal acts against Pierre Vallin, alias 'Perrer', on behalf of the legal right and feudal interest of the Lady of Tournon and the domain of La Tour-du-Pin; and because [Pierre] has done such things which are an evil example, contrary to the faith of our Lord Jesus Christ and in contempt of Christian law, and deserves to suffer the punition and corporal punishment contained in these articles,[10] [the procurator fiscal] asks that he be sentenced and compelled to abandon, for the legal and remedial causes and reasons mentioned above in connection with his forementioned [offences], the benefit of the edict [whose provisions were] to continue for the rest of his life and be entirely for his own good.

[*On 16 March 1431 Vallin was brought before a tribunal of secular judges to hear the charges and make his response. He pleaded guilty to every article and, in answer to the seventh article of visiting a witches' convention, named four others who, he said, were there with him: Pierre Traffay du Pont, Pierre Morelle, Humbert Farod from Arbret, and a woman called Ollieta from La Tour-du-Pin, all of whom had been dead for a long time before the trial. Vallin offered no defence, but asked for clemency, and his case was deferred until 23 March when Vallin appeared once again in court before Etienne de Saint George, the local judge. He was questioned about his accomplices, supporters, and followers and asked for the names and surnames of those who were his partners and accomplices in his crimes, along with the places in which the 'synagogues' had been held and the times they had taken place. Vallin replied that he could not remember more than the five names he had already given, a response ridiculed by the judge who said he had been in the 'sect' for 63 years and persisted in his crimes during all that time, so how could he not remember more than the names of five people who had been dead a long time already? If he was unwilling to revise his statement, said the judge, he would be put to the torture.*]

As a result of this advice, he said that with him there were Guigo and Jean Chanelle, formerly from La Tour-du-Pin; Benedicta, mother of the Allunat family from the district of La Tour-du-Pin, who was the first to make him dependent on these pacts and fatuities; a man called Piccolin from Pont Roujan, and another two whose names he did not remember, both of whom came from Pont; a woman from Pont, whose name he did not know, who had lived there for about the past four years; and Jean Amont from La Tour-du-Pin, who was still alive. He had no recollection of other people, nor was he aware of other women, even though more names were suggested to him. He said that the four from Pont came from Pont on two occasions, even though it was a long way to the meeting place of three roads near Moirans in the district of La Tour-du-Pin where they

10.   Reading *articulis* for *actentis*.

regularly met,[11] because one of them would ride a stick and they used to come like the wind.

Later on, after lunch the same day and year mentioned earlier [*23 March 1438*], the judge came to Pierre, terrifying him by having his hands bound tightly together and [asking] if he wanted to be dragged, put to the question,[12] and strung up, and asked him about his accomplices in the offences with which he had been charged and the people who had been with him. This [took place] in the presence of the honourable and noble Etienne Garin, substitute procurator fiscal of the dauphinate; Jean de Petra, *confirmarius*[13] of the dauphinal court, mayor of Vienne and the territory of La Tour-du-Pin; and Guillaume de Buenco, dauphinal castellan of Avinières, all of whom happened to have come there. With his arms and hands tied, and in much pain, under advice he named names: that is, Pierre, son of the late Pierre Ragis, alias 'Burillio'; Guigona, wife of Jean Pelliand who is still alive; Guillaumette Bone, wife of the late Guillaumet Vecy, alias 'Pic', who is dead; François Rebuffa who is dead; and Jean Motignot who is still alive. All these come from the region of La Tour-du-Pin. He was then questioned further by the dauphinal officials in the presence of the said judge, and said, in the judge's presence, that he knew no others and that they could do what they liked with him, because he did not know the names of any others.

On the following day, 24 March, the judge came again to Pierre Vallin, alias 'Perrer', and questioned him again about [those of] his accomplices he had not named who were with him at those sects and synagogues, saying to him that many of the others were and must have been priests, clerics and nobles [...] as well as rich people. [Pierre] said and asserted under oath that [even] if he could escape by revealing the others whose names he had not named, he could not name anyone else apart from those whose names he had given already.

[He said] this in the presence of Genet Janelle, vice castellan of the said place, Jean Ruffe, Jean de Vacherie, notary, certain others and me [G. Mareschal], notary.

9. Guillaume Adeline, a Benedictine, confesses to taking part in the Sabbat, 1453

Hansen VIa, no. 31 (pp. 467–72)

[*Guillaume Adeline, Master of Theology, was arrested at the instance of the Bishop of Évreux and the Inquisition. His case helps to show how much debate there was during the fifteenth century over the real or illusory nature of flight to the Sabbat and the Sabbat itself, and was used as an exemplum by Nicolas Jacquier and Pierre Marmoris, two French writers on magic, to demonstrate that the flight was actually real, or at least possible. Both knew Adeline and must have*

---

11. Perhaps 30 km along modern roads, and thus further and more difficult in earlier times.

12. I.e. tortured.

13. The official who appended his seal to the court record.

been shocked to find that beneath the surface of theological erudition lurked a heretic and a worshipper of demons. See further M. Ostorero, 2003, 'Un prédicateur au cachot', Médiévales 44, 73–96. The passages which follow are taken from the trial records and consist of the articles alleged against Adeline and then his abjuration.]

1. The said Adeline confessed of his own free will, and not coerced thereto by being shown instruments of torture or in any other way, that on many occasions he went on foot, without the assistance of any kind of transport, to the most damnable 'synagogue of the Waldensians'[14]. The synagogue, as Adeline himself alleges, was then held in the year of our Lord 1438 or thereabout, in August, near Clairvaux in the diocese of Besançon in the *comté* of Burgundy; these days [it is held] in mountainous places and in uninhabited places, quite often at night.

2. This Adeline entered the so-called 'sect of the Waldensians', he said, for two reasons: first, to see what it was like; secondly, to regain the affection of a certain soldier of good family, the temporal lord of Clairvaux who had a deadly hatred for him, and in this way be reconciled with him. He [Adeline] went to this sect almost every month for no other reason than this, he maintains. Those who had gone there were very happy when he arrived, and the presiding demon said to the demon who was escorting him, 'Let him be made very welcome'.[15] Adeline further said that many people of both sexes would come there from various places a mile and more away, some because of the lechery and secret lasciviousness and carnality which they used to practise there; others mainly because of the opportunities to eat and drink a lot. But certain people came to avenge themselves on their enemies or to get something from the demon who used to promise them a great deal if they would obey his orders. [Adeline], however, maintains he got nothing from the demon.

3. On his first visit, he kissed the hand of the demon presiding over the synagogue. [This demon] was called 'Monseigneur'. [His hand] stank, and was rough and cold. He appeared in the guise of a human being and his eyes were extremely savage and glittered and burned.

4. The foresaid Adeline used to proclaim and announce the devil's instructions at the order and command of his teacher, the presiding demon called 'Monseigneur' in this synagogue of Waldensians which (as was mentioned earlier), quite often took place and was held during a time of darkness, with a dim, sulphurous light. When the presiding demon arrived, [Adeline] said to the people assembled there, 'Here comes your lord! Get ready to receive him in appropriate fashion.' He also preceded the demon as he was coming to the synagogue.

5. On the second or third occasion Adeline attended the synagogue, after he had reminded those who were present to obey the synagogue's rules and the

---

14.   The word 'Waldensian', originally describing a member of an heretical sect originating in the twelfth century, quickly became synonymous with 'witch', transferring with it the notion of such a person's being a heretic as well as a devil-worshipper.

15.   These and other words in the passage put between inverted commas are in French.

orders of the presiding [demon], he went down on his knees and kissed the demon known as 'Monseigneur' on the buttocks which were rough, cold and stinking, [the demon] having taken the form of a goat into which he sometimes transformed himself.

6. The foresaid Adeline, who was at that time a Carmelite, swore an oath to the demon known as 'Monseigneur', using the following form of words: 'I, Brother Guillaume Adeline, prior of Clairvaux, renounce my belief in the Trinity, the Virgin Mary, the cross, holy water, the holy Bread and the veneration of wayside crosses and [crosses] everywhere'.

7. This Adeline, as is clear from his signet attached to a letter, promulgated and preached the following proposition in the pulpit at Orbec in the diocese of Lisieux, namely, that women who acknowledge a child born of adultery cannot be absolved by any priest unless, for the sake of the children, they disclose it to their husbands in the presence of witnesses before they themselves die.

As far as the other points are concerned, one should refer oneself to information which convicts him of simony, gross perjury, rape, adultery, incest with his own legitimately born niece, sacrilege, theft and being absent from the Divine Office for many years, [an office] he does not know how to recite according to monastic usage.

[Recantation of Maître Guillaume Adeline, made on 12 December 1453 in the Episcopal chapel at Évreux in the presence of the judge, the inquisitor's vicar general and two public notaries, one of whom recorded Adeline's recantation and the sentence passed against him. The recantation is in French, the sentence in Latin.]

I, Brother Guillaume Adeline, born in the parish of St Hilaire in the diocese of Chartres, now stand before you to be judged, Maître Simon Chenestre, official judge appointed in the name of the reverend father in God, Guillaume, by divine mercy, Bishop of Évreux, to this case which involves the Catholic faith, and Maître Enguerrand Synard of the Order of Friars Preacher, vicar general of Maître Roland La Cozic, Inquisitor General of the Faith in the kingdom of France.

I, wretched sinner, recognizing the great error into which I have fallen, and sincerely and willingly wishing to return to the way and obedience of our holy mother, the Church, sincerely and genuinely abjure, hate and abominate all error, idolatry and all heresy revolting against and contradicting the holy Catholic faith of the Lord Jesus Christ. Especially and particularly, I abjure and detest the damnable sect of Waldensians in which I have had communication with the adversary of the human race, the enemy from Hell, whom I saw presiding over that sect in the likeness and form of a tall man, whose hand I have kissed in homage and, the second or third time I was in that damnable gathering and he had the form of a goat, whose arse I have kissed, on my knees, in reverence and homage.

Item: I acknowledge and confess that in the congregation presided over by the Devil (which I attended as much for the experience of seeing it and [seeing] what it was about as being able, with the Devil's help, to be protected against a knight who wished me ill and with whom I could not be on good terms), I twice proclaimed and pronounced the following words in the presence of those attending the meeting: 'Here comes your lord! Prepare to receive him in the appropriate fashion', and walked in front of the Devil, who told me when I first entered the congregation, that I was welcome and that, if I wanted, I could increase his lordship a lot. He told me that, in order to increase it and calm the well born and the country folk, and bring justice to a halt, I should preach in my public sermons that this sect of Waldensians was merely illusion, fantasy and dreaming, and that I should refer to the canon *Episcopi*.[16]

I confess and acknowledge that in the presence and in front of the said devil from Hell, I swore an oath and renounced by Creator in the following words: 'I, Brother Guillaume Adeline, prior of Clairvaux in la Franche Comté, renounce belief in the Trinity, the Virgin Mary, holy water, the holy Bread, and veneration of wayside crosses and [crosses] everywhere'. For the things here expressed and all the other sins committed by me and confessed during my interrogations, [which] are plainly contained in the legal proceeding against me, I ask mercy and pardon of God, of the Church, and of you, gentlemen, my judges.

Moreover, I swear and promise to the best of my ability to pursue, tell, make known and reveal to prelates, officials and inquisitors everywhere, as far as I shall be able and on every occasion I shall remember and recollect, all those I may know who have done and perpetrated similar things in the past or will do in the future.

Item: I promise and swear to live a good life, to refrain in future and utterly abstain from blasphemy against the Lord Jesus Christ, His glorious mother, and the Christian faith.

I swear to our holy father [Pope] Nicholas and his successors, and to the prelates, officers and inquisitors of the Faith, to obey the commandments of the Church in future; that I shall never give aid, counsel or favour directly or indirectly against the office of the Inquisition but that to the best of my ability I shall give aid, favour and counsel to pursue all those (should I recognize them), who hold erroneous opinions; that I shall pursue, as much as I can in faith, all heretics and idolaters, their supporters and defenders and those who receive them and give them credit. I promise and swear to keep the true Catholic faith which is preached and guarded by the holy Roman Church, and to obey her commandments under the penalty which is due and ought to be imposed according to the laws, canons and statutes of Holy Church upon perjurers, backsliders and those who do the opposite after having sworn an oath, if I fail in any of the foregoing, either in some or in total or in part of what I have promised or sworn, or in any way fall into other errors I have committed before, or [errors] deriving from them, or new ones. Thus I ask help of God and the holy Gospels I have touched, and in affirmation of my sentence and this present abjuration, and in confirmation of my promise, I sign this document with my sign manual thus: G. Adeline.

---

16.   This was the early ecclesiastical text which suggested that women who believed they flew through the air while following the pagan goddess Diana's hunt were entirely deluded.

[This was done in the presence of John, Abbot of the monastery of St Taurin of Évreux, Maîtres Gerard Thomas, Professor of Sacred Theology, Gaufridus Amici, Doctor of Medicine, and several others.]

After they had heard this, the foresaid Maître Guillaume Adeline was judicially sentenced by the forenamed judges to perpetual imprisonment with the bread of sorrow and the water of distress, and he was cut off from the ministry of the altar and deprived of every office and benefice.

10. Four men and four women from Chamonix are sentenced to death for demon worship and apostasy, 1462

Hansen VIa, no. 36 (pp. 477–84)

29 April

[Claude Rup, vicar general of Vittore de Monte, inquisitor in the cities and dioceses of Geneva, Lausanne, and Sion (Sitten) passes sentence on the following:]

Peronette, widow of Michel de Ochiis; Jean Greland; Peronette, wife of Martin Don Bectex; Jean François the younger; Jean de Molarie, alias 'Pesandi'; Pierre de Nant from the parish of Vallée des Ours; Michelle, wife of Ramus de Ville from Vaudagne in the parish of Blessed Mary of Siervo; and Jeannette, wife of Michaud Gillier from the district of Chamonix in the diocese of Geneva.

[They confessed separately and repeated their confessions more than once in open court, saying that]: each one of them individually, out of his or her malice and perverse intention, had treacherously denied and inwardly departed from Almighty God, their Creator and [Creator] of everything, His most deserving mother, the whole Court of Heaven, and everything which comes from God. They had drawn the venerable sign of the cross on the ground and, in contempt of God, had stamped on it; and had moreover paid homage to the enemy of God, the Devil [who is] hostile to the human race. They had kissed his backside and elsewhere, on the shameful parts of the body he had assumed [for the occasion], as a sign of homage and, having cast and thrown away our Lord Jesus Christ, had taken and acknowledged this devil as their true lord and teacher; and at the same time had promised and paid him certain animals as a tax and a more distinct sign of homage. They have continually and abominably become soiled in the same crime over the passage of many years, one person more, another less, by infecting various individuals and their worldly possessions, and have heartlessly and most heinously perpetrated other crimes which are concealed for good reasons by silence.

[Their errors were detected and they themselves arrested, but they have not bothered [non curaverunt] *to return to the Faith. They have been imprisoned and questioned, but have still shamelessly remained impenitent. Each has confessed his or her errors –forcedly rather than voluntarily – although they have tried to conceal and disguise them by various evasions and equivocations. In the*

light of their confessions, therefore, a definitive sentence is pronounced against them, namely, that they be relaxed to the secular arm with recommendation for merciful treatment and that all their property be confiscated. A judicial opinion given by Martin Sostion concludes that five of these accused should suffer specific penalties. Michelle, wife of Ramus, Jeanette, wife of Michaud Gillier, and Peronette, wife of Martin Dom Bectex should be burned alive and their bones reduced to powder. Peronette, widow of Michel de Ochis, should be made to sit on a red-hot iron 'for the twentieth part of an hour' before execution by burning, because she had allowed herself to be buggered by several men; and because he had stamped on a consecrated Host, Jean Greland should have his foot amputated and be made to kiss a cross drawn on the ground before being executed 'alive or dead'. These recommendations were accepted by the court and the sentences duly passed.]

11. Women condemned for holding a Sabbat and for heresy and fortune telling, 1470

Hansen VIa, no. 37 (pp. 484–5)

In 1470, say the Records of Burgundy, Jeanne 'the Chatterbox' and Jeanne Moignon, professed 'branch women'[17] and heretics, were the subject of a sermon at Nuits by the inquisitor of the Faith, had [paper] mitres put on their heads, and were sentenced by Jacques Bouton, baillie of Dijon, the former to be burned, the latter to be whipped and banished. They used to hold their Sabbat under the rock 'Boutoillot'.[18]

Another woman at Dijon, accused of fortune telling [*sortilège*] while the late Duke Charles was alive, was handed over by the inquisitor of the Faith for Dijon to the town court, was the subject of a public sermon by the inquisitor in the Place de la Sainte Chapelle, was interrogated by Jacques Bonne, the town mayor, on the facts and circumstances of her trial, and after her admissions and confessions was sentenced to be burned and then handed over to the Prévôt.

*[Between 1472 and 1475 there were trials of women from Lavone, a municipality north-west of Turin. They were accused of acts of harmful magic [*malefizi*], incantations, acts of witchcraft [*stregherie*], heresy, poisoning, murder and transgressions against the Faith and Jesus Christ. It is worth noting that here* malefizi *and* stregherie *are clearly distinguished from one another as separate offences. In the sentence which handed them over to the secular arm, reference is made to further specific crimes. 'From their confession, willingly made, it appears they are heretical mascae, they have denied God, stamped on the cross, paid homage to a demon from Hell, in token of which they were in the habit of paying him tribute, and they have deliberately committed and perpetrated*

---

17.   *Ramassières*, that is, women who rode on branches or sticks, in this context a reference to their form of transport to a Sabbat.

18.   Reading *roche* for *noche*.

many other different kinds of harmful magic by means of their devilish practice'. Masca *means 'mask', and seems to be a reference to the fact that on several occasions when witches met, a number of them wore masks. For example,* 'Sometimes they take part in this feast [the Sabbat] with their face covered by a mask, a linen cloth or some other veil or facial representation. Usually they are masked', *Martín Del Rio,* Disquisitionum magicarum libri sex ('Six Books of Investigations into Magic'), *Book 2, question 16.]*

12. An acquittal disapproved, 1476

Hansen VIa, no. 40 (p. 487)

31 August

[The General of the Dominicans wrote] 'to Brother Pietro da Pezzano da Vercelli who is said to have acted improperly as an inquisitor and unjustifiably acquitted a female magician [*magam*] called Margareta, to the disadvantage of Master Niccolo de Bugella, [Inquisitor of Como]'.

13. A witch eventually confesses she has attended Sabbats, 1477

Hansen VIa, no. 41 (pp. 487–99)

9 September to 25 October

(i) On 9 September 1477, in the presence of the reverend father, Brother Etienne Hugonod from the Dominican monastery of Plain-Palais in Geneva, Vice Inquisitor General of the Holy Faith against heretical wickedness, [a hearing was held] by the reverend father, Brother Thomas Gogati, by special dispensation[19] General of the Dominican order, Prior of the said monastery in Geneva, and Inquisitor General of the Holy Faith in the cities and dioceses of Geneva, Lausanne and Sedan. There was present, in person, Antoinette, wife of Jean Rose from Villars Chabod in the parish of Saint-Jorioz in the diocese of Geneva. By command of the Vice Inquisitor and the noble and mighty Claude de Belfort, she had been arrested and committed to the prison of Villars Chabod by officials on behalf of the Church, noted, accused and charged with being suspect in her faith and indicted of the damned crime of heresy. She was brought into the Vice Inquisitor's presence, released from her prison shackle, and examined and questioned by the Vice Inquisitor. She took an oath, dictated by the Vice Inquisitor, on [a copy of] God's holy Gospels which he held and she touched. While doing so, she was asked whether she was in any way guilty of the said crime of heresy or answerable for it. The accused replied that she was innocent in every way of this crime. After they had heard her [say this], the Vice Inquisitor questioned her as follows.

---

19.   Strictly speaking, he was not entitled to be Prior and Inquisitor General at the same time except by permission.

First: Does she know why she has been arrested?

Answer: The men who arrested her told her they were taking her on behalf of the Faith.

Item: Has she ever considered she has been talked about as a heretic?

Answer: No.

Item: Has she ever run away from [Villars Chabod] to avoid being arrested for the said crime?

Answer: No.

Item: Has she given any sign of trying to purge herself of the reproach of the said crime of heresy which has prevailed and does prevail against her in the eyes of those who are affected by it?

Answer: No, because she says she did not know she had been slandered of this crime of heresy.

Item: Has she ever used any harmful magic to cause illness or did she ever carry out other evil acts?

Answer: She has not, except in the way she has already confessed in the presence of the foresaid Vice Inquisitor.

Item: Has she ever belonged to any sects or synagogues[20] of heretics in order to carry out, along with her accomplices, the acts usually carried out there?

Answer: No.

Item: Does she know the places in which heretics have been accustomed to hold synagogues?

Answer: No.

Item: Does she know the things heretics usually do, either by hearing anyone speak about them or in any other way?

Answer: No, except for what she heard in sermons while the heretics were preaching. But she doesn't remember what they said.

Item: Does she know there are ['wicked women'?], in general as well as in particular, in her parish, or in the district of Croisilles, or elsewhere?[21]

Answer: She doesn't really know.

Item: Has she threatened anyone, secretly as well as openly, and did harm later occur as a result of this, as is the way of heresy?

Answer: No.

Item: Has she attended any of the general sermons given by the Reverend Inquisitor in which he warned all heretics they had a limited period of time in canon law, and advised them they ought to turn back and confess and disclose

---

20. In this context, the word should be understood as a technical term for meetings of witches.

21. *Mal molles* which Hansen puts in brackets with a question mark. The phrase is more likely to be French than Latin, and if so, has a peculiar local meaning. Since 'mal molles' does not make any obvious sense in this context, it is open to emendation and one possibility is *malvaises*. Miscounting the minims of *va-* and taking a badly written *–is* to be *–ill* will produce 'malmolles'. *Malvaises* is merely a tentative suggestion. I have translated accordingly, but put the phrase in brackets. The 'Croisilles' mentioned here is unlikely to be the modern town of that name, since it is too far away from Annécy, the principal administrative centre with respect to Villars Chabod. One should therefore probably posit a Croisilles which no longer exists.

their error, so that at last they could return to the bosom of Holy Mother Church?

Answer: Yes.

Item: Why has she not returned to the bosom of Holy Mother Church after the foresaid warnings?

Answer: Because she has not left the said bosom.

Once this was over, the Vice Inquisitor held out to the accused, Antoinette, the grace and mercy of Holy Mother Church, and gave her the first canonical warning, with a day [to think about it], her second canonical warning and another day, and her third, with another day after that. The Vice Inquisitor assigned these three days for canonical warnings in case she was willing to confess the whole truth of the crime of heresy for which she is being detained, accused and charged and to return to the bosom of Holy Mother Church. Finally, she was directed to appear[22] before the Vice Inquisitor on 14 September at which time she, the accused, should be seen and heard confessing the entire truth of the said crime of heresy for which she is being detained, or proceedings will be taken against her in a different fashion.

Recorded and dated in the said castle of Villars Chabod, in the hall of the castle keep, in the presence of the noble and mighty Claude de Belfort, the venerable Antoine Declea, curate of (Mumminum),[23] and the venerable Claude Galliard, chaplain, summoned to and present at the forementioned [hearing] as witnesses.

(ii) 15 September 1477. The forementioned accused, Antoinette, wife of Jean Rose, was brought out in person from the forementioned prison into the presence of the forementioned Vice Inquisitor. She was released from all her prison shackles and the Vice Inquisitor asked whether she was willing to confess the crime of heresy with which she was being charged and because of which she was being detained. She answered that she knows nothing about the said crime. After hearing this, the Vice Inquisitor questioned her as follows.

First: Does she recognize Françoise, wife of Jean Tavan?
Answer: She does.
Item: Has she had and does she have a good name and reputation?
Answer: Yes.
Item: Have they been at loggerheads with one another?
Answer: No.
(Challenged by Françoise, she says it's not true).
Item: Does she recognize Claude Vincent Champanay?
Answer: She has a good name and reputation.
Item: Has she ever been at loggerheads with [Claude]?
Answer: No.

22.   Reading *comparendum* for *compendium*.
23.   Where I have not been able to identify a place in this passage, I have put the Latin name in rounded brackets.

Item: Does she recognize Jeannette, wife of Claude Fabre?
Answer: She does recognize her. She has a good name and reputation.
Item: Has she ever been at loggerheads with [Jeannette]?
Answer: No.
Item: Does she recognize Peronette, wife of Jean Missilier, alias 'Buvard'?
Answer: Yes.
Item: Have they ever been at loggerheads in any way with each other?
Answer: No.
Item: Does she recognize [the name] Masset Garin who was drowned for heresy?
Answer: No.

[*François Farod, procurator to the Inquisition, then stood up and asked for an interlocutory sentence, that is, a sentence passed while a trial is still going on, in order to determine some incidental point arising from the proceedings. Antoinette said nothing which could be recognized by the law against such a sentence's being pronounced. The Vice Inquisitor asked her whether she had any objection to the procurator's request, but she said nothing to the contrary except that she was not guilty of heresy. So the Vice Inquisitor proceeded to deliver the sentence.*]

Interlocutory sentence
    I, Father Étienne Hugonod, Vice Inquisitor General against heretical wickedness, judge and commissary in this region, have seen the evidence of your bad reputation and the verdicts against you, Antoinette, wife of Jean Rose from Villars Chabod in the parish of Saint-Jorioz in the diocese of Geneva, who have been accused by the Office of the Holy Inquisition of the Faith. I have seen the charges laid against you, and the inquisitorial proceeding by the said Office of the Holy Inquisition of the Faith, in the presence of the procurator of the Holy Inquisition. It must be declared that these are against you, together with the discrepancies [in your answers], the many perjuries you have made during the said legal proceeding, and everything else which must be taken into account by law. I have taken advice from [law] books and those experienced in these matters, and have waited until the due process of law has come to an end; and [now], by use of my ordinary power,[24] and by this my interlocutory ruling, I invoke the name of Christ from whom all right judgement proceeds and, inclining neither to the right nor to the left, but weighing things in equal measure, having God and the Holy Scriptures before my eyes, I say, pronounce and ordain that you, the said accused, Antoinette, be shown the instruments of torture and be tortured and questioned until the truth be brought to light from your mouth, [although] I expressly forbid any shedding of your blood or mutilation of your limbs. In the name of the Father and of the Son and of the Holy Spirit, Amen. I commit execution of this my sentence to the noble castellan and the prison officers of the

---

24.   That is, the power he has, of his own right, to exercise immediate jurisdiction in ecclesiastical cases.

forenamed Claude de Belfort of Villars Chabod, under pain of automatic excommunication under the law.

This my interlocutory sentence was delivered and read in the hall of the keep of the castle of Villars Chabod in the presence of the venerable Antoine Declea, chaplain and curate of (Mumminum), and the noble and mighty Blaise, son of the noble and mighty Claude de Belfort.

In conformity with this sentence, she was taken by the said officers to the place of torture, her hands were tied behind her back, and she was raised three cubits[25] from the ground on a rope, and there she stayed, without any extra weights being added,[26] for about half an hour. She was not willing to confess anything on that occasion, but asked for [a period of] reflection and a stop to the torture. She was immediately released from it and given remission until the next day to think about things.

Recorded in the place of the said torture in the presence of those named above.

(iii) 20 October 1477. The forenamed accused, Antoinette, was brought from the forementioned prison personally into the presence of the foresaid Vice Inquisitor. She was released from all her prison shackles and asked by the Vice Inquisitor whether she was willing to confess the crime of heresy of which she was accused and defamed, with which she was charged, and for which she was being detained. She answered she knew nothing about the said crime and was not willing to confess [to it]. When she had said this, the procurator of the Holy [Inquisition of the] Faith stood up and once again produced the written records and documents in the present trial of the said accused by the [Holy Inquisition of the] Faith and, once these had been seen, asked that the torture be continued in accordance with the [interlocutory] sentence delivered earlier. After looking at [the records] and hearing [the procurator], the foresaid Vice Inquisitor, in accordance with the sentence delivered earlier, ordered the foresaid accused to be tortured according to [the requirements] of the law; and in accordance with this sentence, the accused, Antoinette, was taken to the place of torture, her hands were tied behind her back, the rope was put in position, three weights were added, and then she was hauled up. Once this was done, she stayed where she was for a short time, but then asked to be taken down, promising to confess the whole truth of the said crime. The accused, Antoinette, was taken down and brought to the audience chamber, where she was not willing to confess to anything and was given until the next day by the Vice Inquisitor to think about things and [decide] to tell the whole truth.

Recorded in the hall of the castle of Villars Chabod in the presence of the noble and mighty Claude de Belfort, etc.

25.   About 1.37 metres.
26.   *Nulla tamen cavallata sibi data*. A *caballata* was a horse's burden, hence the notion of weight: see illustration of the strappado with a weight added to the feet.

Another session

(iv) 21 October 1477. The forementioned accused, Antoinette, was brought from the forementioned prison personally into the presence of the foresaid Vice Inquisitor, released from all her prison shackles and asked by the Vice Inquisitor whether she was willing to confess the truth of the crime of heresy of which she was accused and defamed, with which she was charged, and for which she was being detained. She replied that she was, and humbly implored grace of God and mercy of the Church.

She said and confessed that 11 years previously, or thereabout, one feast day during summer, she was coming from the chapel of Poisy, sad and depressed because someone called Jacquemart who lived in Annécy had seized pieces of land from her, on the authority of the honourable President of Geneva (that is, Maître Bertrand de Dereya), because she owed him money. She had obligations to both men because she and her husband had paid for their lord's assent to transfer a fief or holding, and the foresaid President had released Jean, husband of the accused, from his tenantry.[27] While she was on the road, she ran into Masset Garin who had been punished for heresy and, full of wails and tears, explained the reason for her distress.

When Masset heard this, he told her, 'Don't worry. We'll find a good remedy. I'll find you a man who will give you money and allow you to buy back your lands. It'll be fine, as long as you have confidence in me'.

[Antoinette] replied, 'I'll have complete confidence in you as long as you do what you say'.

Masset said to her, 'I shall do what I've said, and more, but you will have to do what I tell you. Please come with me this evening to the place I'll take you to'.

When she heard this, [Antoinette] was afraid of meeting him, but after a while, because of lust and greed,[28] she was happy enough to go with him to the place he was eager she should go.

Once it was evening (between 9 and 10 o'clock), this Masset came to the house of the accused and quietly called her and said to her, 'It's time; let's go'.

The accused left her husband and family and went with the said Masset to a place called 'Laz Perroy' which is next to the mountain torrent below Champagney. There, a synagogue of heretics was being held, and she found a large number of men and women who were screaming as though they were mad,[29] and dancing in a circle [*coreabant*], which they did backwards.

When she saw them, she was terrified, but Masset said to her, 'Don't be

27. Payment for such a transfer is expressed by a single term in Latin, *laudemium*. The whole sentence ends, 'who, in place of his wife, had come to the said Antoinette's house'. It is not clear to whom the 'who' should refer, nor what 'in place of/instead of his wife' means in this context.

28. *Cupiditatis causa*. 'Cupiditas' includes both meanings.

29. *Galabant*. This is a verb derived from 'Gallus', a noun referring to priests of Cybele. The *Rhetorica ad Herennium* attributed to Cicero describes someone who, 'like a eunuch-priest of Cybele, shouts and raves', 4.62.

frightened, because here we shall find anything you will [ever] have wanted. But you'll have to do as I say'.

The accused said to him, 'I'll do whatever you want'.

Then he pointed out to her a demon called 'Robinet' who looked like a black human being.

'There's our master', he said. 'You must do him homage if you want to have what you desire'.

The accused asked him how to do this and what he wanted her to say.

Masset replied, 'You will deny God, your Creator and the Catholic faith, and that red-haired woman[30] called the Virgin Mary, and you will take this demon called Robinet as your master and teacher. You'll do it in any way you like and [then] you'll have everything you desire – gold and silver in great quantities'.

When she heard this, the accused started to feel distressed and at first refused to do it, because when she saw the demon and he began to talk to her, urging her to do it and promising he would give her many good things – gold, silver and much else besides – he spoke to her in a hoarse voice which made him difficult to understand because the sounds were distorted and she could scarcely make out what he was saying.

[But] at the earnest importunity of this demon and of the others who were present, she then denied her Creator, saying, 'I deny my Creator and the Catholic faith and the holy cross as well, and I take you, the demon called Robinet, as my lord and master'.

She paid homage to this demon by kissing his foot and, at the demon's request and Masset's insistence, she [henceforth] gave him every year, as an annual tax, one 'vienne',[31] paying him round about Pentecost in the place where the synagogue was being held. (This year, it was held at the lower end of open tracts of lands belonging to someone called Jacquemod, next to a mountain torrent near [Planchia]). [When she paid her tax] she would say to the demon, 'Teacher, here's your tax', and the demon would then grab it.

She confesses further that the said demon, her teacher, marked her on the little finger of her left hand, and for ever after [the finger] felt dead; and that at his eager insistence, she gave the demon her soul. Then she trampled on a cross made of wood and laid out on the ground and broke it into pieces in contempt of God. When she had done this, the demon handed the accused a purse full of gold and silver, but when she got home and opened it, she found nothing inside. He also handed her a stick a foot and a half long, along with a small box full of ointment with which she would have to smear the stick [when she wanted to go] to the synagogues. Once she had smeared it, she used to put it between her thighs and say, 'Go, in the name of the Devil, go!' and immediately she would be carried through the air quickly to the place where the synagogue was being held. She further confessed that in the foresaid place, they ate bread and meat and drank wine (but she does not know what kinds of meat because, she says,

30.   Red hair was a sign of loose morals (Mary Magdalene) or treachery (Judas Iscariot) in Mediaeval iconography. Hence the blasphemy in calling the Virgin Mary '*la rousse*'.

31.   A low-denomination coin from the archiepiscopal mint of Vienne.

on that occasion she ate only bread and cheese).[32] Then they danced in a circle once again, and afterwards the demon transformed himself from their teacher in the likeness of a human being into that of a black dog to whom they showed respect and reverence by kissing him on his anus. Then the fire, which had been lit to illuminate the synagogue and [burned with] a green light, was put out and the demon shouted, 'Have sex! Have sex!'[33] Men took part [in this] with women in animal fashion, and [Antoinette] herself had sex with the said Masset Garin. After they had done this, everyone left, each to his or her own home.

She was asked [the names of] those whom she knew at the said synagogue, and answered that she saw and actually recognized Masset Garin, Peronette Bernardaz and Antoinette, wife of Pierre Rose from Villars in the parish of Bellecombe, who once tried to kidnap the son of Michel Rose at night and would actually have done so had not Michel wounded her in her left arm (as this Antoinette told the accused). She further confessed that she had attended another synagogue held in the direction of (Pereria) in a place called 'Es Publex', and that during that synagogue they ate bread and meat and drank wine, danced in a circle and yelled and screamed while they did their dance backwards. There was a large number of men and women along with a demon, their teacher, who was walking hither and thither among them, and after he had transformed himself in the manner described above, they paid him respect and reverence by kissing him on his anus. There was a green-coloured fire there, and when it had been extinguished, the demon shouted, 'Have sex! Have sex!' and men took part [in this] with women in animal fashion. Once they had done this, everyone left, each to his or her own home.

She was asked [the names of] those she knew who were at the said synagogue. She says she saw and actually recognized Pierre Guerron; Antoinette, widow of Girard in the parish of Saint-Jorioz; and Peronette, widow of Jean Grenod. But she says she did not recognize the others who were paying honour and reverence to the demon, their teacher, by kissing him on the anus as she herself, the accused, did too.

Next, she confesses she was at another synagogue held in the harbour of the lake below the vineyard of (Ochia) belonging the priory of Saint-Jorioz, along with the demon, her teacher, [who was] in the likeness of a black dog, and a large number of men and women. After this, she confesses she was at another synagogue held for the sake of doing harm[34] to our lord, the Comte de Genève, with the demon, her teacher, [who was] in the likeness of a human being.

---

32.   The perfect tense of the verbs indicates that Antoinette was talking about one particular occasion, presumably her first visit to the Sabbat, rather than giving an account of what habitually happened at the assemblies.

33.   *Meclet, meclet.* The word also appears as *meslet*, which probably represents the French *meslez*, itself a translation of the Latin *miscete*. *Misceo* means 'I mix, blend, entwine, exchange, embroil', and is a common Mediaeval euphemism for having sexual intercourse.

34.   *Empra mala.* I read *empur* for *empra.* If this reading is correct, the assembly could have been held in order to put right by counter-magic evils done to the Comte by some other magical operators, but since the contexts of these assemblies always suggests wickedness done by the participants therein, I have chosen a translation which will be in keeping with that idea.

Item: She confesses she was at another synagogue held in the meadows next to Lake [Annécy] in a place called (In Sogetis), where fishermen hang up their nets to dry.

Item: She confesses she was at another synagogue held in a place called [Les Croisettes?], near a spring, along with the demon, her teacher, [who was] in the likeness of a human being, and a large number of men and women.

At these synagogues they drank and ate and danced in a circle, shrieking and jumping with the demon, their teacher, and paid him honour and reverence by kissing him on the anus. Then they had sex [*mecletum fecerunt*], men taking part [in this] with women in animal fashion, and did the rest of the usual things mentioned in connection with the foresaid two first synagogues.

Later she confesses that she, along with her other accomplices, promised the demon, their teacher, that one of them would not make the other known, but would keep him secret.

Furthermore, she confesses that for the most part heretics go to the synagogues on a Thursday.

She confessed nothing else on that occasion, but was sent back [to prison] by the Vice Inquisitor to think about things and how she could make her confession complete, otherwise legal proceedings would be set in motion against her.

Recorded in the hall of the castle in the presence of the noble and mighty Claude de Belfort, lord of Villars Chabod, the venerable Claude Galliard, chaplain, the noble Jean, son of the foresaid noble Claude de Belfort, and Vincent Chevalier (de Calces), summoned and present as witnesses to the foregoing.

Another session

(v) 22 October. The forenamed Antoinette, the accused, was brought from prison and personally appeared before the Vice Inquisitor who asked her whether each and every thing she confessed before was true. She replied yes, both in respect of what she had done and other people had done.

She confesses further that at the synagogue held in [Les Croisettes?], she saw and actually recognized a woman called Bovetaz, mother of Claude Bovet, and her brother [who came from] Villaret; Jeannette, wife of Pierre Guerron; a man called Aymonet Petex from the parish of (Calces) – he was older than anyone else – the father of Jean Petex and his brothers and their sister, Françoise, a woman [living] in the house of Jean Rolet and married to his son Jean Rolet.

She confesses further that at the synagogue held below Dereya she saw a serving woman from Talloires, who during harvest time, by the love of God, used to glean grains of wheat. There were about 60 there altogether.

Later, she confesses that at a synagogue held in the harbour of Lake [Annécy], along with her other accomplices, she saw and actually recognized Colet Garin from the parish of Saint-Jorioz; Aimonette, wife of Albert, a convert, from Saint-Jorioz; and at the synagogue held for the sake of doing evil, [she recognized] Jeannette, wife of Jean Besson from Le Noiret; a man called Piciorti from the house of Pierre Colet from (Nanton Coterie) in the parish of Saint-Jorioz – he is the younger of the brothers in the house; Beatrice, wife of Garbil, a son from the same place; the widow of Merment Clément from Dereya, whose actual name [the accused] does not know; and Jean Jacquemod the Elder from Villars Chabod, who married a woman from their house in (Sales). The demon, their teacher, was there in the likeness of a black dog, and they paid him honour, homage and reverence by kissing him on the anus, and did everything else they usually did on these occasions.

She confessed nothing else on that occasion and was sent back [to prison] until the next day in order to complete her confession.

Recorded in the great hall of the castle of Villars Chabod in the presence of the venerable Antoine Declea and Claude Galliard, chaplains, the noble Jean de Belfort and Vincent Chevallier from (Calces), who had been summoned and were present as witnesses to the foregoing.

Another session

(vi) On 23 October [...]. She further confesses that at a synagogue held for the sake of doing harm she saw and actually recognized Raymund from (Sales) in the parish of Saint-Jorioz – he was the synagogue's cook; Pierre Millet, son of Pierre Espagnier from the parish of Saint-Jorioz; Jean Tavan from Villars Chabod – he was one of the important people in the synagogue, and wore a horn over his mouth [?] so that he might not be recognized; and Jean Besson senior from Le Noiret, who was also a cook there.

Then she confesses that on the Thursday before the interlocutory sentence was pronounced against her, the demon, her teacher, came to her in prison and told her not to confess, saying that if she did so, he would beat her. Antoinette, the accused, said to herself that the demon who could appear to her while she was undergoing imprisonment could liberate her from it. But the demon refused to do so (she said), and once again told her not to confess, saying he would keep her safe from every torture and any other kind of harm. The demon then transformed himself into a loathsome shape and suspended himself from the prison timbers, saying that hanging there did not bother him and he was not suffering pain because of it.

Next, she confesses that she did not engage in curing *mal de crid(s)* before she paid homage to the said demon, her teacher, but that after paying homage she would cure it by means of the demon, her teacher, saying the following words (or words to similar effect), 'There are three who lock you in, and three who unlock you. They are the Father, the Son and the Holy Spirit,' shouting,[35] then saying in a low voice, 'Robinet, Teacher, if you have any power to cure this child, please cure him;' and then she would make (a reverse cross).[36]

---

35. *Baliando*, i.e. *clamando*?

36. *Malum cridi* presents a difficulty. Hansen says he does not know what kind of illness this was. *Cridum* means 'proclamation' and so makes no sense in this context. It may be possible, however, to suggests that *malum cridi* represents a French *mal de crids*, to be translated as 'the illness [known as] crid'. Ambroise Paré refers to an illness in children, called *cridons*. 'There is another illness called "cridons" which happens to small children, annoying

Moreover, she confesses that on several occasions she saw pieces of human flesh, or [the flesh] of small children brought to synagogues where it was eaten, and she confesses that she, too, along with her other accomplices, had eaten it. It was sweet and soft (she said), adding that she had not seen the heads of the actual children carried in the said synagogues, but [participants] used to say that when they were digging up small children in the cemeteries, they left their [heads] because of the holy oil of baptism.

Item: She confesses that the demon handed the heretics an ointment to give to the sick, and that she received some of this ointment from the demon, her teacher, and with it touched the hand of Louis Fabre's daughter from (Fillioz) in the parish of Saint-Jorioz, who was aged four, and who immediately contracted an illness from it, growing physically weak for 15 days, after which she died. This happened six years ago, or thereabout, because Louis kept on asking the accused to pay a dowry.

Item: She confesses that powders to do magical harm and cause illness in humans and animals were made from the bones and guts of children.

Item: She confesses that Raymund from (Sales), Jean Tavan, and another fat man at a synagogue held below Saint-Jorioz in the harbour of Lake [Annécy], made powders from the bones of one of Pierre Millet the Younger's children, whom Masset Garin took and dug up in the cemetery of Saint-Jorioz one Wednesday. The boy had been buried in that same cemetery the Tuesday before and was taken to the synagogue the next Thursday by Masset in order to work harmful magic and cause illness.

Item: She confesses that in a basket in her chest she used to keep, and still does keep, her stick and the box of ointment given to her by the demon, her teacher, so that she can go to synagogues.

Item: She confesses that with powders given to her by the said demon, her teacher, she touched one of Pierre Jacquemod's cows which died as a result of that contact, and killed three more of Pierre Jacquemod's cows by means of the same harmful magic. She did this because he had beaten a nanny goat which belonged to her.

Item: She confesses that by using powders given to her by the said demon, her teacher, she performed harmful magic [*maleficiavisse*] on one of Pierre Girard's cows because he had deprived her of some oats which belonged to her.

Item: She says the said demon, their teacher, told them during the said synagogues that they should not worship Christ in church, nor pay Him honour either during the elevation of the Lord's body or in any other way, and that at the elevation of Christ, they should deny Him; and when they took holy water, they should sprinkle the holy water behind them. She also says that whenever she (the confessing accused) used to take holy water, the said demon, her teacher, would not appear to her. Furthermore, the demon used to tell the heretics attending the

them and causing them great pain as though they had thorns in their back', 6.23. 'Reverse cross' is my guess for Hansen's *mediam crucem* which does not make sense. We have references elsewhere to someone's making a *versam* or *inversam* or *reversam* crucem, but *mediam* cannot be emended, at least with much conviction, into any of these three versions.

synagogues that if they passed in front of crosses, they should not worship Christ but rather deny Him who was crucified upon the cross, and spit out the Lord's body on Easter Day. (But she says she couldn't do this.)

Finally she confesses that the most sacred Body of Christ was once brought to a synagogue held in the harbour of Lake [Annécy] by Peronette, wife of Jean Massilier: Jeannette, wife of Pierre Guerron: and Antoinette, wife of Antoine Girard. They dragged it on the ground and everyone present stamped on it – the accused with her left foot – and then they tried to grind it into pieces by jumping up and down [on it]. However, they could not succeed and while they were doing this, it vanished from their sight with a great burst of light. The demon was standing at a distance.

On this occasion she did not confess anything else, but was sent back [to prison] until the Vice Inquisitor's next arrival, so that she could make her confession complete.

Recorded in the castle hall of Villars Chabod in the presence of the venerable Claude Galliard, chaplain, the noble Jean de Belfort and Vincent Chevallier, who had been summoned and were present as witnesses to the foregoing.

Another session and the conclusion of legal proceedings

(vii) On 25 October the accused, the forenamed Antoinette, was brought from the prison and personally appeared before the Vice Inquisitor. All her prison shackles were removed and the Vice Inquisitor asked her whether each and every thing she had confessed earlier, was true both in respect of what she had done and in respect of what other people had done. She answered yes.

She confesses further that on Thursday last, 23 October, after the Vice Inquisitor asked to see her again and after she returned [to prison], the demon, her teacher, came to her there in the likeness of a fat, disgusting-looking man and told her she had denied him. The accused replied she had done so and that she had returned to the bosom of Holy Mother Church by giving herself back to God, the blessed Virgin Mary, and Saint Bernard, and by offering three *deniers* in honour of Saint Bernard so that the demon might not harm her or tempt her. At which point the demon left without saying anything else and (she says) she has never seen him since.

She said that all this would turn out to be, and was, genuinely true without any equivocation, and swore it on the holy Gospels of God, which were held by the Vice Inquisitor and, on peril of her soul, said that she had spoken the entire truth about this crime. She maintained she did not know anything else, and humbly and devoutly, weeping, upon her knees and with clasped hands, asked God to grant her mercy and the Church to give her grace concerning these things. She also asked for sentence to be given, concluded and declared in her said trial and confession, as is recorded by this present [document].

In response, the venerable Claude Galliard, chaplain, procurator of the Holy Inquisition of the Faith, appeared and sought and asked for [sentence] to be concluded and announced in the said trial, the law to be stated and a definitive sentence to be delivered. After both sides had had their say, the Vice Inquisitor brought the said legal proceedings to an end and appointed a day for the parties [concerned] to hear the law and his definitive sentence anent the said trial.

Recorded in the castle hall of Villars Chabod in the presence of the venerable Antoine Declea and Pierre de Con[…], chaplains, and the noble Jean de Belfort and Vincent Chevallier, summoned and present as witnesses to the foregoing.

14. Decisions in a trial of five accused witches, 1485

Hansen VIa, no. 46 (pp. 500–1)

22 August

We, Jean du Pré, graduate in law, lieutenant of my lord the Governor and Baillie of Chauny, and Guillaume le Normand, also graduate in law, councillor to the Duchess of Orléans and her procurator general in her land and lordship of the said Chauny, certify that, by order of the said Duchess and her council, we have charged and do charge Jean de Lié, Prévôt of Chauny, the sum of 20 *livres tournois*[37] for certain expenses made by him at the command of the said Duchess and her council in criminal proceedings against Henriette Huette and Perrée Rogière, both deceased witches who were executed and burned by the official executioner quite near the law court of Chauny according to the sentence and judgement of the councillors and vassals of the said Duchess, as [the record of] the trial on this charge makes perfectly clear; also [in the criminal proceedings] against a woman called Marie Jaquenette, a defendant in the said case of witchcraft, who, according to the judgement in the said case above, was whipped and beaten with rods by the said executioner at the crossroads in Chauny and, after that, branded on both cheeks with a *fleur de lis* and banished from the lands and lordships of the said Duchess.

Simonette Rousselle and Gillon, her sister, who were defendants in the said case, have been sent back to Lâon, in accordance with the instructions of the [law-]court of the parlement, to have the rest of their case tried; and with regard to the expenses of the Inquisitor of the Faith, who came to Chauny at the Duchess's command for the business of the said witches, and the salary of some councillors from Lâon [who came] at the Duchess's command, as well as the charge [of 20 *livres*], the said Prévôt asks letters and we have granted them to him [in the form of] this present document.

Given under the counterseal of the said bailliage, 22 August 1485.

---

37.   That is, money from the mint at Tournois. The sum is not a large one.

15. Wolfgang Heimstöckl is commissioned to suppress all forms of magic and divination and undertakes the task, 1491–1499

Hansen VIa, no. 53 (pp. 506–10)

(i) Ratisbon, 10 March 1491

Heinrich, by the grace of God Bishop of Ratisbon, to our dearly beloved man of religion in Christ, Wolfgang Heimstöckl, overseer of the granary and professed monk of the Monastery of the Blessed Virgin in Rohr, member of the canons regular of the Order of St Augustine in our diocese, greeting in the Lord and a call upon your diligence in the things entrusted to you.

It has come to our notice that in many places of our said diocese an error is growing little by little, with the result that several people of both sexes are taking upon themselves 'divine' honour and, contrary to the prohibition of Holy Mother Church, are claiming to be adepts in magic [*divinos*] or sooth-sayers and, in pursuit of monetary gain in particular, are promising physical health to livestock as well as human beings by means of incantations, amulets and [magical] bindings, [all] mixed up with the semblance of sacred words and other superstitious things. Thus they lead many simple-minded people astray, delude them and extort money from them, and perpetrate very many other acts of harmful magic. So we, wishing to counter the scandals and dangers to souls, as vigilant care for our duty demands, commission you by the contents of this document, strictly enjoin you, under the penalty of excommunication, and order that when people have assembled for divine worship on a Sunday or feast day, you or the rectors of other parish churches under your control bring authority to bear, from the pulpit, on priests or purveyors of this kind of superstition[38] by means of a like penalty; and that you interrogate and summon to court not only each and every person who is perpetrating the things mentioned above, but also those who have approached the foresaid adepts in magic [*divinos*], enchanters or enchantresses and superstitious individuals for their pretended help, so that within eight days of your making this public pronouncement they appear before you to disclose the error of superstitious practices of this kind, and denounce and make known both those who carry them out and those who are suspected of these things and have a bad reputation because of them.

These people we constrain and compel to desist from superstitions of this kind and all other acts of harmful magic by our ordinary[39] authority [expressed] in the contents of this document, and by the penalty of excommunication and removal of the sacraments of the Church; and we wish and command that they be constrained and compelled by you. If any of them, having been inter-rogated as mentioned earlier, offers you resistance or is unwilling to turn aside from the foresaid error and make it known, you are to send him or her to our presence as someone suspected of heresy, and you may call upon the secular arm if necessary.

---

38. Reading *superstitionum* for *superstitiones*.
39. That is, episcopal authority sufficient for dealing with a particular case.

(ii) Ratisbon, 18 February 1493

Rupert, by the grace of God, Bishop of Ratisbon, to our dearly beloved brother in Christ, Wolfgang Heimstöckl, professed monk of the monastery in Rohr, greeting in the Lord.

Although the darkness of the foolishness of idolatry has been cut off by the illumination provided by the light of the truth of the Gospel so that no longer, as before, does each nation wander off after its own deities, nevertheless, the ancient serpent, swelling with the poison of ancient pride, busies himself with usurping the honour due to God alone who (we believe) is the only originator and dispenser of every good thing. He is, at least implicitly, getting himself worshipped and honoured as a god, and because of this he continues to urge certain human beings, especially of the female sex, partners in his wickedness through certain tacit or openly expressed pacts, to call themselves by the insolent word 'divines' [*divinos*] and (their prime mover being the Devil), to present themselves as helpers (male and female) in any difficulty. But since inquisitors of heretical wickedness do not bother themselves with this kind of 'divination' and sorcery [*sortilegiis*] unless they clearly smack of heresy, lest evils of this kind remain unpunished and increase day by day we commission you and strictly enjoin upon you our order to summon and interrogate magical adepts [*divinos*] of this kind, sorcerers [*sortilegos*][40] and workers of harmful magic and their accomplices, helpers or clients in places subject to the spiritual or temporal authority of the monastery in Rohr. You are to constrain and compel them, under the penalty of excommunication which, by our authority, you will be able to bring against them and any one of them, to abjure their errors and disclose [the names of] other people who have a bad reputation [on this account], as well as the kinds of help they provide. You may discharge, do and enforce each and every thing which is necessary and appropriate in carrying out the business of this kind of inquiry and which inquisitors of heretical wickedness do or are able to do in accordance with law and custom. If anyone, having been interrogated by you, offers you resistance, you are to send him or her to our presence as someone suspected of heresy, and you may call upon the secular arm if necessary.

In this regard, we urge each and every faithful person of whatever social rank or status, and we enjoin and command those subject to us in virtue of their obedience and under the said penalty of excommunication, faithfully to assist the foresaid Brother Wolfgang in the foregoing with aid and advice as soon as and as many times as they have been asked, and to show themselves quick to respond and faithful, as they will want, not without good reason, to be commended for the sincerity of their faith.

(iii) Rohr, 4 July 1497

[Heinrich Institoris, inquisitor, commissions Wolfgang Heimstöckl, now desig-nated prior of his monastery, to proceed against 'the heresy of female witches' [heresin maleficarum] *and any other heretics in the diocese of Ratisbon.]*

40.   Or fortune-tellers.

(iv) Rohr, 2 July 1499

[Wolfgang Heimstöckl writes to Erasmus Rambein, parish priest in Abensberg, a town a few miles south-west of Ratisbon (Regensburg).]

A rumour has reached [me] from trustworthy sources that the city of Abensberg of which, by God's agency, you are the parish priest, is full of the filth of idolatry because (it is said), there are many workers of harmful magic there, especially women, who carry out their acts of harmful magic to the detriment, and no small one, of their fellow citizens. If this is so, I am absolutely astonished, since you are a learned and well-known preacher and an intelligent man, that you do not take a stand against such notable crimes, even as far as [shedding] blood. For if you do not unceasingly cry out and raise your voice, like a trumpet, against silliness, crimes, etc. and do so effectively, because you are silent on the subject of this very great crime of idolatry, you have become in effect a dumb dog which is unable to bark. I believe you are particularly afraid to be stirred to action in case the female witches [*maleficae*] work harmful magic against you, etc. If this is so, your faith is pretty weak and you are more afraid of elderly women than of God, since it is quite certain that witches [*malefice*] can do nothing against preachers and the other people who administer justice; or perhaps you have no hope that the foresaid witches will be saved, because they are completely hostile to God and your words may not be enough to bring them back [to Him]. But listen, I beg you, to the words of St Augustine in his sermon on auguries [...][41] and if you cannot convert these hostile women, at least counsel the innocent by your salutary exhortations, so that they can beware such things for themselves.

You will grant me your indulgence for speaking at such length, because if I were not afraid for my soul by reason of my duty to investigate the wickedness of harmful magic – which you know I am bound to do – at any rate I should refrain from being especially silent. So get ready to fight and be brave; stand in battle line for the Lord God of battles – He Himself will be your helper – cleanse your hands of the blood of these people[42] – a thing which happens (if you don't fail to do it) – when you tell them all their crimes. It would redound (believe me), to your shame if, because of your negligence, I or one of my subordinates were to send a sickle to your harvest which, however, I could do, as is perfectly clear in the letter of commission made out to me. It will not be enough to cry out and raise your voice against such a great evil as this in a single sermon. [It will take] more after that one, so that the deaf ears of the witches are burst open by your continual shouting. In this you will do something very pleasing to the Lord God and acceptable for your sins. Goodbye.

Given in Rohr on the day of the Visitation of Mary.

41. Omitted by Hansen.
42. *Eorum*, masculine, so this now includes men as well as the women he has been emphasizing before.

16. Sabbats in the Val Camonica, 1518

Hansen VIa, no. 59 (pp. 511–12)

[Carlo Miani, the castellan of Berno in the Val Camonica, reports what he has been told about witches in his area.]

24 June

Some people in this valley who had the great Devil as their god and caused the death of a good many women and men were burned. Then, giving an account of the ceremonies of those 'goat people', he says, young women, urged on by their mothers, make a cross on the ground, spit on it, trample on it, and lo and behold there appears to them a noble horse ridden by its groom, a demon, [and] thus they find an open space on the summit of the Passo Tonale where they hold vivacious dances and brilliant banquets. Next they are very kindly received in a dazzling room covered in silk draperies, and pay homage to the king who is seated on a very precious throne, and at his command they insult the cross. Their reward is to be escorted by extraordinarily good-looking young men.

Some of these deluded women, under barbarous torture, confessed they had caused death by means of powders they had received from the demon, and when [these powders] were sprinkled in the air, they raised storms. Other women smeared their distaff or a stick with some fantastical[43] ointment, climbed on and were carried to the top of the mountain.

17. Definitive sentence passed against a widow who had attended a Sabbat, 1527

Hansen VIa, no. 69 (pp. 513–15)

(i) 13 April

In the name of the holy and undivided Trinity, Father, Son, and Holy Spirit, Amen.

I, Brother Etienne de Geul, Doctor of Holy Scripture, Dominican from the Plain-Palais monastery, Inquisitor against heretical wickedness, specially deputed by Apostolic authority, in the city and diocese of Geneva, to each and every person who will see what follows, make known and manifest that in the year of our Lord 1527, on 13th April, I saw the inquisitorial proceedings against you, Claude, daughter of the late Etienne Lyane, widow of Guillaume Bastard from the parish of Copponay in the diocese of Geneva. From their contents we think it legally plain and clear that you have treacherously denied Almighty God, the Virgin Mary, His mother, the Catholic faith, holy baptism, the holy cross and everything to do with God. Moreover, you have paid homage and reverence to

---

43. *Fatato.* The adjective implies that the ointment came from the fairies. A connection between fairies and demons or the Devil himself is not uncommon in witchcraft accounts from all over Europe.

the Devil, the adversary of God and the long-standing enemy of the human race. You have kissed this demon in disgusting fashion on the backside of the body he constructed [for himself]; you discarded and rejected our Lord Jesus Christ and took this same demon as your lord and teacher. You also gave and paid a certain annual tax to this demon as an overt token of homage to him. You trampled on the venerable sign of the cross, ate and devoured pieces of human flesh which had been brought to the synagogues, and did and perpetrated other appalling crimes which are dreadful to hear about and which I pass over in silence lest they offend the ears of the devout.

Because of these and other reasonable causes, therefore, which could and should have been able to affect our mind and that of any other person of proper sensibility, by this my definitive sentence, with the agreement of those experienced in the law and after mature consultation of [law] books and experts in these matters, in my official capacity according to long-established custom, having God and the Holy Scriptures before my eyes and making the sign of the cross with the words 'In the name of the Father and of the Son and of the Holy Spirit, Amen', so that my judgement may proceed from the face of God and my eyes may see impartial justice, and having earlier taken my ordinary power which has duly committed its full force to me, I convey in this written document, pronounce, decree, say, command and decide that you, Claude, should have been and are to be sentenced; and I do sentence you as faithless, idolatrous and impenitent. By the contents of [this document] I relinquish and hand you over to the secular arm as an impenitent, a murderess and a rotten limb of the Church, so that your wrongdoings may not remain unpunished and so that no morally depraved individual may become more depraved because his or her crimes go without punishment. I ask that same secular arm, with as much feeling as I can, to restrain the sentence against you so that you do not die, shed blood or suffer mutilation of your body.[44] By this my definitive sentence, I say and declare that each and every one of the goods you have, have had and can have had from the time you committed the foresaid crime, should have been and are to be confiscated; and I do confiscate them and declare them confiscated, to be divided as the law wishes and as customary practice [says] they should be distributed.

(ii) *[The charges are formally repeated by the secular authorities who then say:]* All of these are worthy of serious punishment. Therefore, so that justice may be done and an example given to everyone else, we sentence you, Claude, to be burned and devoured by fire and consumed thereby in such fashion that death follows therefrom, your soul departs from your body and your body is changed and reduced to ashes.

(iii) 15 May

[A note in French, however, says that] you are to be taken to the usual place in Champel, and there your head is to be cut off, your body fixed to the gibbet and your head attached and nailed with an iron nail above and near your body.

---

44.   *Membrorum mutilationem. Membra* may mean 'limbs', but may also refer to any parts or organs of the body.

PART IV

TRIALS OF WITCHES AND OTHER WORKERS OF MAGIC
(B) CONDUCTED BY SECULAR COURTS, 1304–1540

1. A dead body vanishes from the field of battle, 1304

Hansen VIb., no. 1 (pp. 516–17)

18 August

On this day there fell about 4000 armed men from the Flemish army. Among them was the distinguished Wilhelm von Jülich who died while he was chasing the enemy.[1] [The cause] was either suffocation because he could not breathe and fell – he was of a slight build, even though he was brave – or (as the French say), he fell down dead while he was coming after them with a small troop of about 80 men. The Flemings, practically without number, agree that right up until the French turned tail he was in good health and also uninjured, [but] he was surrounded and hemmed in by their (that is, the French) cavalry, and killed along with all his companions while they were putting up a very brave resistance and inflicting physical damage. But because later on neither the French nor the Flemings could find distinguishing marks to identify his body or his armour, the common Flemings long afterwards used to maintain that he had been carried away by the art of magic of which he used to avail himself, and that at some future time, when it suited him and when they were in rather great danger of war, he would return. This, however, is just a silly story. It is certain he died that day, even though marks to identify his body or his armour could not be found, because that happened to many noblemen in Courtrai.

It is said that a very wicked enchanter [*incantator*] from a wicked family, who was with him at the time, deceived him because he promised that whenever he wanted or needed, he would be rendered invisible to his enemies and anyone else[2] by means of a magical incantation he taught him. But [Wilhelm] uttered the incantation and it did nothing to save his life. I don't know if it helped at all to conceal his body, because it is easy for demons to conceal any dead body. Consequently, after a short time the said enchanter [was brought] to Brussels by Johann, Duke of Brabant, a kinsman of Wilhelm, because of the said crime, which he confessed. His forearms and shins were broken and he was bound to a wheel raised high above the ground. The said incantation could not help him in any way.

2. A question of legal proof in a case of murder by magic, c.1350

Hansen VIb., no. 2 (pp. 517–18)

Concerning the prosecutor and the defendant when women are said to have brought about murder by means of incantations and magical objects.[3]

---

1.   The battle in question was that of Mons-en-Pévèle, one of a series between the French and the Flemings at the beginning of the fourteenth century.
2.   Reading *aliis* for *alias*.
3.   *Experimenta*. Almost any small object could be used as a vehicle for preternatural power. Sometimes they were engraved, often they were not. They could be concealed under or over the threshold of a house, or in the roof or walls, the aim being to allow a maleficent potency to pass through them, unseen, and to target a named or intended individual.

A young man was lying ill in Lautzchen [in Saxony]. He summoned his father and men of upright character, and in their presence testified that he was being made ill by the incantations and acts of harmful magic (or by the magical objects) of two women whom he named. [He also said] he was going to die soon. So after his death from that illness, his father brought an action against those women, just as though they were murderesses, complaining that his son had died because of their incantations. But (the women ask), since they have preserved their respectability and worthiness as women all their lives and have never been accused of such a disgraceful thing, and since eyewitnesses have sworn that neither wound nor weal has appeared on the young man's body as should happen, in principle, in cases of murder, should they be obliged to answer the complaint lodged against them as though [they had committed] a murder? On this point a ruling was given that, notwithstanding the young man's testimony and his father's complaint, if the women's representations were found to be true, it is not reasonable [to require them] to make answer as they would be legally obliged to do in a case of murder. But, because the general rule of state law says that a defendant must answer every complaint by acknowledging or denying [his or her] guilt, it is sufficient for the women to reply yes or no, and purge themselves by a simple oath.

Therefore, since criminal cases require the clearest proof, much more so than civil, [and] since we are dealing with incantations and similar pretended inanities which have usually been done not openly but in complete secrecy, we must fall back on things which give rise to a presumption: for example, if a woman has been another man's concubine, and if, with reference to that man, she happened to say in front of trustworthy people who heard her say it, 'Unless he does such and such ' or '[Unless] he stops doing such and such, I shall contrive a death for him', especially if it has been her habit to swindle [others] with incantations and if she has ever been arrested in [the commission of] such an act.

The kind of woman in the case such as the one we are dealing with, who has been deliberately dragged before a judge, lacks the means of purging herself as a murderess by means of witnesses. Therefore not all cases require proof of equal strength, and actually proof and purgation quite reasonably differ from one another because of the difference in the circumstances [which call for them].

3. Conjuring the Devil in an act of hostile sex magic, 1390

Hansen VIb, no. 3 (pp. 518–20)

30 July–24 August, Paris

[Marion, a prostitute, was once the lover of Haincelin. He, however, left her and married someone else. In order to win him back and prevent him from having sex with his wife, Marion asked Margot, another prostitute, to bewitch him for her. Both women were arrested and tortured, Marion twice, Margot five times. In their confessions, they said they made two garlands and then invoked the Devil.]

'Demon, I invoke you in the name of the Father and of the Son and of the Holy Spirit to come to me here'. Then, while the woman who was giving evidence held the two garlands in one of her hands, a demon[4] appeared to her in the shape and form of the demons people make for Passion plays, except that he had no horns. He said these words. 'What do you want?' The woman giving evidence said, 'I give you this garland which you see [and] which I'm putting on this chest. I'm asking you to beat Haincelin (named above)[5] (a friend of Marion who is here), and the woman who has just married him, in such a way that they can't have use of their limbs until they've accounted to Marion for the harm and damage they've done'. Whereupon the demon left her house, taking with him the garland she had put on the chest. The woman giving evidence saw him, the demon, leave by an open window in her room, and while he was leaving the house the demon made a noise like a whirlwind. The woman who was giving evidence was very frightened and agitated by this.

She said that [before] making the invocations of the Devil, she laid a spell on [*conjura*] the two garlands by [repeating] the following three times. 'Devils, help me and see to it that Haincelin cannot have sex with anyone but me'. She crossed herself, making the cross upside down and saying these words, 'In the name of the Father and of the Son and of the Holy Spirit, devils, come here!' This done, and in Marion's presence, the woman giving evidence handed over the two garlands to Marion.

[At the final session, on 9 August, the court was unusually crowded, with 17 conseillers, several advocates, and the presiding officer, the Prévôt.]

After this was done, the Prévôt asked the advice of the *conseillers* who were present on how best to proceed against the prisoners. Having considered the evidence and the women's denials, the herbs found in their houses and in their chests – items which give rise to suspicion – the women's confessions, the spell cast at Marion's request by Margot (who was known to have set Haincelin and Agnescot, his wife, free from the spell), and Margot's invocation of the demon while she was calling upon our Lord Jesus Christ, they deliberated and came to the conclusion that Margot and Marion were worthy of death as witches [*sorcières*], and that as such they were to be executed as follows, namely: they were to be drawn to the pillory in Les Halles, turned there,[6] and the misdeeds and crimes for which they were being pilloried publicly proclaimed. Then they were to be drawn or made to walk to the piggeries outwith the city of Paris and there burned for their misdeeds and crimes which they had acknowledged and confessed. Exceptions [to this judgement] were the captain of the watch [and] Messieurs Pierre de Lesclat, Robert de Tuillieres, Nicolas Chaon and Geoffroi Le

---

4.   Reading *ennemi* instead of *annenni*.
5.   Presumably the secretary's note which has made its way into the text. The following reference to 'Marion who is here' indicates that Margot was the magical operator and that Marion her client was standing nearby while the interchange took place.
6.   *Tournés.* Other records speak of 'turning' on the pillory, and it appears there was some mechanism which allowed the device to be turned so that everyone had a good view of the person confined therein.

Goybe, [who] deliberated and came to the conclusion that in Marion's case she should not be burned, but that after she had been turned on the pillory in the manner described above, she should be banished for ever from the city, viscounty and provosty of Paris, on pain of being burned.

Having heard these opinions, and in view of the said trial, the Prévôt condemned Margot and Marion to be turned on the pillory in the manner described [above] and afterwards burned on account of their faults and confessions.

[On 11 August, Margot was burned, and in spite of the repeated pleas of the above-named conseillers *that she be reprieved, Marion was burned on 24 August.]*

4. Magic with toads and a wax image, 1390–1391

Hansen VIb, no. 4 (pp. 520–3)

[This is the first recorded witch trial held at Le Châtelet in Paris. There were two accused women, Jeanne de Brigue alias 'La Cordière' and 'Macette' unhappily married to Hennequin de Ruilly. Jeanne appears to have specialized in recovering lost or stolen items and her talents had actually been used about six years before her arrest and trial by the priest of a neighbouring village. She also cured the sick and made healthy people ill by means of magic. Her interrogations began on 29 October 1390, and on 9 February the following year she was found guilty and sentenced to be burned. Macette, her friend and colleague in magic, was questioned on 4 August 1391 and confessed everything immediately. She was condemned on 5 August. Both women were executed on 19 August.]

Macette also says that, at the time stated earlier, she was heard and understood by the said women, her neighbours, to say that if the woman would do or wish to do the things she had planned, with the intention of hurting her husband more severely, or the person or person she wanted and intended to hurt or have hurt, she would have to capture two toads and put each of them separately into a new clay pot. Then she would have to take them, look at them, call three times upon Lucifer for help, recite three times the Gospel of St John, Paternoster, and Ave Maria, put [the toads] back in the pot, and keep them under control with a bit of white bread and some breastmilk. When she wanted to hurt her husband, or the person or persons she wanted and intended to hurt, and when she had a [suitable] place [to do so], she called Lucifer to her aid three times above each of the earthenware pots containing the toads before she uncovered them. After that, she recited the Gospel of St John three times, and Paternoster and Ave Maria. Once she had done this, she opened the earthenware pots and stabbed the toads hard with long needles or small iron spikes, and the person she intended to hurt would suffer the same way the toads suffered, or something similar, and would not be able to rest anywhere, even though there was no danger of his dying, only becoming weak and sick … .

She also says that about four or six months after she, the accused, married
[Hennequin] de Ruilly, and when she came to live with him, her husband,
among the other property she brought for their household in the town of
Guérart where she and her husband were going to live and stay, she bought,
in the rue des Lombards, about half a pound of pure white wax and a small
quantity of pitch, with the intention of doing or taking care of what was
mentioned earlier [i.e. harming her husband] and being able to help herself
without putting herself in anyone's power and without anyone's noticing what
she wished and intended [to do]. Not long ago, she and her husband lived
together in Guérart, and kept a tavern and hostelry for a period of four years
near the Madeleine. During that time she and her husband quarrelled and
argued frequently because her husband criticized her and beat her, and because
she was unwilling to do what he wanted, and because she answered back very
loudly and rudely, telling him she was as good as he was. For this reason he
led a very hard, tough life, which is why he hit her as [opposed to behaving]
in any other way.

Therefore, seeing she could not go on living with her husband because of the
beatings he gave her, she remembered and thought that some of the things her
neighbours from Rilly in Anjou said to her were true and wanted to try to find
out whether the other things they said to her (mentioned above), were equally
true – that doing the things they had spoken about involved no danger of death.
One day (she does not remember which), she was alone, locked in her room in the
hostelry in Guérat while her husband was away attending to his business. Three
times in succession she called, begged and asked Lucifer to be willing to help her
put her husband in such a condition that never again would he be able to beat
or abuse her. While she said this, held the pure wax and the pitch in her hands,
and then recited the Gospel of St John, Paternoster and Ave Maria three times
over them. The accused did and said these things with the help of a little warm
water which she had in front of her and heated in her room. She mixed together
the wax and the pitch and, after they were mixed, once again called Lucifer to
help, advise and comfort her, repeating the Gospel of St John, Paternoster and
Ave Maria three times in succession – last Candlemas, or thereabout. From the
wax and pitch the accused moulded an image in the form of a child and, while
making it, called three times upon Lucifer for help. She also recited the Gospel of
St John, Paternoster and Ave Maria three times each, and then put a brass pot on
the fire with plenty of water and the wax image. While she did this, she called on
Lucifer three times, begging him to come to her aid, and also recited the Gospel
of St John, Paternoster and Ave Maria three times. Then she put the wax image
in the pot with the water to boil long and hard, and while doing so made three
crosses over it with the point of a knife, and several times turned and tormented
the wax image in the water in the pot, using a brass spoon and sometimes the
sharp end of the knife.

She says, in answer to a question, that every time she put the said pot and
water on the fire, along with the image, she would do secret things each time
and torment the image as well. This she did several times, and saw, realized and
perceived that the said [Hennequin] from Ruilly became very ill and would often

complain to her every day that wherever he went, he used to feel and endure many severe pangs, illnesses and stabbing pains which came over him.

5. A thief evokes a devil to act as a source of information, 1401

Hansen VIb, no. 12 (pp. 524–6)

This is the investigation and summary or record of the proceedings of an investigation which is taking place and is intended to take place in Geneva in the court of the vidame[7] of Geneva, [recorded] by me, Johann Estuer, clerk of the vidame's court, against and in opposition to Jeanette, daughter of Richard Charles lately of Geneva. It is taking place because it is the simple duty of the court [to deal with it], and also because public opinion says [it should], evidence of the deed is widely known and there is rising complaint against her, as follows.

[1. She has boasted she is able to uncover secret thefts and protect livestock so that it will not be eaten by a wolf or stolen by a thief. 2–4. She has used these abilities to put names to specific thefts.]

5. On Shrove Tuesday, in a room, by means of her incantations and magical practices, she made a devil come to her. He had been transformed into the likeness of a man wearing a large houpland *[long-skirted tunic]* of black velvet. By having a conversation (which she wanted to do) with this devil, the woman under investigation committed heretical wickedness and the crime of heretical wickedness.

[6. She has given the names of the thieves to various people, including the vidame's deputy and Johann Estuer, clerk of the court.]

[7. The women she named were arrested and have now been shown to be innocent.] Consequently, since the foresaid things have been committed wickedly, in a most evil fashion, have been done contrary to the Faith, give a bad example, and should not be left unpunished, the court has proceeded and does proceed to inquire into the truth of the foregoing, so that the said Jeanette, who has been found out, may be punished by due process of law; and so that we, having noted the nature of the crime, may have the truth more clearly from her mouth, the procurator asks, insists and requires that as far as you are able, gentlemen, while declaring the law on these matters, to pronounce and ordain that Jeanette here be examined and tortured with the express aim [of getting her] to say and reveal what practice and what spirit induced her [to do these things], what was her purpose, who is giving and has given her the said practice, knowledge and power and how well she knows and knew that Guechard and the others were involved in the above-mentioned thefts, so that, were she by some chance to frustrate [the law] and be released and sent heedlessly on her way, she may not return to those same things and tear pieces from her neighbours with her stake.[8] So once torture

---

7.   Someone holding lands from a bishop in return for being his representative and advocate in secular affairs.

8.   *Suo ligno*, that is, the wood to which she should be tied and with which she should be burned.

or other means have got the truth from her, let this Jeanette be found guilty and, having been found guilty, let her be punished as justification dictates, so that she may provide an example to anyone else in future who puts up with such things.

10 May

[Jeanette was interrogated by the vidame's deputy, two procurators and two citizens of Geneva. She confessed that those who had been robbed consulted her and that she believed her magical practice was genuine.]

She had a fire lit in the fireplace of the front room of the house, a cloth put on a table in the room and bread on top of the cloth. Then she made everyone leave the room, and she alone made the responses[9] and remained there undisturbed. She confessed that while she was making the responses, holding a small open book, she was saying and said certain words which caused a devil in the likeness of a clothed human being (as is contained in the record of the investigation), to come into the room. He said to her, 'What do you want of me?' She answered the devil and said, 'I want you to tell me who has stolen the saffron from Guillaume de Rotul's house and the money from Vincent Crocho's workshop'. The devil told her the money had been stolen from the workshop during the Thursday night before Shrove Tuesday, etc. etc. Asked what words she had said to make the devil come, she says she can't remember.

[Several witnesses testified they had consulted Jeanette. The vidame's deputy and Johann Estuer said under oath they questioned her and, as a result, she was accused and arrested.]

[Jeanette] was furnished with a copy of this interrogation and given ten days to prepare her defence, if she wanted to make one and believed it was in her interest [to do so]. The said woman refused to take this copy and refused to undertake to put up a defence. She was appointed [to appear] before the said procurators on the Monday after the octave of Corpus Christi (if that was going to be the convenient date), to hear the court's decision and definitive sentence.

6. The execution of the Chancellor of Savoy on a charge of attempted assassination by magical means, 1417

Hansen VIb, no. 24 (p. 528)[10]

(a) Sentence of death and confiscation of property, pronounced by the appeal judge of Bresse against Jean Lageret, Doctor of Laws, on 29 September 1417, for having attempted numerous acts of witchcraft [*sortilegii*] by means of various

---

9.   This is an ecclesiastical term, as is *mantile*, the cloth on the table = 'altar cloth'. The language illustrates how imbued ritual magic was with ecclesiastical terminology.
10.   I have inverted these two passages because taking Hansen's (b) before his (a) seems to make better sense.

images engraved on gold ducats and pieces of wood against the person of Duke Amadeus of Savoy. This sentence was ordered to be carried out at once.

(b) [The treasurer] paid the costs [of keeping under guard] Monsieur Jean Lageret, Doctor of Laws, knight, incurred in the town of Le Bourget from 4 September when he was brought early in the morning by the baillie of Bresse's people, to 28 September when he was sent on to Laurent de Brenax, depute governor of Chambéry, for execution of the sentence pronounced against him. He was taken by Laurent to Chambéry, and from Chambéry to an open space, there where he was beheaded. Then his body was taken to the gallows.[11]

7. The activities and subsequent prosecution of sorcerers, fortune tellers and similar workers of magic in the bilingual territory of Valais (Wallis), 1428–1434

Hansen VIb, no. 39 (pp. 531–9)

(a) [Thomas Venech, baillie of Valais (German Wallis) has noted the decisions made by a public meeting called because the inhabitants of Valais, concerned for the reputation of the Church in Sion and the whole region of Valais, do not want the practice of sorcery (ars sortilegii) *and the acts of harmful magic* (maleficia) *performed by certain people to go unpunished. Valais/Wallis is a canton in the south of Switzerland, almost completely surrounded by mountains. Sion is its capital. It was, and still is, dominated by two castles situated above the town.]*

First: It was decreed that if anyone, or more than one person, of any rank or position, in any place, whether in the mountains or the plain, is found to have been slandered of [magic] in the distant past, or has had a recent similar complaint or grouse made about him[12] or them by the public talk or slander of three or four neighbours, he [*sic*] or they are to be arrested and imprisoned by the castellans and ecclesiastical judges who have authority and jurisdiction over them. The same should happen in the case of noblemen who have authority and jurisdiction in the foresaid places, and legal proceedings should be brought against people of this kind.

Item: It was decreed that any such person, male or female, found to have been slandered by five, six, or seven or more persons, up to the number of ten, who were qualified to do so and not under suspicion themselves, should likewise be arrested and put to the torture.

Item: It was decreed that once legal proceedings had been started, if the

---

11.   *Ad furchas.* This may mean that his body was suspended from the gallows as a warning to other wrong-doers. But *ad furchas* could also mean 'to the crossroads'. The bodies of executed criminals were often buried at such a place both as a sign that they had been expelled from their community, and to confuse the ghost so that it would be less likely to return and trouble the living in the places it knew during life.

12.   *Ipsum.* Venech here uses the masculine form of the singular pronoun. It is not clear whether he means to be gender specific, or whether 'him' stands for 'him or her'. Later in the passage, he writes of men and women, so it is likely that his *ipsum* is meant to be inclusive.

public utterance and reputation of their neighbours should count against them, and they were unwilling to confess their faults, such people should be put to the torture.

Item: It was decreed that in the case of persons conjoined in marriage, the man and the woman who are found [to be] innocent of this practice in the forementioned circumstances may have the right which [each] has or ought to have with regard to the property of the other [kept] safe and reserved by whatever right and in any way for one or both, but only until such a man or woman takes an oath and swears on the holy Gospels of God that he or she knew nothing about the practice carried out by the man or woman, and this [oath] is true. If he or she refuses to take an oath, he or she is not to be allowed to avail him or herself of the forementioned [privileges] contained in this article.

Item: It was decreed that if our lord of Sion or his baillie, castellans or other officers arrest any person on account of the practice of sorcery [*artis sortilegii*], and after being arrested he or she is found guilty: on condition that (a) he or she, having been found guilty because of the crimes and misdeeds he or she has committed, has been judicially condemned in body or money by court decision and personal confession[13] to be burned or to lose part of their body or property: [and] (b) the condemned person has property, fiefs or feudal property deriving from other lords and nobles in fief: [and] (c) [no such person and his or her property] comes under [those lords' and nobles'] jurisdiction, those nobles, whoever they may be and whatever their rank and standing (i) should and ought to make a proportional and equal contribution by their fiefs to the costs and expenses which have been incurred or which will be incurred by the lord or his officers and (ii) take a proportional part (as granted above to them) of what the judgement says should be paid as a penalty, notwithstanding that the lord or baillie or his officers carry out the sentence upon the body. The reason for this is that another person neither should nor can prejudice these nobles by incurring a proportional penalty (as above), as granted to them, after the expenses have been paid equally (as above).[14]

Item: It was decreed as above, that if by chance any person not slandered long ago in general, and by chance recently is slandered in public by a single person judicially burned to death, such a person should not be arrested but first an inquiry should be held in secret to find out whether he or she [has committed] any crime or not and secondly to condemn or acquit should [a crime] be uncovered.

Item: Likewise, it was decreed that if any person [is slandered] by two or more other persons arrested for the practice of sorcery and judicially sentenced to be tortured or to death by burning, he or she, no matter what his or her rank or position, should be arrested and detained, public investigatory proceedings should be undertaken and he or she put to the torture.

---

13.   *Per sententiam cognitionem*. I have added *et* between the nouns in an effort to make some sense of the phrase.

14.   The Latin is badly garbled, so this translation represents an approximation (I hope close) to the intended sense of the passage.

Item: It was decreed that the foresaid arrested persons should be given defence advocates and copies of the proceedings and investigations undertaken against them, along with their defences according to what they believe is to their advantage.

Item: It was decreed that any person accused by three persons who had been tried and sentenced to death for the practice of sorcery should be arrested and put to the torture and, according to the merit of the case, condemned and executed, or acquitted.

Several people present at the said council and assembly, together with the castellans, mayors, magistrates and other officials in the foresaid places, who have our letters of attestation which we have granted to them, and copies available when wanted for confirmation and testimony of the foregoing, have petitioned us regarding each and every one of the points listed above.

Given and enacted at Leuk, 7 August 1428, under our seal and the manual dispatch of Antoine de Platée (squire) and Jean de Lapis, public notaries.

(b) [In the tenth century, the Valais (Wallis) was a diocese governed by the Bishop of Sion, who was also a temporal ruler of part of the territory. In the west, however, it was the Duke of Savoy who was the temporal lord. Responsibility for the suppression of magic and heresy was also divided between the bishop in his diocese, and Dominican inquisitors in Savoyard territory. Johann (Hans) Fründ, c.1400–1469, wrote his account of witches and their activities soon after the events described here in an extract from his chronicle.][15]

In the year of our Lord 1428, there was discovered in the territory and diocese of Wallis (Valais) the malice, the murders and the heresy of witches and workers of magic, female and male, who are called *sortileii* in Latin. They were first discovered in two vales of Wallis (Valais), one called the Vale of Anniviers, the other the Vale of Hérens, and a number of them was brought to trial and burned. Then, the same year, many more were discovered in this same region, to begin with particularly among the Romansh and German speakers. In addition, many were also discovered among the people who lived in that same diocese of Wallis (Valais) and were under the authority of the Duke of Savoy. Many of them confessed their great malice, several murders, their heretical beliefs and other vile things, and they also confessed they had committed those acts which are called *sortileia* in Latin. I shall describe several of these acts later, but I shall keep quiet about others so that no one may be corrupted by them.

The most important thing to know is that these people, women as well as men, who were capable of committing these acts and had proved their malice, had done as they had been taught by an evil spirit. When he knows that people doubt their faith in holy Christ and are [therefore] vulnerable, he tempts them and gives them to understand he wants to make them rich and powerful, that he wants to teach them many skills and that they will be able to avenge wrongs

15.   I follow the order of the text given by Kathrin Utz Tremp in *L'imaginaire du sabbat* because the text given by Hansen is badly garbled.

done to them and make the people who have harmed them pay and suffer. With similar wicked tricks, he convinces these same individuals, relying on the arrogance, greed, jealousy, hatred and enmity one person can feel towards his or her neighbour. The evil spirit also gets the upper hand over people who are prone to such feelings and do not live in fear of God, and in the region I mentioned earlier he gained the upper hand over very many people to such an extent that, as I have said, they turned to malice.

Before the evil spirit was willing to teach them, they were obliged to dedicate themselves to him and therefore to deny God and all the saints, holy Christian baptism and the Church, and so enter into his service. [They also had] to pay taxes and much else every year, namely, a black sheep or lamb, a measure of oats, a part of their body, [payable after death] and other things in accordance with the pact they made with him and he with them, and to which they subsequently swore. The evil spirit appeared mostly in the shape of a black animal, such as a bear or ram, and also in dreadful, evil form, and spoke to them (so one gathers) about evil. When he was successful [in corrupting them], he forbade them to go to church, take part in the Mass, listen to sermons or confess to a priest. [He also said] they must not confess to any priest what they did with the 'art', so that no one could accuse them because of it.

Some of these people knew better than other coarse individuals how to comport themselves after they had been arrested and would call upon God and His saints sooner than the others. They all did this so that people would think they were innocent. [But] some made no confession at all and quite a few allowed themselves to be tortured to death rather than let themselves confess or say anything. Several, [on the other hand], confessed lightly and were very repentant of their sins.

Note this.[16] They said they had given people poison and many other bad things to eat, and that several of them had died as a result or become lame and very sick.

[They also said] that it was the evil spirit who had taught them these wicked practices and methods of killing, and that if they threatened or harmed the people with whom they were at variance or against whom they entertained anger, the evil spirit had given them the power to inflict harm on them straightaway. One became sick, another paralysed, another mad; several became blind, many others lost their children because their wives went into labour at the wrong moment or [the husbands] became impotent. They bewitched [*verzouberten*] many women who became barren, and did many other things of the same kind to which [people] bore witness and of which they were accused. They likewise did many other things to which they themselves confessed and which no one had known about until then. They likewise confessed how the evil spirit would carry them at night from one mountain to another, how he would teach them the way to make ointments which they smeared on chairs, and [said that] afterwards they would ride on them from village to village [and] castle to castle, and

---

16.   *Nota.* This does not appear in Hansen's text. It occurs again, later, written in red in the left-hand margin of the manuscript.

that they would end up in the cellars of those who had the best wine. There they would have a good time and then afterwards once again go where they wanted. They were asked if, after that, there was less wine, in accordance with what they had drunk, and they replied that there *was* less in the barrels from which they had drunk, and that the wine became less good because they put several nasty substances in it, which people used not to notice.

There were among them many whom the evil spirit taught the way to turn into wolves, something they thought actually did happen to them. They were quite convinced they were wolves, and those who saw them believed that such and such a person really was a wolf at that moment. They would run after sheep, lambs and goats which, in their guise of wolf, they ate raw. When they wanted to, they would become human again, just as they had been before. The evil spirit also taught several of them how to use plants to make themselves invisible so that no one could see them. There were also some among them who could free people from harm laid on them by other workers of magic [zoubrer] – such as paralysis or a similar kind of illness – and transfer it to others. In this way, they would set people against each other.

There were also among them those who would go at night to 'schools' [i.e. Sabbats] which were held in secret places. Then the evil spirit would come there and behave like a teacher [in eins meysters wyse], preach a sermon against the Christian faith and forbid them to practise confession and penitence. They would then tell him how many times they had gone to church and what good they had done – acts for which the evil spirit gave them a penance and [told them to do] many wicked things which they carried out at once. What these things were I shall not describe. There were also those among them who used to kill their own children, roast them and eat them, [or] cook them and take them to their meeting and then eat them. They would then take rags or other nasty things of the same kind to church and everyone believed that these were the children. This way, they actually left them at home and would eat them later when they wanted. Some of them were so wicked that they would assault their children, or those of others, at night. After the children had been ill for several days, [the witches] would squeeze them and they would end up dead. Then they let their neighbours see them and where they had touched [the children] with their evil hands, the children were black or blue because [the witches] had spread an evil substance on their hands. They would give people to understand that blessed souls had come to look for these children and they would lament a great deal. [But] when the children were buried, [the witches] would come and dig them up at night and eat them in secret.

Many confessed to having committed these murders and wicked deeds about which no Christian should even know; and no one could believe it, had [the witches] themselves not demonstrated [that it was true]. In fact, they themselves provided proofs which bore witness to the truth of such deeds, and they said they had committed much harm of the same kind. There were also many who, while not being guilty of such great wickedness, of this heresy, or of these murders, nevertheless committed other misdeeds and made themselves guilty of wickedness, heresy and magic [zauberei] and were also brought to justice and burned. There were also those who voluntarily confessed they had partly destroyed the fruits of the earth, especially wine and corn, by means of curses and other wicked deeds, and they used to claim they had received power from the evil spirit, and were perfectly able to do [these things] because they had devoted themselves to him. Likewise, several of them took away people's milk – that is to say, their cows would no longer give milk, or it was unpleasant when they drank it. Others could also cause carts and ploughs to stop working, in such a way that they became unusable. There were also many among them who neither would nor could confess, even though there was plenty of evidence against them and other people had denounced them and could prove [the truth of their accusations]. They would say their minds had been thrown into confusion and that they could not talk about other witches [*hexsen*]; and even when they were subjected to severe torture, many were never willing to confess and allowed themselves to be tortured to death. They were, nevertheless, tried and burned, whether they were dead or alive.

The legal proceedings lasted more than a year and a half, and in the territory of Valais (Wallis) more than a hundred individuals, as many men as women, were tried and executed. Many of them had been committing crimes such as these for very nearly nine years, and several people who had been initiated, had been active for a long time, and had given up [their activities] for years, had taken them up again nine years ago.

Note: They were so numerous, they thought that if they could hold out for a year, they could elect a king from among them. The evil spirit gave them to understand that they ought to become so strong so that they would not fear any power or any court, and that they themselves should create a court and rein in Christianity. They also thought that if they survived the year in which they had been made prisoner, their number, already considerable, would be further increased (and they had confirmed that their society amounted to seven hundred individuals). Of that number, 200 were burned in a year and a half. Every day they were put on trial and burned, when they could be caught.

Many were also burned in the French-speaking country and valleys of Lower Valais (Wallis) and near Mount St Bernard, but I don't know how many. It is thought they were so numerous because God wanted to demonstrate their great wickedness and their false, dirty beliefs, from which God very much wants to protect every Christian's faith. He also wants to strengthen [that faith] and divine law, too, so that, thanks to this, we may have eternal life after this life. May God and the Virgin Mary, His mother, come to our aid, in the name of the Holy Trinity who always has been and will be, without end, amen. Amen.

[*Written in another hand*] The person who wrote me had the name Hans Fruünd.

(c) 13 February

In the name of our Lord Jesus Christ, Amen. In the year 1434, in the 12th year of the indiction,[17] on the 13th day of the month of February, the noble and

---

17.   A recurring period of 15 years, originally referring to a fiscal period first instituted by the Emperor Constantine in 313 AD and reckoned from 1 September 312.

prudent men, Rudolf and Johann Asper, mayors of Raron,[18] [and 34 men from the municipality], in their name and that of the whole community of Raron for their part, were constituted as a body representing the community (and for this reason made such a body). [They met] individually and in person at Raron in the heated rooms of the mayor's house,[19] in the presence of me, the public notary, and of the witnesses whose names are given below, because certain persons of both sexes have been accused and slandered (so it is claimed, at any rate), of the practice of sorcery,[20] divination, incantations and suchlike, and the presumption is that the community itself and individuals are putting up, openly and secretly, with many scandals, losses and injuries in many different ways in their own persons, animals and property. They met again a second time in order to investigate these things and to fulfil, administer and implement justice (saving the earlier agreements and arrangements they had made and recorded in writing earlier), being of one harmonious mind and without any disagreement. [Their conclusions were] as follows.

First, anyone who is or has been accused by anyone who has been brought to justice and burned, or could otherwise and in another way be accused or inculpated by three or more trustworthy witnesses (for example, for eminently true and likely reasons which result in a judicial sentence), should be and are considered to be suitable on the grounds of the law as it now stands and as it should be obeyed, to pay surety into the hands of the said mayors. If they refuse to do this, then they ought and should be obliged to leave or go away from the parish for a while, or until the said mayors and their councillors show them clemency.

Item: Anyone who could be accused (as written above), ought and may be obliged to pay and make provision for his pertinent and relevant costs and expenses according to to his wrongdoing and the merit of his case.

Item: Under the penalty and proclamation prescribed elsewhere, *[word missing in the text]*, no one in this parish should agree or dare to assist any such culpable or guilty person to escape legal proceedings, or in any other way – by word, deed, action or token – draw him away from legal proceedings or show favour to him in any way unless a judge has actually told him [to do so] in return for the objections and rejoinders he would be making in the legal proceedings; [and neither this nor anything else] should be done fraudulently.

Item: For the duration of the court proceedings, any person publicly

---

18. A municipality in the canton of Valais (Wallis).

19. From the thirteenth century onwards, the great hall of an important building with its central hearth and high roof, was abandoned more and more for small rooms heated by a fireplace with a chimney. Leroy Dresbeck observes, 'In northern Europe the heated house not only offered refuge from harsh climate, but also furnished a place where more work could be done in the wintertime. In all occupations, from government service to the production of simple items in the home, the fireplace and chimney helped to overcome the cold. Rooms, more and more often equipped with fireplace and chimney, were now reserved for various functions'. L. Dresbeck, 1971, 'The chimney and social change in Mediaeval England', *Albion* 3, p. 22.

20. *Artis sortilegii*, which could also mean 'the practice of fortune-telling', although the inclusion of divination in the list renders this less likely in this context.

denounced and accused as above, can and must come and go freely and securely to court and legal proceedings in person with his supporter and advocate in order to make each and every one of his objections and rejoinders against everything which has been deponed against him.

Item: Any person who is obliged to leave his parish can and should, if the said mayors and parishioners are willing, demand justice of [those who have made them leave] under the jurisdiction of another court in order to bring legal proceedings against such persons.

Item: Any such person of either sex who has removed himself and fled from legal proceedings and the foresaid parish, and who might return to that parish and be unwilling to pay appropriate surety into the hands of the forewritten mayors, according to the law as it stands, would and might by that act be committed and devolved in person and money to the said mayors, because his running away would be proof of his guilt and the accusation [against him] (saving always the mercy of the forewritten mayors and community in the forementioned circumstances).

Item: The rights and jurisdictions of the mayors and foresaid community are reserved in respect of the foregoing, so that there may not be prejudice to either party, nor prejudice to these [rights and jurisdictions] in future.

These same parties promised each other to consider authoritative, pleasing, reliable and valid etc., each and every one of the above-written and below-written points, on their own part and that of their heirs, by oaths made in person and under liability of all their property, movable and immovable, present and future, and [those] of the said community. Then they asked that two public documents be drawn up (one for the purposes of either party), with exactly the same contents – or more [than two], if members of the council asked for them.

The following persons, having been summoned, were present as witnesses to these things. Their names are Jodocus Owling, castellan of Châtillon; Jean de Platée from Visp; Schaninus, legitimate son of the priest at Raron; Jacques Lampertner, who lives there; and I, François de Ryedmetton from Schovsum, clerk, citizen of Sedan, public notary by Imperial authority, etc.

8. The crimes and sentence of Jubert of Bavaria, tried for witchcraft, 1437

Hansen VIb, no. 40 (pp. 539–44)

[The judge in overall charge of this court appearance by Jubert was Claude Tholosan (died c.1450), who was chief prosecutor for the Briaçonnais from 1426 until 1449. He had ten years' experience in witchcraft cases and conducted more than a hundred of them during that time. The conclusions to which he came as a result of these experiences are contained in his book, Ut magorum et maleficiorum errores *(1437), which expounds his conviction that witches were members of a diabolical sect and met at intervals to worship the Devil. This made them both heretics and apostates, but because their crime could also be classed as treason against their lawful rulers, Tholosan maintained the importance of involving secular as well as ecclesiastical courts in the trial and sentencing of*

individuals accused of being witches. All these points are well illustrated in the following document.]

In the name of the Lord, Amen. In the year of our Lord's nativity 1437, and on 28 November, at Briançon in the place recorded below, in the presence of the noble and wise Constant Bochard, dauphinal procurator fiscal of Briançon, [and] in the name of the Dauphin, Jubert of Bavaria from the city of Ratisbon in Lower Germany, a skinner, was handed over to hear a definitive sentence in final, itemized form with respect to certain criminal proceedings held and constituted in the greater dauphinal court of Briançon against the aforementioned accused Jubert. [This was done] in accordance with the duties of that court, on the instruction of the said Master Procurator Fiscal, [and] in accordance with what the records of the said case and proceeding agree about his being handed over.

So on the day and in the placed designated above, in the presence of the noble, esteemed man, Master Claude Tholosan, licenciate at law, dauphinal adviser and chief prosecutor of Briançon, the aforesaid Master Procurator Fiscal appeared, seeking and requiring, in the Dauphin's name, with respect to the said interrogatory proceeding, the items [recorded in the indictment], and the judicial proceedings, that a sentence be decided and recorded on behalf of the Procurator Fiscal, and that the aforesaid accused be condemned, admonished and punished according to and in accordance with what is demanded by the offences and crimes committed by the accused, and [that he may be punished] in such a way that he provide a deterrent to anyone else who commits extraordinarily great offences of this kind.

The said Jubert appeared, asking [the court] to take pity on him and deal with him mercifully.

The said parties appeared in court. The said judge heard them and then proceeded to his definitive sentence as follows:

I, Claude Tholosan, the aforesaid judge, have seen and considered the manner in which the accused, the said Jubert, was charged with sorceries and unmistakeable acts of magic,[21] and also the preliminary statements and verdicts. Jubert was brought into the dauphinal castle at Briançon, and there I questioned and interrogated him. I also examined him very carefully on many other occasions about those same sorceries and acts of harmful magic. Then, once I had seen the said process of interrogation (which I did by virtue of the office I occupy), a case was drawn up against this same Jubert. The tenor of what he confessed is as follows.

First. The said Jubert said and confessed by means of his own free oath, with touch manual.[22] The said Jubert declared the truth during a number of interrogations held on separate occasions, [saying] that he is 60 years old, and that more than ten years ago he was servant in Bavaria to a very influential man whose

---

21. Reading *facturis* instead of *fachuris*.
22. Oaths were made by placing the hand on a copy of the Gospels, or a reliquary, or an object under dispute (such as a piece of land), or the hand of another person.

name was Johann Cunal, a priest and rural dean from a city called Munich [which is] in Bavaria, near Böhmen.

Item. He further said and confessed that the said Johann Cunal had a book of necromancy and upon his (Jubert's) opening the said book, three demons immediately appeared to him. One devil was called 'Lecherous', another 'Arrogant' and another 'Miserly'. The first appeared to him in the shape of a pleasing young woman, aged 12, who slept with him that night. He enjoyed himself and had a delightful time.

Item. He used to worship that devil as a god, going down on his knees at night and turning his arse towards the east. He used to make a cross on the ground, spit on it three times, stamp on it three times with his left foot and piss and shit on it; and whenever he saw a cross he would spit at it and deny God three times.

Item. At dawn he would worship 'Arrogance' in similar fashion. [This demon] used to appear first in the form of a mole[23], then in the shape of a middle-aged man wearing black clothes; and 'Miserly' would appear to him at the hour of Compline in the form of a very old man in filthy clothes, carrying a purse full of money. [Jubert] would worship him as above and offer him all the money he used to make on feast days.

Item. When he was eating and drinking, he used to give 'Arrogance' whatever food he had left over, and on the Holy Friday before Easter he would give 'Lecherous' three or five pennies. Likewise, he made them a gift of his limbs, body and soul [to be surrendered] after he died. The said devils wanted him to deny the God they called 'cursed prophet'. When he used to worship the demons as gods, he would turn his face to the west and his arse to the east and say what he [has been described as saying]. When he used to have sex with 'Lecherous', the others would laugh.

Item. He further said and confessed that the devil 'Miserly', one of his keepers,[24] once gave him three ducats from a secret store of money and started to urge him to kill himself.

Item. He further said that when he used to walk through the streets, and the demons were with him, and he came upon a cross, the devils would run away from it and take the long way round. They also forbade him to do good or to worship the sacred Host and [would tell him] to shut his eyes during the Elevation. They would also forbid him to take holy water, or to kiss the cross and the pax,[25], maintaining that they alone were all-powerful gods.

23.   Reading *talpie* for *tapie*.

24.   *Magistris.* The word has a number of different meanings, one of which refers to someone who has charge of animals, such as a shepherd or goatherd. Hence 'keeper' seems to be an appropriate translation for this and the other contexts below in which it appears.

25.   The Elevation is the point during the Mass when the newly consecrated Host is lifted up by the priest so that the congregation can see it clearly. In older rituals of the Mass, the priest stood in front of the altar, not behind it, so the congregation could not see the moment of consecration. The Elevation was thus the first chance they had to see the sacred Host. The *pax* was a metal or wooden tablet with a cross painted or engraved on it. It was offered to the congregation to be kissed at the appropriate point of the Mass.

Item. He further said and confessed that on Sunday 17th of this month, all three demons were in prison with him. Their eyes were glowing like sulphurous fire. They told the accused they would have taken good care of him if he had not revealed what he had spoken about earlier. He had sex with his [lover], the said 'Lecherous', on that same occasion. He said further that the demons would have freed him from prison had he not revealed what he had spoken about earlier.

Item. He further said and confessed that on that occasion the devils told him he would be interrogated in great detail the next day, and would be obliged to tell the whole truth. He would then be put to death; and by describing the distinguishing marks which identified him, they let him know who had been sent ahead to carry out [the sentence].

Item. He further said and confessed that on one occasion he and his keeper were walking through a wood when robbers attacked them, [but] a large number of devils who appeared in the shape of armed men came to their assistance and made them run away. He declared further that the world is full of people who invoke demons, and that the devils chase after them a lot, principally because the world is full of sins, wars and factions.

Item. He further said and confessed that in a single night his keeper made a bridge for the use of demons in Bavaria over a river and a place where there is said [to be] a hermit in [the chapel of] Santa Maria.

Item. He further said and confessed that, because she had displeased him, he had proposed blinding Jeanne, the widow of Jean the Countryman from Briançon, by drawing her picture with two keys. (The way he did this and the drawing he made have been described in the trial record.) He drew this picture on a Sunday, below the names of devils. (The things he did and the materials he used have been described in the trial record). He used the same procedure in the case of someone called Johann the Carpenter [who came from] Vienna in the dukedom of Austria (as indeed he revealed before his arrest, and bragged about doing it.)

Item. He further said and confessed that he is a necromancer, and that, with his devils, he picked out a boy for his keeper in the city of Monaco without being seen. They also picked out a child in his cradle, killed him, roasted him and mixed him with blood from the corpse of a boy who had died without being baptized. This mixture included nocturnal emissions, menstrual blood and a woman's pubic hairs, which is what necromancers are accustomed to do. They summoned up inauspicious children (who are demons) and put them in the place of the children they had taken away. These [changelings] look like the original children, but they have a swollen stomach, a large head and are always making a racket. When they want to, they vanish, as he saw and learned from experience in Germany.

Item. He further said and confessed that the foregoing happens to those who put their children in cradles without a cross and a blessing.[26]

---

26.   This could mean that the parents make the sign of the cross over or on the child along with the blessing, or that they put a small cross in the cradle as an apotropaic against invasion by demons.

Item. He further said and confessed that this takes place on Thursday and Saturday nights when he and others of the sect would be carried, with the help of devils, in the twinkling of an eye, upon mule or horse shit to the usual place. Here they would render accounts of the evil their demons had done with other members of the sect, and on this occasion the person who had committed more acts of harmful magic would be the more commended by the Devil and would sit in the Devil's place. On that occasion, too, they were taught how to commit worse evils and the circumstances in which they should be committed.

Item. He further said and confessed that two years ago, or thereabout, he was on holiday in Vienna, a city in Austria. (It was actually a Thursday.) There were three drunken cooks in a tavern there, who had refused to give him a drink; and when it was late and they were starting to leave, one said to the other two, 'Get up, in the Devil's name, and let me pass!' Immediately, at the request of Jubert's keeper, three demons seized hold of those three men. They threw one in a well, one in the Dominicans' drain or lavatory and one in the lavatory of the Franciscans. The one who had been thrown in the well was stone dead, but the other two were rescued by monks at the hour of Matins.

Item. He further said and confessed that with the help of the devils, they make poisons with which he and his keeper can kill people, either with the demons' help – this [death] happens quickly – or by means of a slow, wasting exhaustion, just as the person who administers them wishes. Secondly, [this can be done] to greater or lesser effect by administering a poison taken from a basilisk, a toad, a snake, a spider or a scorpion, in the name of the poison's devil. The manner and class [of poison] are contained in the trial record.

Item. He further said he gave some of the said poison in some food[27] to someone called Conrad in the city of Munich in Bavaria.

Item. He further said and confessed that while he was going through the streets he would see images of the Virgin Mary or the cross, and spit at them three times out of contempt for the Father, Son and Holy Spirit; and that on the feast of St John the Baptist [24 June], he would collect certain herbs for medicines whose names are in the trial record. First he would kneel down and venerate them, and then he would pull them up in the name of his devils and in contempt for Almighty God, the Creator of everything.

Item. He further said he was egged on by devils to have sexual intercourse (this pleases them a lot) and carry out rape and commit every kind of wickedness. They would call the cross 'a shameful piece of wood which can't do anything'. While he was rambling about through the world, with the help of devils he used to recognize in the smoke of smelting furnaces those [who belonged to] the sect and those who had no religious belief. How he did this and how he recognized them are described in the trial record.

Item. He confessed the foregoing in legal form, on more than one occasion, entirely of his own free will and, with his own free oath, he maintained that he would be telling the truth. In fact he lost his case because of these pieces of evidence.

---

27. *In quadam scutella.* This literally means 'in a dish', but may also refer to a meal.

Item. It appears from the foregoing that he was delated a long time ago, and that he has been a necromancer, a worker of harmful magic, a diviner, a poisoner, an apostate, a murderer, an invoker of demons and an astrologer.

We have seen the many summaries [recorded] above. The deeds of the said accused have been written down in a record of these proceedings, along with what he has been seen to do. [We have considered] the manner in which the said accused has unwaveringly persevered in the foresaid confessions he has made, and his resolute adherence [to them]. Finally, we have seen and given careful thought to the legal proceedings against this same accused. We have diligently watched him[28] and visited him, and on this day and [at] this time have seen and heard every single statement the said parties wanted to make. We have come to a decision and have made up our mind in these same matters, and [he] is to hear our definitive sentence. The proceedings in this case have been held, reported, brought to a conclusion, and [witnesses] have been produced, together with the lawyers and the documentation. By sacred custom we sit in open court. The Holy Scriptures have been placed where we can see them, so that our impartial judgement may proceed in the face of God, and so that our eyes may always see impartiality in these things and in everything else, not inclining more to one party than the other, but weighing this kind of case with balanced deliberation and just language.[29]

First we invoke the name of Christ our God, defend ourselves with the sign of the venerable, holy cross, and say 'In the name of the Father, and of the Son, and of the Holy Spirit, Amen.' As a result of the things we have seen and gathered from the progress of the said trial and its results – [things] which disturb us and can and should disturb[30] the mind of anyone who makes up his mind in accordance with the facts – by this definitive sentence, which we utter with our own mouth, we say, pronounce, decree, declare and pronounce sentence as follows.

As a result of the way this trial has gone, it is quite apparent to us, the foresaid judge, and is clear from the personal confession made by the said accused on his bodily oath, often without [any] discrepancies that he, the accused, has committed and carried out the foresaid things in a detestable fashion with deliberate intention and in an obstinate frame of mind: that he is a magician and a worker of harmful magic and, in consequence, wherever he may be in the world he is an enemy of God and humankind, as far as this point is concerned. Moreover, in many ways and according to divine and human laws, he has incurred the penalty of the ultimate punishment. We cannot close our eyes

---

28.   This is unlikely to mean that Jubert was deliberately deprived of sleep in order to render him more liable to confess the truth of the accusations against him although this is a common interpretation of 'watching'. Evidence from elsewhere suggests much more strongly that he was watched in case he called upon his demons to rescue him and carry him out of prison, or changed his shape into some tiny creature which could then escape via the window or a crevice in the wall.

29.   Reading *voce* for *lote*.

30.   Reading *movere* for *moveri*.

to this[31] and ignore it without gravely offending Almighty God and without [incurring] the vengeance both of God and of the minister of the law; and zeal for justice [will not let us] fail to exact retribution. Therefore, by this our definitive sentence which we speak with our own mouth in these present writings, we condemn the said accused to be burned alive in public in the place prescribed by us – the usual [place] for the execution of justice – and killed by a devouring flame upon a pile of wood constructed there. By this same sentence we confiscate and appropriate his goods to the dauphinal exchequer and treasury, so that he may serve as an example to those who wish to do similar things. Finally, with the approval[32] of the noble castellan of Briançon or his depute for the execution of our present sentence, we must certify it, as is proper, by a document which will be available to the public.

The present sentence was delivered, read and published in the year and on the day [noted] above, within the court house at Briançon, in the presence of the noble Humbert de Nevache, the noble Reynand Rainlis, the noble Gonet Durand, the noble Jean Medici of Briançon, the noble Ponezon Scrivian of Château-Queyras and a number of others.

M. Sager, clerk.

9. An accused woman found not guilty, 1431

Hansen VIb, no. 41 (p. 544)

[This case comes from Faido, the capital of Valle Leventina, an Italian-speaking region is Switzerland.]

27 August

Giovanni Orsi di Airolo, Antonietto di Nante, and Zanoretto di Airolo have accused Giacomina of perpetrating certain acts of harmful magic [*malefici*]. This has come to our notice via a written accusation, extremely hostile to her, drawn up by the notary, Antonio da Deggio. The accused woman, however, presented reasons for considering that their denunciation was without foundation and their accusations slanderous – [more than any other], the one which said that she, along with another woman of her acquaintance, had wrought an act of harmful magic upon one Zano Guillelmi Beleni di Nante, 'and it is believed he is bound to die'. The accused, Giacomina, demanded to be set at liberty and found not guilty. The document which she set out entirely in her own words is stuffed with legal citations. As for the rest, one must consider that the confession extorted from her is not true. Finally, letters arrived from the Duke of Milan [addressed] to the municipality and people of Leventina, [saying] that Giacomina was to be acquitted, 'if in some fashion she were found guilty, because she is actually innocent and guiltless'.

31. Reading *quod* instead of *quos*.
32. Reading *committente* for *commictente*.

10. The costs of guarding prisoners and execution in Fribourg, Switzerland, 1426–1442

Hansen VIb, nos. 37, 47–8, 50, 53 (pp. 530, 545–6)

1426

[Payment of] 40 sous to Folliet for guarding the carpenter who was held prisoner for eight weeks and five days because he was alleged to know how to put an end to the enchantments [*sortilèges*] from which a husband and wife were suffering. *Item*: for guarding a woman from Thun for seven weeks and two days. She was alleged to have made enchantments against the crossbowman's son.

January–June 1437

[Payment from the town treasury of] 63 sous to Jean Bugniet, burgess, sent to Grasburg where the woman who used to make people ill was detained: 28 sous to Monsieur Ruff, executioner, sent over to Grasburg with the executioner of Berne to execute the woman. She has been burned.[33]

July–December 1437

[Payment from the town treasury of] 28 sous to M. Ruff, executioner, sent over to Schwarzenburg with the executioner of Berne to execute a woman: 40 sous paid to the said M. Ruff in compensation for his expenses, and also for those he employed on another occasion for the torture ordered by the authorities.

1438

[Payment from the town treasury of] 28 sous to M. Ruff, executioner, to execute and burn Cuno Godin who was strangled in prison [after being] arrested for 'Waldensianism' [*witchcraft?*]; 48 sous for 12 wagonloads of wood when they wanted to burn Katharine, wife of Jean Coppellin of the tracts near the castle of Aigremont.

1442

[Payment from the town treasury]: (1) to M. Willi, executioner, to burn Stolloz and his wife, and Liebi's sister, and La Granta: 112 sous: (2) to M. Willi to burn Peter Buntzen: 28 sous: (3) to Willi, executioner, to burn La Stuckina and Peter Stuckis, her son: 56 sous: (4) to the carpenter to make and put up a stake[34] to

---

33. It is impossible to give any exact equivalent of value for this early fifteenth-century sou, but we can gain some very rough idea from comparison with other wages. In 1432, the poet Michault Taillevent attached to the ducal court of Burgundy was paid 6 sous a day, increased to 7 by 1435, and in 1420 a priest was contracted by the church of St Martin in Vitré to produce a missal and a psalter in 18 months, and was paid 80 livres for the job, and 30 sous (a day) for bread and wine. So the executioners were clearly being paid quite well. See J.H. Watkins, 2006, 'Michault Taillevent: a "mise au point"', *Modern Language Review* 46 (1951), p. 362. D.E. Booton, 'Notes on manuscript production and valuation in late Mediaeval Brittany', *The Library: Transactions of the Bibliographical Society* 7, p. 127.

34. Reading *colonna* (i.e. *colonne*, 'column') for *colunda*.

burn the said 'Waldensians': 13 sous: (5) to M. Willi, executioner, for his wages when they burned Agnilla Morschina: 28 sous.

11. Paying a fine or being burned in Perugia, 1445

Hansen VIb, no. 58 (pp. 547–8)

[This extract is taken from the Diary of Graziani *which was incorporated in the* Chronicles of Perugia, *1309–1491.]*

22 February

At Monsignor's request, one 'Santuccia' a fortune teller and sorceress [*faturaja*] who came from Nocea was seized. She lived in the hills between Assisi and Nocea and was arrested there.

6 March

On Saturday the said Santuccia, a fortune teller from Nocea, was burned on the Campo della Bataglia. She was willing to pay 200 florins if they let her off. When she came to her execution, she was brought riding a donkey, with her face turned to its rump and a mitre on her head. There were two demons [on the mitre], one on each side.

20 March

On the 20th of the said [month], three priests were put in prison. Two were sorcerers who used to meet the said Santuccia, and the other was seized in the convent of Santa Giuliana, in spite of the fact that it had been decreed that they could not go into any convent. Afterwards, the two priest-sorcerers were sentenced to perpetual imprisonment and the other monk was sentenced to six months in prison, after which he paid 50 florins and was set at liberty.

12. A man blinded by magic, Berlin, 1446

Hansen VIb, no. 61 (p. 548)

28 April

One woman called Glunekynne and another called Pauwel Siferdynne performed acts of poisonous magic [*venefica*] and made incantations because of ill will and spite. According to their public confessions, they more or less deprived a man called Hans Weneger of his sight, as they confessed in public. On the above date, they were tried and burned for this reason.

13. The case of Anna Vögtlin: theft and abuse of the Blessed Sacrament for the purposes of harmful magic, 1447

Hansen VIb, no. 62 (pp. 548–51)

16 June

To each and every adherent of orthodox belief, Hermann von Russegg, Lord in Büron, [sends] greeting and an invitation to have implicit faith in this letter.

Since mortal life is lost and forgotten, and the things which are done while time exists pass over with it, it seems to me one should not regard it as of no consequence that the deeds of Christians which particularly illumine the Faith lie hidden when old people no longer receive a hearing, but rather become known through the light of literature as deeds worthy to be remembered by the present as well as the future. Consequently, I make known by this present document to everyone in the future who wants to know, that in the year of our Lord 1447, on Wednesday 23 May, in the parish church of Ettiswil near the town of Willissow in the diocese of Konstanz, the most precious and most holy body of our Lord Jesus Christ was stolen from the tabernacle. After a fairly short time it was found, by God's merciful disposition, by a young female swineherd called Margaretha Schulmeistrin, near a hedge not far from the said church, thrown away and scattered like a white, shining flower. This misfortune brought great distress and ruin to the parishioners of the said church and threw them into confusion (as might have been expected), as they laboured and tried, like tracker dogs,[35] to find the individual who had tried, not without great prompting from the Devil, to carry out this appalling crime. They sent their spies to various places and eventually two of the church's parishioners, acting upon reliable inferences and information, by disposition of the Most High, laid hands on a woman in the village of Triengen. Her name was Anna Vögtlin, from the town of Bischofingen, and they brought her prisoner to the castle of Büren. There in front of me, Hermann, lord and judge of the forementioned district, and in front of other witnesses whose names appear below, she spoke, of her own free will and accord, not tricked by deception or any other evil device[36] nor compelled by force, and remembered the truth and began to confess.

First [she said] a peculiar man[37] came to her in the region in which Anna spent her childhood, at a time when she was suffering great poverty and wretchedness, and spoke to her as follows.

'If you are willing to find comfort in my words, I shall teach you how you can inflict harm on anyone you like and damage their property as well their body;

---

35. *Omni sagacitate*, literally 'with all keen-scentedness'.

36. *Machinatione*. Since *machina* refers to some kind of apparatus, the implication is that she was not shown the rack or other instruments of torture.

37. *Homo perversus*. The adjective means 'reversed, distorted, wrong-headed, depraved, ill-tempered, abnormal'. Some of these are not applicable in the context, although they may express the *post eventum* opinion of Helmann and the witnesses. But if it is the translation of an adjective used by Anna herself, 'odd' or 'weird' seems likely to catch the kind of person she meant.

and I shall buy you a nice dress straightaway, so that you're not going about in these torn, really cheap clothes'.

Although she was going to be persuaded (she said), not because of his malice but because of [her] poverty, and would acquiesce in everything, the peculiar teacher said to her, 'You must give yourself into the hands and power of malign spirits, and I pass on to you one of the first importance, called *Light*, to rule, direct and govern you'.

After he had done this, so that they could transact their business, they would meet on quarter days in certain places next to where more than one road turned into a single one. When Anna was first taken to a meeting by her devil on a Wednesday, everyone unanimously declared that she must enter the parish church of Bischofingen and there steal the precious body of our Lord Jesus Christ, which should be reverenced above everything. Anna completed her task and was taken to her peculiar teacher, and thus they performed their most iniquitous treacheries (which one is not permitted to utter), with the most holy body of our Lord Jesus Christ.

Secondly: she maintained and said that they met again ten weeks after that appalling outrage and passed a resolution similar to their previous decision, that Anna should steal the most holy sacrament once again from the same church in Bischofinger. After she had done this, they destroyed the crops of everyone they hated and made them perish completely; and they inflicted many another harm on people, which could not be cured by other people's remedies, only theirs. For, as she resolutely maintained more than once, they were able to restore to their former health, whenever they wished and as often as they wanted, people who had been ruined by their treachery.

Thirdly: now that her conscience had been thoroughly pricked, in floods of tears she asked forgiveness of the Most High, and publicly confessed that, at the urgent request of some individuals who were afraid that the theft was becoming public knowledge because it kept on happening in a single place, she went, at their expense, and lived among people outwith the locality, so that she could steal the most noble sacrament of the Eucharist. After she came to the village of Ettiswill (she said), she stayed there for quite a long time, awaiting her chance to steal it. At last she seized an opportunity and, through an iron grille in the parish church of Ettiswill, pulled from the tabernacle the venerable and worshipful sacrament of the magnificent body of our Lord Jesus Christ, wrapped in a corporal,[38] and then immediately fled the church. However, while she was carrying it outwith the walls of the graveyard, its weight gradually increased until finally it grew so heavy that she could no longer carry the burden, regardless of the pact she had made, and no longer had the strength to go back or go further forward. She was therefore obliged to stay in the same place and at length, because of the enormous weight, threw the life-giving sacrament under a hedge among nettles. Keeping the corporal for herself, she escaped, made her way to Büren, and at last came from Büren to Triengen with the aim of going

---

38.   The linen cloth on which the consecrated elements are laid during the Mass and which covers them afterwards.

back home. There she was arrested by the two parishioners from the church of Ettiswill, whom I mentioned earlier, and confined in chains. Upon her detention I, Hermann von Russegg, together with the others assembling [to try] her, then came to the conclusion, from the various pieces of evidence which were perfectly clear, that this Anna was the thief who removed the body of the Lord, which is to be glorified, and the most noble sacrament, from the said church of Ettiswill.

Fourthly: she said and acknowledged that she would have received a large sum of money if, by her subsequent activity, she had effectively carried out her intention and taken the most venerable sacrament home. [She also said] that the rest of them would have completely destroyed and deprived [people] of grain, grapes, vegetables and fruit, as well as carrying out other abominable, dreadful acts of treachery with the magnificent, sublime body of our Saviour, just as they had done more than once already. As for those acts, I think it best – and I have taken advice on this – to omit them and pass them over in silence rather than provide a detailed account for everyone.

Each and every one of these enormities and appalling crimes (which had been conceived in advance, not through error, but with ripe and careful consideration), the said Anna confessed in front of me, the judge, and in front of the witnesses whose names are given below. She persevered in this confession, with great heartfelt contrition, right to the end of her life and (so it is devoutly believed) she died happily in the intense fire[39] with great devotion.

14. Punishments for witches and their cronies, 1448

Hansen VIb, no. 67 (pp. 552–3)

18 May

On 18 May a woman was burned as a witch [*sorcière*] in Gorze [in Lothringen]. Another who had admitted to being a witch was branded there with a hot iron in three places on her face. A man who was in cahoots with the said women was banished to a distance of ten miles from Gorze and his property confiscated.

15. Els from Merspurg and her dealings with the Devil, c.1450

Hansen VIb, no. 68 (pp. 553–5)

The following has been confessed by Els from Merspurg:

1. First, she knows the art and has taught it to more than one woman so that men will have to be kindly disposed to them and not beat them.

---

39.   *In igne valido. Validus* may also mean 'legal', indicating that the capital sentence had been duly delivered in a court of law. But it would perhaps be rather odd for the presiding judge to feel he had to explain that Anna had not been lynched, so it is more likely that *validus* here refers to the comparative mercy of dry wood and a quicker death granted because Anna expressed sincere remorse and repentance.

2. *Item*: She has often forcefully uttered evil curses when she has been angered. These have come true for people, and she believes she had wished [the evil] upon them.

3. *Item*: She confessed that, on the Monday when the last hail came, she had been between Malters and the town. A beggar approached her and wanted her to marry him and have sex with him. She became angry and stepped over some water and threw it into the air behind her with both hands in the name of the Devil and particularly in the name of Beelzebub and Krutli who is a captain among the devils. (He is the one to whom she gave herself.) She cursed the beggar wishing that evil might overtake him and that hail and lightning might strike him. (This is what she would have liked.) Then indeed hail came, and she had done it.

4. *Item*: After she had given herself to the evil spirit, he met her for a third time and she wanted to ride away [with him].

5. *Item*: She had lived publicly with the priest of Kilchberg for [2]6 or 27 years. It happened like this. He used to be her husband, but after she separated from him he became a priest and she moved in with him again. She lived in the house for many years, and in all the years he spent in Kilchberg, right up to his death, hail never fell. [It was] as though he could bless it to keep its distance. But after his death, there were massive hailstorms there.

6. *Item*: Her master, the Devil, is called 'Krutli', and she has belonged to him for some time. He came to her in the shape of a goat.

7. *Item*: She also confessed that 40 years ago, when she was still a little girl [living] with her father, there was a woman in Mersperg who used to cause massive falls of hail. Her name was Else Schiesserin and she is now in Erdfurt (as far as the accused knows). Else came to her with many kind words and taught her what to do and what to say to assign herself to the Devil during [the Church's] fast days. [Els] did this and gave herself to the Devil so that he would help her to get worldly goods and give her what she asked for. This same teacher [Else Schiesserin] also taught her how to make the hail which hit the people of Konstanz and Mersperg very badly.

8. *Item*: The people in Konstanz had hurt her and her family. That is why she wanted to take revenge on them. With the help of her master, the Devil, she produced a great hailstorm which did a lot of harm to the people of Konstanz. This was 30 years ago.

9. *Item*: Forty years ago, she also raised a hailstorm in Frawenfeld, but it was not big and the people did not suffer much.

10. *Item*: (N.B. ask her about the witches who are believed to live on the Rumliker).

11. *Item*: (Ask if she knows anybody else.)

12. *Item*: (N.B. about the big hailstorm).

13. *Item*: Note that three of them met at Strassburg and talked about a few things to each other. She told them she wanted to leave them and go to Mulhausen to her family and to stop doing such things in future.

14. *Item*: She and these same women produced the big hailstorm seven years ago. This, as ten of their acquaintance complained, was because the Swiss

confederates had ruined them, and so that is why they had to be ruined [in their turn]. This happened in Mentznow. She is called one of the Wissenbachen of Strassburg. They were seen behind Wechters Lane in Mentznow during the fast days. *Item*: She has ridden a dog and a wolf. *[This is crossed out and the words 'they are burned' added].*

15. Note. Two beggars are apparently living or have settled in Escholtzmatt or in Entlibuch. One of them has a little daughter. The one with the child is called Anna Stellin. The other is called Grett Jegerin. The latter also has a little daughter in Langnow. She was a weaver and is also a witch. She was with [Anna], but has escaped.

16. *Item*: [Els] has also confessed that she and the others cannot do these things when they are alone. It was the Devil who did it.

17. Note. Twelve have been seen together within the cloister garden in Than. When they are together, the grass is lush. This was on a Thursday morning during the fasting days. They fenced and fought with hemp stems. They rode. Many of them rode on dogs. They do not know if these were wolves or dogs.

18. *Item*: The master of the witches is called Angnese from Lipenheim

19. Note: [Els] advises that beggars be driven from the country.

20. *Item*: There is a tall, beautiful woman in Schaffhausen, who is supposed to be one of the principal masters. *Item*: This woman's landlady is called Els from Mundelheim. The beautiful woman lives at the cattle market. She has been there for 14 years.

21. *Item*: When the others smeared their sticks with [magical] ointment and rode them, she wanted to ride her stick as well, but it did not work.

22. *Item*: There are two witches at Siplingen. One of them is called Anna Böschin, the other Els Schudin. Her father has been hanged.

23. Note. When they are arrested, they should receive special treatment. Their own and other things should be taken away.

24. *Item*: As soon as they give themselves back to God and His Mother again, they cannot practise magic.

25. She has thrown her stuff into a stream.

16. *Children, Waldensians and the witches' Sabbat, 1452*

Hansen VIb, no. 73 (pp. 556–9)

18 August

[In July 1452, a foreign woman turned up at the Hôpital de Provins in Paris.[40] *There she was bitten by a dog and, promising vengeance, hit the female janitor and told her she would die within three days. She was arrested, brought to the Prévôt, and, when the janitor did indeed die within three days as the woman had threatened, interrogated.]*

40. Provins is a commune in the department Seine-et-Marne in the region of the Île-de-France.

Later, the said interrogatee confessed in prison that her master (that is to say, the Devil), had been to speak to her in the tower where she was being kept prisoner. He asked her why she was distressed, and she replied, 'Why haven't you released me from here and taken care of this woman, as you promised?' Her master replied that he no longer had power to do so unless she hanged herself, but that if she did hang and strangle herself, he would bring her outside. So she asked for one of the bags they used to bring bread to the prisoners, tore it into strips to hang herself and asked her master where or from what she should hang herself. Her master showed her and told her [to do it] from an iron bracket which was set into the prison [wall]. She hanged herself from the bracket and believed she was strangling herself, but while she was doing this, the gaoler came in and found her hanging and in distress. He rescued her and was very afraid, so he undressed her completely so that [it did not look as though] she had hanged herself with her clothes and then he alerted the justice.

The justice came and questioned her, and she acknowledged and confessed several murders she had committed in like manner – even several other murders of children killed in their mothers' wombs, which were defended in secret and which she would not dare to make known to the justice – and several other murders of other children while they were lying in their beds, [whom she had killed] merely by touching them. While she was doing this, she made herself invisible to see if she liked these children and to touch them and make them die. When they have been buried, she digs them up again (as do others belonging to her sect), to take them to their 'free-for-all',[41] where they roast and eat them. She further confessed that members of her sect go to cellars wherever they want and drink the best wine they can find there, after which they refill the barrel with water or else piss in it. Afterwards, when they want to cast their spells, they make three rings one on top of another and one inside another. The first they call 'Balsebur', the second 'Satan' and the third 'Lucifer'. Once they have given them names, their masters appear to them and ask what they want, [and then the members of the sect], together with their devil, can damage and strike with lightning a district, a region or wherever they want.

She also acknowledged and confessed that the Devil cannot strike with lightning or do damage at all unless a Christian man or woman helps him. She said further that she recognized members of her sect who came from a distance, and that when she wants to damage a district with fog, members of her sect make the three rings described above and call their devils, saying, 'We want' or 'I want such and such a district to be damaged by a fog'. The devil replies, 'Shove your stick in the ground in the middle of these three rings'. Then he makes them walk round the stick, making the hole bigger [as they go]. He then makes them pull the stick out, and through the hole comes a large black cat which they pull out and bring to the end of the stick. It asks what they want and they tell the cat, 'We want such and such a district to be damaged'. Then the cat agrees, on condition they insult God, His blessed Mother, and the chrism they received [at

---

41.   Mescle = mêlée, i.e. the Sabbat.

their baptism]; and from the hole through which the cat appeared there immediately comes a great fog which goes away after the black cat.

Item: She confessed that members of the Waldensian sect [*Vauldois*] make sleet change into stones and sand whenever they want, such things, she said, having been done often in France and Burgundy.

Item: This woman acknowledged that there are as many members of her sect in France as in Burgundy – more than 50 or 60 – most of whom wear mirrors in their hats. One of them has a very thick, fat right leg. He is a tall man and one of the sect's principal instructors.

In view of this deposition by the said woman, three men and two women wearing mirrors in their hats were arrested in Provins. They were all interrogated, and they all confessed everything which has been described above – or things which are similar – and worse, and which would be too long to repeat. Among these people was a young servant boy aged about 10 or 11. He acknowledged that he had been to a Sabbat [*mescle*] twice, brought by his father and mother. In order to recognize [members, he said], they should be completely undressed and it will be found that the men and women have a mark, a white stain, on their arms or on other parts of their body, looking like a burn or a scald, about the size of a pea or larger, with the flesh raised round it.

Item: The woman said these people had been in their sect for about two months, and that because they were annoyed with a man from Talent, who had displeased one of their sect, they had called up a storm and ruined Talent's vines. She also said there is a priest from near Dijon (she did not know his name) and a very rich man from Dole, both of whom were members of their sect.

When this came to the ear of the Archbishop of Sens, he asked for custody of these prisoners, saying that this was a Church matter. But [the Provins authorities] did not want to hand them over, because the Archbishop told them that the justice had to surrender them to him by a certain day; and when this was not done (because he was not willing to post bail), the Archbishop excommunicated them. So the *procureur du roi* went off to the President of the Parliament of Paris and explained the situation to him. The President replied that the business had been handled well, and wrote to the Archbishop, sending him a specific instruction. Now, after the Archbishop had been shown this instruction, he was told that even though he wanted them handed over without bail's being posted, they would be handed over to him on condition they would be sent back. They were taken out of their prisons. The Archbishop interrogated them, but was unwilling to post bail, and because no one was willing to post bail for him, he excommunicated those he had already named [in his previous excommunication]. Consequently royal officials arrested the Archbishop in Provins and summoned him to appear in person in court in Paris on 3 September following.

[Signed by J. Rabustelli, Procurateur of Dijon, who declares that all the papers and documents dealing with the case were drawn up by him personally and are therefore authentic.]

17. *Mob rule as an epidemic is blamed on female witches, 1453*

Hansen VIb, no. 74 (pp. 559–61)

Charles VIII, King of France, etc. Let it be known (July 1457) that we have received the humble petition of Jean de Sompère and Jean de Guinhon, merchants, inhabitants of our town of Marmande in the seneschalsy of Agenais, as follows.[42]

In the year 1453 there was great mortality and widespread illness in the said town of Marmande to such an extent that several people died from the epidemic. At this point the townspeople began to grumble a lot, saying that the mortality was caused by female witches [*femmes sorcières*], and that there were several people in the town who were employing the devilish practice of witchcraft [*sorceries*] and making these people die. Because the petitioners, along with their companions, were town councillors for Marmande this year, someone called Gaubert Chamfré from Marmande came to them and spoke to them more or less as follows. 'Master Councillors, there's a man in my house who comes from Armagnac. He says there's a female witch under arrest who's accusing Jeanne Canay of being a witch, so be warned'.

Then the petitioners and the town baillie took themselves off very late in the evening to where Jeanne Canay was, arrested her and put her in prison without any further information; and while they were taking her to prison the towns-people came to their windows, asking what was going on. Someone told them it was a witch who had been arrested, so then the townspeople came out and told the said petitioners and baillie that there were several other female witches in the town, and that they should be arrested; and at night, armed with weapons and sticks and thoroughly excited, they demanded that the baillie and petitioners let them arrest [those women]. The petitioners, seeing the people so excited, left them, since it was night time, and went home. Then the townspeople, who numbered 200 and more, divided themselves between two parts of the town, appointed two leaders, and throughout the whole night seized other women, to the number of 10 or 11, and threw them in prison with the said Canay. After these women were arrested, the townspeople made the two petitioners come and talk to them to see what should be done with these women, saying they were witches. They said the women should be guarded by more than one person and told the petitioners to have some of the townspeople guard them. These townspeople also decided that the next day a woman called Péronne de Benville should be arrested since she too was said to be a witch, and that a bell be rung to assemble the townspeople to see how they should proceed against the said women. The petitioners disagreed with this and resisted strongly, because [Péronne] was the godmother of one of the petitioners.

Next day, however, at the sound of the bell and against the petitioners' wish, the people assembled at the town priory, two or three hundred of them, including the petitioners, and agreed, in front of the petitioners and without their consent,

---

42. Marmande is now in the département of Lot-en-Garonne in south-west France.

that the women who had been arrested would be tortured and interrogated. (This was decided by those who had arrested the said Péronne. The petitioners did not agree to it at all.) After one or two days, the women were tortured and interrogated without any interlocutory sentence or other advance warning. Because of the severity of the torture, or for some other reason, a woman called 'Cachette', another called 'Franque Joffre' and another called 'Languairande' confessed that they were witches and that they had used witchcraft and had caused the deaths of several children – for which they were sentenced by the baillie and others. The said petitioners were in favour of the three witches' being burned, and this was done.

[But] because Péronne de Benville and Jeanne Canay did not continue to say what they had said under torture, the baillie did not sentence them to death and was unwilling to do so, and the petitioners were not minded they should die, either, because the women had not persisted in their confession. At this, the townspeople were extremely angry and indignant at the petitioners and the baillie and wanted to kill the baillie. In fact, the people took Péronne de Benville and Jeanne Canay and put them to the stake where they were burned as the others had been, to objections from the petitioners. Because a woman called 'De Beulaigne' and another called 'Du Condon' were unwilling to confess anything, they were tortured by the townspeople (or on the townspeople's instructions). The petitioners were present but did not dare object, and because of the severity of the torture, the women died one or two days later. The other women who had been arrested were tortured and then set free because they did not confess anything. They are still alive.

Because the petitioners were present, as has been described, at the trial of the said women and at the other events described above, and failed to observe the law in any way, they were summoned to appear in person before Our seneschal of Argenais, or his deputy, at the request of Our *procureur* in that seneschalsy, and their property has been inventoried and confiscated by Us. Every day they have been tortured in the presence of Our said seneschal for the reason given. They expect to be so more and more, and proceedings will be conducted vigorously against them and their property unless Our grace and pity be accorded them.

18. A boy's evidence convicts several witches of destroying vines, 1456

Hansen VIb, no. 83 (pp. 565–6)

[Extract from the Chronicle of Metz *by Philippe de Vigneulles.]*

22 April–18 May

On 22 April in the said year 1456, the vines round Metz looked extremely fine with an abundance of grapes, just as they had the past 40 years. On the said day, at about four o'clock in the morning, there arose a great mist and cold, and for this reason most of the vines were destroyed and frozen. Several people began to say that this sprang from the diabolic practice of male and female witches [*sorciers et sorcières*], and in fact there was a young boy living at Pont-à-Mousson who said he had been with these female witches [*sorcières*] several times, especially when the said vines were thus destroyed and frozen; and he gave the names of several men and women he said he had seen. Several of them were arrested: namely, in the town of Pont, four men and women; in the town of Nomeney, three women and one man; in the city of Toul, three women. They arrested one man in the town of Vic, who was said to be one of the 'masters'. [He was known as] 'The Old Saint'. He was burned on 18 May, declaring publicly that this mist had happened because the said male and female witches throw into a fountain near Desme a mixture made by the Devil's art, and out of it comes that mist which lays waste the vines. He said this was why a priest from Pont-à-Mousson had lost half of his. He [also] said he had killed a small child and caused several serious mishaps and great losses. He had been a witch for more than 40 years.

19. A female magical practitioner, specializing in weather magic and freezing water, 1456

Hansen VIb, no. 84 (pp. 566–9)

[The first passage is taken from the Chronicle *of Cornelius Zantfliet and deals with events in Köln. It was written after passages (ii) and (iii) which are an exchange of letters between officials in Köln and Metz the previous month.]*

(i) August

At that season, two sorceresses [*mulieres sortilegae*] were arrested in Köln and burned. One of them confessed she had killed a man with poison; the other may have come from Metz. Rumour was that this woman, along with her cronies, could raise winds, rain, hailstorms and suchlike weather, and she confessed that in May she had raised a hailstorm and such icy blasts that for two miles round the city of Metz the vines and other fruit trees perished completely and there was no hope of their sprouting any more. But a townsman from Köln wanted to find out whether this was true or not and asked the said sorceress to give him a plain demonstration of a piece of magic, if she knew one. She got him to bring a cup full of water and immediately made her invocations and did some magic [*magiis*], and in the space of two Paternosters (in the month of May!) froze that water so hard and thick that one could scarcely make a hole in it with the tip of a very strong knife or dagger.

(ii) [8 July]

[A short letter from the burgomeister and council of Köln to their equivalents in Metz. Its import is summarized in the following reply from Metz.]

(iii) 18 July

From the honourable, wise burgomeister and council of the city of Köln to the principal magistrate and 13 magistrates of Metz, affection and esteem.

We have received the letter you have been pleased to write to us, saying you have arrested and are holding a woman called Ydette, who says she comes from our city, for certain maleficent practices of hers which she has used to raise bad weather and bad air, [and you say] she is talked about and well known for it. You say, too, that we are holding prisoner her husband and daughter, and that the sister of the said Ydette is a prisoner in Toul, and you ask and desire that, via the messenger who brought us your letter, we may be kind enough to inform you about what she does and says, as your said letter makes clear. Please be informed that about six months ago in Briey which is situated near our city, a woman was taken and arrested because she was talked about and well known for certain acts of heresy, etc. This woman testified and confessed that she had been a witch [*sorcière*] and had on several occasions murdered children, caused storms and frosts and done other diabolic things recently; and after she had been interrogated, she was punished for them and burned.

At her death, she said that Ydette used openly to practise this kind of witchcraft and the works of the Devil, and that she [Ydette] had taught her and been her instructor in this case. So then, as a result, we had Ydette arrested and detained her in our prison cell as suspect in this situation; but we have not been able, as a result of any interrogation to which she could be subjected before this, to find that she is willing to testify to practising heresy or the works of the Devil at any time. [She says] only that she knows nothing about them, and in consequence we have released her from prison. After this, we had two women and a girl aged about 14 arrested. They belong to our jurisdiction and are talked of and well known for wicked practices of this kind. We still have them in detention, and they know Ydette well. After interrogation, these women and the young girl told and testified to us that Ydette came and went with them several times recently through the air, thanks to the enemy from Hell, and that the three of them have been to several places where they committed several crimes and offences against children as well as doing other things. The two women have also testified to us that Ydette gave each of them a box of ointment so that they could anoint themselves and be helped in this activity. Immediately after we had had these two women and the young girl arrested (who are still being detained), Ydette, being in no doubt that the two women and the young girl would accuse her of doing these things, left our city and has not, to our knowledge, come back.

As for the said Ydette's husband and daughter, we had them arrested to find out from them where Ydette was or could have gone. Furthermore, for your information, it is true that in several places near our city and within the jurisdiction of the reverend father in God, Monseigneur, the Bishop of Metz, several men and women have been arrested, accused of sins and offences similar to those described above. Officers of the said reverend father in God, Monseigneur, the Bishop, interrogated them, and they have been punished and burned publicly; and to inform you even more plainly, out of our affection for you and to please you in this matter, we brought your messenger, the bearer of this [letter], into the presence of the officers of Monseigneur, the Bishop of Metz, so that they could inform and tell him that those people they interrogated did not accuse Ydette of the said crimes. According to what your messenger may report to you about them and this case, you may wish to interrogate and examine[43] the said Ydette and decide how to proceed as may be appropriate in this case.

This we hope you do, honourable, wise, dear and special friends. May the Son of God bless you and have you in His holy keeping.

20. More male and female witches executed in Metz, 1457

Hansen VIb, no. 91 (pp. 569–70)

July

On Saturday 1 July, round about midnight, the youngest child of Jean de Wassoncourt, the notary, was fiercely attacked by male and female witches [*sorciers et sorcières*]. Next morning, so that the truth could be ascertained, one man and three women were arrested and taken to the Palais [de Justice] on suspicion of being involved. They were interrogated and held in prison until 28 July, then taken to the Bishop's court at about 9 o'clock in the morning and handed over to Monseigneur, the Bishop's, officers. They confessed they had done a lot of harm and renounced our Saviour, Jesus Christ, the Virgin Mary and their own anointing and baptism and had taken the Devil as their lord. They were then handed over to The Thirteen who had them taken by the executioner [to a place] between the two Ponts des Morts where the said man and three women were burned.

21. Punishment for blasphemous superstition, Augsburg, 1469

Hansen VIb, no. 115 (pp. 578–9)

There was a shoemaker aged 80, Leonard Gutt, who had taken a very young woman to be his wife the previous autumn, and when, because of his age, he became frigid and impotent when it came to doing his [marital] duty to his wife, he tried to resuscitate Venus quite ineffectually, by making use of other remedies on the advice of elderly enchantresses. The deranged [old man] set about the situation as follows. He removed the wooden cross from the grave of a murdered man (for poor people use such a sign in place of a memorial on their tombs). On Good Friday he bored holes in it, threaded beads through, made a number of invocations and on three nights urinated [over it] at the head of the bed. Then, while it was still dripping from its 'bath', he put it under the bed, hoping that, by means of such frivolities, he would be a man and pleasure his wife. But when these things did the stupid man no good and his randy wife at long last made public his deficiency and her husband's every outrageous action, the shoemaker was thrown in prison and because of his sin of idolatry was sentenced in the county court to death by drowning. But because he had led a more respectable

43.   *Examiner*, which implies the use of torture.

life earlier on, and because of his present advanced age, not to say mental derangement, the city council, as a favour, fined him 50 gold pieces towards [the upkeep] of a house for abandoned children. In the ecclesiastical court, they imposed a more ample penance on the old man, [namely], that on the second Sunday after Pentecost, once Mass had been celebrated, when every crossroad in the city was filled and thronged with people, he was to carry a wooden cross, half-naked, from the Mary chapel of the Abbey of St Ulrich and St Afra to the cathedral through the middle of the city, followed by an ecclesiastical butcher[44] (that means a cowled Dominican, of course), and this wretched man would thrash his back with rods.

22. Payments to Meister Hans, executioner of Freiburg, 1454–1477

Hansen VIb, nos. 77, 93, 103, 124 (pp. 561, 570, 576, 580)

(i) 1454. To Meister Hans, the executioner, to execute Willhelm Gigniol who was burned: 25 sous. To the said Meister Hans, to execute Hugo le Borgognon, who was burned: 28 sous. To Meister Hans, the executioner, to execute Alix Buchser and Nesa, her companions, Waldensians: 56 sous.

(ii) To Meister Hans, to hang Le Williser who knows how to foretell the future [*deviner*] and is a thief.

(iii) 1462. To Meister Hans, the executioner, to execute Antoinette, wife of Nicaud from Cloz, who was burned; and to execute Girard, baillie of Sorepierre, who was burned.

(iv) To execute Pierre Dey from Morsens, who was sentenced to be burned for his offences (at the constant entreaty of the nobles and burgesses of Gruyère and the authorities of Wippens, he was granted reprieve), and to execute Claude Estevenant from Mollon, who was burned for his offences.

23. Witches and bad weather, 1481

Hansen VIb, no. 130 (pp. 581–2)

[*An extract from the journal of Jean Aubrion, burgess of Metz.*]

June–July 1481

Item: It rained the whole month of June and all the flowers perished, as did the fruit on the trees. There was no fruit. The weather was such that on 8 July one no longer saw any flowers on the vines, which was strange. People presumed this

---

44.　*Spiritali carnifice. Carnifex* also means 'executioner' and could be used as a term of abuse such as 'scoundrel' or 'villain'.

was being done by female witches [*sorcières*], and in fact several were arrested. The first one was arrested and burned in Bouxières in the district of Chamenot.

Item: Monsieur Renault de Gornais had one arrested in his district (called Chabontel), in Ciey. Her name was Marguerite, Jean Willemin's wife. Sieur Renault did not have any space in his district which was not covered in vines and orchards. This meant they were at a loss how to execute the said Marguerite without doing great damage to the vines and orchards. So he borrowed space from the chapter of the great church of Metz above the steps of St Quentin. The chapter lent it to him so that he could not make difficulties in future for the parties involved. They made a [written] legal agreement which was kept in a box belonging to a good friend of Metz. Geoffroi was the notary [who drew up the document] and Poincignon de la Haie was the good friend.

Item: One [female witch] was burned at Remilley, one at Chastel in front of Metz, one at Mairange. They said there were still several throughout the district who were doing a lot of harm day after day.

Item: 19 July. They wanted to burn two female witches at Salney, but one of them retracted everything she had confessed, and the result was that she was brought back and not burned on that occasion. But the other was burned.

Item: Good weather began on 6 July. It was fine and warm and made good hay.

Item: On Saturday, 21 July, they burned two women at Wappy for being witches.

Item: A woman was arrested in Vignuelle for being a witch and was strangled in prison. They said she had slept with her master.

Item: Two women were arrested in Mairange, apart from the one who was burned. One of these two was strangled in prison.

24. The effect of hydromancy in Jülich, 1486

Hansen VIb, no. 144 (p. 584)

[A resolution of the theological faculty of the University of Köln.]

5 July

Enacted in the congregation, with regard to remedies against the rising tide of superstitions in the territory of Jülich [encouraged] by hydromancy. It was concluded that a letter be sent to the Duke of Jülich, entreating him to take action against so many insults and injuries to Christianity, to be vigilant against people who do this kind of thing and, after warnings have been issued, to order that people such as this be handed over to judges for interrogation and chastisement.

25. Record of executions and deaths, Metz, 1488

Hansen VIb, no. 149 (pp. 586–7)

Item: In that year, because of the bad weather, people began to grumble loudly against female witches [*sorcières*]. One was arrested in Rouserieulle and burned.

Item: A man was arrested in Vantoul as a witch. He was taken to the Dean's house in Metz and there he died.

Item: Three female witches were arrested in Mairange and burned on 17 June.

Item: Three women were arrested in Maizières as witches. Two were burned on 25 June, the feast of St Eligius. The other was set free because she was innocent of the charge.

Item: Three women were arrested in Chastel-sous-St Germain and burned as witches on 26 June.

Item: Six women were arrested as witches in Metz. Three were sentenced to be burned. One of these three died in the law court, and they had to take the others to be put on public display in the Bishop's courtyard. The other two were put on display in the said courtyard and taken back to the law court. Straight away they were put in a cart (that is to say, the one who was dead and the other two), and all three were burned in front of the bridges on 1 July that year.

Item: The weather was constantly rainy and extraordinarily dangerous with storms and thunder, and it was scarcely hot for two days before a storm came again. They had to keep on ringing the bells night and day,[45] and large hailstones fell in the territory of Corney and Nouvion on 28 June and did great damage.

Item: A woman was arrested at Salney as a witch and burned 3 July the said year.

Item: On 12 July, three women were in court again. Two of them were burned as witches, the other was banished because she had believed in some of the charms one of the women had made for her.

Item: On 19 July, three women were in court again and were burned the same day, as witches, in front of the bridges.

Item: A man was arrested in Preuvillers as a witch. His case was heard there. He was put on public view [*chaffaudé*] in Preuvillers and handed over to [the authorities] in Briey to be executed.

Item: On 19 August, two women were burned as witches in Juxey.

Item: On 23 August, two men and three women were burned as witches in Thionville.

Item: On 2 September, a woman called 'La guriatte de chambre' was burned as a witch in Metz.

Item: On 15 September, they burned a woman as a witch in Vigny.

Item: On 22 September, they burned a woman as a witch in Juxey.

---

45.   This was regularly done in order to ward off the evil spirits who might be causing the bad weather.

26. A woman, imprisoned as a witch, set free, 1492

Hansen VIb, no. 161 (p. 590)

15 November

[In Metz] a woman who was accused of being a witch [*sorcière*] and was sentenced to perpetual imprisonment, and had already been [in prison] four years and more, was set free and left.

27. The Devil's sect, 1493

Hansen VIb, no. 162 (pp. 590–2)

On Tuesday, 20 August 1493, in the presence of the sagacious, wise and discerning councillors of Fribourg, [namely] Jean Musillier, Pierre Ramus, Jean Cordez, Hans Espagniod, Gaston Gastrod, Wilhelm Reiff and Hans Techtermand, a magistrate[46] in Fribourg, Jeanne Relescée from Estieven in Vacheresse[47] confessed:

Item: Because of great despair she felt because her husband used to beat her, she went at night to a rock in a wood and began to call on God or the Devil to be willing to help her. Then there came to her a [man], deep black in appearance, who called himself Satan, and asked her what she wanted and what was the reason for her distress. She answered she was at the end of her tether because her husband never stopped beating her. At this, Satan told her that if she was willing to trust in him and take him as her master and God, he would console her and her husband would not beat her any more. So then she denied God and took Satan as her master and did him homage, kissing his backside and giving him three hairs from her head.

Item: She also confessed that later on, for two years, she went to and frequented the sect which they used to hold in an old castle called 'Des Roches' which was in Bernex.[48] Their master Satan used to summon them to this sect twice a week on Wednesdays and Fridays, and would give them sticks on which they would ride to the sect; and if by chance they were unwilling to go, he would beat them severely. When it was time for them to leave, they would ride on these sticks, each person returning home.

Item: She and her accomplices (named afterwards) would attend the sect on the days mentioned above at about midnight, and when they were all gathered together, first of all they would begin to dance and have a good time, and then later their master Satan would bring them food. A member of the said sect, called Pierre Sessel, from Larrengez, was their cook.

46. *Grosoutier*. Perhaps 'burgomeister'.
47. A commune in Haute Savoie.
48. A commune in Haute Savoie, not far from Vacheresse.

Item: One of her accomplices, Jean Villic, once kissed a fat young woman on her middle and squeezed her in such a way that she gave birth to a son. He was not baptized, and when he was buried they came secretly, dug up [his body] which was still fresh, and took it to the sect where they roasted and ate it. They used to eat several other children at the sect, not knowing whose they were. But [the children] had not yet been baptized, because [members of the sect] have no power over children who have been baptized.

Item: When they were at the sect, they would 'mingle' but never contrary to Nature.

Item: Several members of this sect have been burned and legally executed.

Item: One of her accomplices called Jeanne Livret (who has been burned) knew how to cause illness in people and in animals, all because she would hit them. She would hit them with a stick and immediately they fell ill and if there was no remedy, they could die. But when you brought them to her, she knew how to cure them by means of [certain] words she knew. After she was in the hands of the law, however, [these words] had no power.

Item: Her husband, who very recently lived in this town, knew perfectly well she was a heretic. (When he worked for people in their houses, he would use woollen shoes. He collected a large number of these and sold them to several people in Moudon.)

[The names of] those who belonged to the said sect are given here: Pierre Morat, Berthet Damon, the wife of the fat butcher from Larrengey, the woman in Magniens, Jean Guillaume (Maître Buaz), the son of Nicod de la Vernaz and several others who have been legally executed, of whom there is no record.

This woman [Jeanne Relescée] who was brought to court on 22 August was sentenced to be burned.

28. A witch executed in Konstanz, 1495

Hansen VIb., no. 172 (p. 595)

3 July

On the Friday before St Ulrich's day, Adelheit from Frowenfeld was taken for questioning. She has yielded herself to a devil called Krüttel with whom she has often had dealings. She has also raised hailstorms and other things. She was put on a cart and then burned.

29. *Two witches beheaded at Hildesheim, 1496*

Hansen VIb., no. 173 (p. 595)

Two witches had their heads cut off in front of the city of Hildesheim. By means of their devils' tricks, they could make any women and young women fall.

30. *Terms of a contract with the Devil, 1501–1505*

Hansen VIb, no. 182 (pp. 597–8)

[Extract from the trial record of male and female witches in Cavalese in the Tyrol. This was under the secular jurisdiction of the Bishop of Trent. Torture was used extensively, one woman being tortured no fewer than 18 times. Those found guilty were either drowned or burned.]

(a) A long period has gone by already, during which people have openly and constantly been talking and gossiping about witches [*strigis*] both in and outwith Val Fiemme, [saying] they and the Devil their lord are able to create and cause storms, and [that] they eat adults, children and animals. In consequence, judicial proceedings have actually taken place against these treacherous witches,[49] (especially when anyone[50] has always been regarded with suspicion and has been the object of public talk and gossip), in order to root them out,[51] to the honour of Almighty God and Holy Mother Church and the undoing of the Devil's activity.

(b) Judicial proceedings against devilish female and male workers of harmful magic (*maleficas et maleficos*), treacherous male and female witches (*strigones et strigas*): Urged to it by a very wicked spirit, they have renounced and denied Almighty God, the most blessed Virgin Mary, the whole Court of Heaven, Holy Mother Church and our Catholic faith. They have accepted a devil from Hell as their lord, promised to be his servant, and have given themselves for ever, soul and body, to the abyss of Hell by not showing mercy to human existence – the righteous, the unrighteous, innocent blood in its mother's body or their own blood relatives. To win his approval, they give and commit themselves to the Devil their lord to eating every available bit of human flesh, and not only this, but also to devastating and completely destroying our life's substance – that is, corn and animals; and by their devilish practice they bring into being storms, cold weather, droughts and floods with a view to the harm, destruction and rejection of human existence.

49.   *Contra ipsas perfidas strigas*. The Latin specifies that they are female.
50.   *Aliquam*, again feminine.
51.   *Illas*, feminine.

31. *Three workers of harmful magic burned at Worms, 1509*

Hansen VIb., no. 196 (p. 600)

13 August

The Monday after, three wicked female workers of harmful magic [*böse wiber zauberische*] who lived in Pfeddersheim were burned. They did a lot of evil magic and [weather] magic, and made a great display of their knowledge.

32. *Diatribe against a murderous witch, 1514*

Hansen VIb, no. 207 (pp. 602, 603–6)

(a) [*Four couplets written on the same subject, the execution of certain local witches.*]

Concerning six workers of harmful magic [*maleficis*], burned in the year of our Lord, 1514.

1. The Abbot of Laach had the butchers from Crufft, cunning women [*sagas*] and much-hated female witches [*strigas*], burned.
2. The monks of Laach, confident of their sound independence, acting with zeal, burned the witches from Crufft.
3. The men of Laach, confident of the law they had on account of their powerful merits, killed the butchers from Crufft.
4. Quite properly this year, Laach put an end to the plague-bearing cunning women in Crufft with a good and valid law.

(b) [*Dom Johann Butzbach, Prior of the Benedictine monastery of Laach in Andernach, had travelled quite extensively in Europe before deciding to enter religion. He was immediately struck by his first sight of Laach and by the character of the monks he found there. During his youth he had had a brush with a witch, as he recorded in his autobiography, and this may have left its mark since his language in the four epigrams commemorating the burning in 1514 of six workers of harmful magic –'butchers' [lanias], 'loathed cunning women' [strigas perosas], 'plague-bearing cunning women' [pestiferas sagas] – is emotionally charged, as is his long poem about the murder of his abbot by a worker of harmful magic who had been working in the monastery's hospital. To begin with, he designates her a wise woman [saga], but later describes her shape changing into a night owl [strix] and flying to demonic assemblies, two of the classic signs of a witch [strix].*]

[Title] Against a dreadful abbot-murdering female worker of harmful magic, the most treacherous woman in charge of the hospital[52] in the monastery of the Blessed Virgin Mary at Laach

---

52.   *Nosocomii*, a Greek borrowing. The word *nosos* means 'disease' or 'illness', and a *nosokomeion* was a place for care of the sick.

In the year 1512, a ghastly looking cunning woman [*saga*] gave Simon of Patra, lord and abbot of the monastery of the Blessed Virgin Mary at Laach, aconite in some cheese and killed him. He was aged 42 at the time when as a man in robust health he succumbed, as it happened, to poison and undoubtedly became a witness of the terrifying Styx. Rightly I weep: I grieve with good cause. My abbot, whom a spiteful cunning woman slaughtered by administering poison, was struck down. That wicked woman, who struck her lord with a dreadful death, was receiving alms from our cloister. The woman, the worst possible kind of cunning woman, struck down a lord remarkable for his abundant devoutness and fervent enthusiasm.

On one occasion, while Father was placing his possessions at the disposal of the poor, he found fault with her. She hated Father and not long afterwards got hold of poisons. Alas! There fell a remarkable man, generous, devoted to God, and died, killed by trickery. For this reason, she was dragged along the ground by her breasts and tortured with white-hot tongs, after which she was burned to ashes. About three years after Father's death she was burned alive and died, along with other butchers [*lanias*]. O would that this evil woman who was not afraid to commit so great a crime had never been born!

Alas, how much harm she did to us by killing Father, a very wicked piece of deceit, worse than evil demons. Whatever good intentions he had in mind to accomplish, had he lived longer, that woman removed; new choir stalls, new bells, new buildings which could have been used to provide food and refreshment, that woman removed. She robbed that church of many things which would have enhanced its beauty and she stole many things which were beneficial to my monks.

[The 72 verses which follow, praising the abbot's many virtues, are here omitted.]

This very wicked woman alone was not afraid of him at the time when she tried so hard to overthrow him. For she was worse than any demon; a worse woman was never born and never existed. This old woman, disgusting, misshapen, meretricious, repugnant, talkative, loud-mouthed, treacherous, stupid, out of control, spiteful, disparaging, caustic and disturbing all those who love peace – she used to go to where the wind of her defiling evil could bring its seeds. Shit would stink in her throat. Her teeth were filthy. She was completely ghastly. In broad daylight she was unable to look at a font. [This] pungent woman would often weep with her dry eyes.

This woman had a demon as a suitor and a husband who would lie with her as often as she wanted; and because she was highly sexed and absolutely insatiable, [this] false lover of fleshly vice used to burn not simply for men, but for the thing which belongs to a man and indeed also enjoyed Satan in a disgusting way.

She put herself at his service; she vowed her soul to him as a sacrifice, and accomplished many dreadful things according to her vow. For as well as [her] lord whom she destroyed with poison when, alas, she had been on the lookout [for an opportunity] for a long time (as she confessed), she did the following very many wicked things, dreadful deeds, to our people, things which it stuns me to write. First of all, unwilling or unable to listen to anyone, this lover of Christ [...] who had been washed in the sacred font, fell in love with those whom we all hate, that is, the hellish enemies of the human race. She solemnly and openly proffered, I'm telling you, the excuse of excessive lust for these black spirits. This lecherous woman, reckless from despair, denied our faith's baptism and our salvation. First of all, when she came to church early in the morning, she would pretend, with devout prayers, to be virtuous. But whenever the priest, according to custom, prayed for the people's salvation, she responded by saying offensive things. Whenever she saw our Lord's body being raised on high, she sneered and vomited very wicked words. She stuck out her tongue, as naughty children do, and hid her hands under her gown behind her back, beneath her veil which hung down quite a long way in front, so that no one would notice. A demon taught her to do this. Blasphemy in church such as this was often the least [thing she would do]. Anyone who saw her might believe she was virtuous, but actually she was worse than a Turk is believed to be. Behaving like a savage, hostile to God, ingratiating herself with demons, she diverted to her own use the food destined for Christ's poor, the sick and pilgrims; and that thief gave what she took to her relatives. Thus, the ill-fated woman who had been offered alms was vexed at another [member] of the cloister. Whoever did good to the poor, she hated. This woman in charge of the hospital was miserly to all wretched people. Because of her, few used to come here for refuge. Each poor person would avoid [someone] worse than a demon. She had no faith, no serenity, no amity, no love of peace: she was often quarrelsome. Therefore the whole neighbourhood used to steer clear of her and, like a lamb, avoid the savage she-wolf at close quarters.

She made it her business to set the peaceably minded at variance, upset people, rupture friendships. I think scarcely any viper which has been split open can pour out a deathly poisonous secretion to the same degree this woman could. She would often pour out abominable whispers to the priest as though she were making her confession, while skipping over serious matters. She would often take away the sacred body of Christ during the year and then, having removed it, utter blasphemies. She brought about numberless storms which caused financial losses, and destroyed the gifts of Bacchus and Ceres. She killed several farm animals and took away their milk. She often took revenge, [even] when she was [only] slightly provoked. This depraved, pitiless woman had so much viperish hatred and so much enmity. She became a night-bird resembling an owl while she flew in the dark night (I mean, of course, as an owl), to troops of demons like herself. When it had fallen to her, as it usually did, to lead their dances, oh who then jumped so high (ghastly creature), by throwing up her arms and feet? Afterwards she was accustomed to lie wantonly with demons; scarcely satisfied, she flew back home.

Whenever she chanced to pass a venerable cross, she would turn her back on it in a disrespectful manner and mock the figure of the crucified Christ by showing it her backside. In addition to this, she killed a woman in childbirth, namely, the wife of her own son.

These and many other things this very wicked witch did. Love of brevity prevents [me] from writing about them.

At length, so that she might pay the penalty for these deeds of hers, she was accused by her partners-in-crime; and so she paid the penalty which the people's verdict wanted. She was bound and lying prostrate on the ground, was dragged through ploughed fields to the death which Vulcan was preparing for her in the middle of a wide open field, after she had been torn by tongs. To this extent she paid the debts of a fate which did not deserve anyone's compassion. She was burned, about to be the pine torch of a hellish pyre. The woman, filled with iniquities and evil tricks, received rewards of such a kind for the 'merits' of her lot. Oh, how better it would have been had she never been born! If this woman was going to be so vile a harlot, she merited enduring every kind of pain and distress a woman has suffered or will endure. She did not deserve bread; she did not deserve any kind of liquid; she did not deserve any kind of gift from God.

Every kind of painful torment, every kind of anguish now torture this wretched woman and cause savage [pain]. Now she feels the torment of the black vulture, the distress of Sisyphus and the liquid of Tantalus. Furies tear her in earnest and whips burst open and exhaust her arms with frequent wounds. She alone pays the penalty of Erebus, no matter of what kind, and [this] viper suffers the torture of everyone else in Orcus. Just as Erigone's throat, tied with a rope, hung, so *her* abominable neck cracked by the use of halters. This woman is thought to have been changed into a rock, like Niobe, and her spiteful soul into running water, like Byblis. Now her ghost fights the spirits of the dead with her hands; a menacing ghost attacks her and makes her its own. This witch, more wicked [than any], who scorned Christ and worshipped Satan, deservedly suffers the very worst evils. She who did very many evil deeds of such wickedness, and would have done more had she survived, will properly endure [her] pains. Indeed, she confessed this while life still remained to her – that she killed as many people as she could, 'hateful brethren who wear the habit', and her own husband.

More than anything else, she had the economy of the monastery in her sights. God deprived her of this by benevolently preserving us from the snares and wicked traps she had laid. Let the Lord spare her if she seem worthy of pardon and if, while dying with a groan, she prayed for this. Although she deserved much greater torments than those she received, she suffered things sufficiently degrading here; and if she endured them willingly with a contrite heart, may she have peace after a thousand thousand years until her most offensive cauldron, which made this world loathsome with every kind of crime, be cleansed. But if black bile overcame this wretched butcher and, after being tortured, she put an end to my distress, then may she rest without peace, suffering every kind of evil, in blazing hot pitch and on a funeral pyre of sulphur. Whatever kind of person this witch was, I tell you this, reader, in brief: she killed the abbot before his time.

33. Magical damage to crops, 1518–1519

Hansen VIb, no. 220 (p. 608)

[Entry in the Brauweiler Chronicle.]

1518. The crops were flattened by a bolt of lightning and a violent hailstorm between Brausweiler and Kirdorp. [The damage] extended in a straight line between Bockelmunt on the Rhine as far as [...]. This damage was said to have been brought about by the activity of female workers of harmful magic [*maleficarum*] who had employed poison. Consequently in 1519 four or five were arrested in Dansweiler and burned.

1519. Several female workers of harmful magic [*maleficae*] were arrested and thrown in prison. After some time they were found guilty by their own confession, sentenced to death and burned between Brauweiler and Weddersdorp, although one of them died in the fire next to the tall wheel between Glessen and Sinteren.

Select Bibliography

Anglo, S.
1997   'Evident authority and authoritative evidence: The Malleus Maleficarum', in S. Anglo (ed.), *The Damn'd Art* (London: Routledge and Kegan Paul), 1–31.

Bailey, M.D.
1996   'The Mediaeval concept of the witches' Sabbath', *Exemplaria* 8: 419–39.
2001   'From sorcery to witchcraft: clerical conceptions of magic in the later Middle Ages', *Speculum* 76: 960–90.
2002   'The feminization of magic and the emerging idea of the female witch in the late Middle Ages', *Essays in Mediaeval Studies* 19: 120–34.
2003   *Battling Demons: Witchcraft, Heresy, and Reform in the Late Middle Ages* (Pennsylvania: Pennsylvania State University Press).
2007   *Magic and Superstition in Europe: A Concise History from Antiquity to the Present* (Lanham, Maryland: Rowman and Littlefield Publishers).
2008   'Concern over superstition in late Mediaeval Europe', *Past and Present*, Supplement 3: 115–33.

Bailey, M.D and E. Peters
2003   'A Sabbat of demonologists: Basel, 1431–1440', *The Historian* 65.6: 1375–96.

Bechtel, G.
1997   *La sorcière et l'occident* (Paris: Plon).

Behringer, W.
2005   'How Waldensians became witches: heretics and their journey to the other world', in G. Klaniczay and E. Pócs (eds.), *Demons, Spirits, Witches* Vol. 1: *Communicating with the Spirits* (Budapest: Central European University Press), 155–92.

Bowd, S.
2008   '"Honeyed flies" and "sugared rats": witchcraft, heresy, and superstition in the Bresciano, 1454–1535', *Past and Present*, Supplement 3: 134–56.

Bozoky, E.
2003   *Charmes et prières apotropaïques* (Turnhout-Belgium: Brepols).

Broedel, H.P.
2003   *The Malleus Maleficarum and the Construction of Witchcraft* (Manchester and New York: Manchester University Press).

Burke, P.
1977   'Witchcraft and magic in Renaissance Italy: Gianfrancesco Pico and his Strix', in S. Anglo (ed.), *The Damn'd Art* (London: Routledge and Kegan Paul), 32–52.

Caldwell Ames, C.
2008   *Righteous Persecution: Inquisition, Dominicans and Christianity in the Middle Ages* (Pennsylvania: University of Pennsylvania Press).

Cameron, E.
2010   *Enchanted Europe: Superstition, Reason, and Religion, 1250–1750* (Oxford: Oxford University Press).

Chène, C and M Ostorero
2000   'Démonologie et misogynie: l'émergence d'un discours spécifique sur la femme dans l'élaboration doctrinale du sabbat au xve siècle', in A-L Head-König and L. Mottu-Weber (eds.), *Les femmes dans la société européenne: 8e congrès des historiennes suisses* (Geneva: Société d'histoire et d'archéologie), 171–96.

Cohn, N.
1975   *Europe's Inner Demons* (London: Book Club Associates).

Decker, R.
2008   *Witchcraft and the Papacy*, English trans. (Charlottesville and London: University of Virginia Press).

Duni, M.
2007   *Under the Devil's Spell: Witches, Sorcerers, and the Inquisition in Renaissance Italy* (Florence: Syracuse University).

Elmer, P.
2007   'Science, medicine, and witchcraft', in J. Barry and O. Davies (eds.), *Palgrave Advances in Witchcraft Historiography* (Basingstoke: Palgrave Macmillan), 33–51.

Emmerson, R.K.
1981   *Antichrist in the Middle Ages: A Study of Mediaeval Apocalypticism, Art, and Literature* (Manchester: Manchester University Press).

Fudge, T.A.
2006   'Traditions and trajectories in the historiography of European witch hunting', *History Compass* 4: 488–527.

Gaskill, M.
2010   *Witchcraft: A Very Short Introduction* (Oxford: Oxford University Press).

Hansen, J.
1901   *Zauberwahn, Inquisition und Hexenprozess im Mittelalter und die Entstehung der grossen Hexenverfolgung* (Munich: R. Oldenbourg Verlags).
1901   *Quellen und Untersuchungen zur Geschichte des Hexenwahns und der Hexenverfolgung im Mittelalter* (Bonn: Carl Georgi).

Herzig, T.
2006   'Witches, saints, and heretics. Heinrich Kramer's ties with Italian women mystics', *Magic, Ritual, and Witchcraft* 1: 24–55.
2010   'Flies, heretics, and the gendering of witchcraft', *Magic, Ritual, and Witchcraft* 5: 51–80.

Iribarren, I.
2007   'From black magic to heresy: a doctrinal leap in the pontificate of John XXII', *Church History* 76: 32–60.

Jones, W.R.
2007   'Political uses of sorcery in Mediaeval Europe', *The Historian* 34: 670–87.

Kamerick, K.
2006   'Shaping superstition in late Mediaeval England', *Magic, Ritual, and Witchcraft* 3: 29–53.

Kieckhefer, R.
2006 'Mythologies of witchcraft in the fifteenth century', *Magic, Ritual, and Witchcraft* 1: 79–108.

Lopez, F.A.
n.d. *Arte mágica y hechicería medieval: tres tratados de magia en la corte de Juan II* (Valladolid: Deputacion Provincial de Valladolid).

Mikolajczyk, R.
2005 'Non sunt nisi phantasiae et imaginationes: a Mediaeval attempt at explaining demons', in G. Klaniczay and E. Pócs (eds.), *Demons, Spirits, Witches* Vol. 1: *Communicating with the Spirits* (Budapest: Central European University Press), 40–52.

Mormando, F.
1999 *The Preacher's Demons: Bernardino of Siena and the Social Underworld of Early Renaissance Italy* (Chicago and London: University of Chicago Press).

Olsan, L.
1992 'Latin charms of Mediaval England: verbal healing in a Christian oral tradition', *Oral Tradition* 7: 116–42.
2003 'Charms and prayers in Mediaeval medical theory and practice', *Social History of Medicine* 16: 343–66.

Ostorero, M.
2003 'Un prédicateur au cachot, Guillaume Adeline et le Sabbat', *Médiévales* 44: 73–96.
2008 'The concept of the witches' Sabbath in the Alpine region (1430–1440): text and context', in G. Klaniczay and E. Pócs (eds.), *Demons, Spirits, Witches* Vol. 3: *Witchcraft Mythologies and Persecutions* (Budapest: Central European University Press), 15–34.

Ostorero, M., A. Paravicini Bagliani and K. Utz Tremp (eds.)
1999 *L'imaginaire du sabbat* (Lausanne: Université de Lausanne).

Page, S.
2004 *Magic in Mediaeval Manuscripts* (Toronto and Buffalo: University of Toronto Press).

Paravy, P.
1979 'À propos de la genèse médiévale des chasses aux sorcières: le traité de Claude Tholosan, juge dauphinois (vers 1436)', *Mélanges de l'École française de Rome: Moyen-Âge, Temps modernes* 91: 333–79.

Pastore, F.
1997 *La Fabrica delle streghe* (Pasian di Prato: Campanotto Editore).

Po-Chia Hsia, R.
1997 'Witchcraft, magic, and the Jews in late Mediaeval and early modern Germany', in J. Cohen (ed.), *From Witness to Witchcraft: Jews and Judaism in Mediaeval Christian Thought* (Wiesbaden: Harrassowitz), 419–33.

Pócs, E.
1999 *Between the Living and the Dead*, English trans. (Budapest: Central European University Press).

Porter, R.
1999 'Witchcraft and magic in enlightenment, romantic, and liberal thought', in B. Ankarloo and S. Clark (eds.), *Witchcraft and Magic In Europe: The Eighteenth and Nineteenth Centuries* (London: Athlone Press), 219–82.

Purkiss, D.
2000 *Troublesome Things: A History of Fairies and Fairy Stories* (London: Allen Lane).

Rider, C.
2006 *Magic and Impotence in the Middle Ages* (Oxford: Oxford University Press).

Riha, O.
1994 'Gilbertus Anglicus und sein Compendium Medicinae: Arbeitstechnik und Wissenorganisation', *Sudhoffs Archiv* 78: 59–79.

Stoudt, D.L.
1995 'Probatum est per me: the Heidelberg Electors as practitioners and patrons of the medical and magical arts', *Cauda Pavonis* 14: 12–18.

Sullivan, K.
1999 *The Interrogation of Joan of Arc* (Minneapolis: University of Minnesota Press).

Tavuzzi, M.
2007 *Renaissance Inquisitors: Dominican Inquisitors and Inquisitorial Districts in Northern Italy, 1474–1527* (Leiden: Brill).

Utz Tremp, K.
2008 *Von der Häresie zur Hexerei: 'Wirkliche' und imaginare Sekten im Spätmittelalter* (Hannover: Hahnsche Buchhandlung).

Veenstra, J.R.
1998 *Magic and Divination at the Courts of Burgundy and France* (Leiden: Brill).

Waite, G.K.
2003 *Heresy, Magic, and Witchcraft in Early Modern Europe* (Basingstoke: Palgrave Macmillan).

INDEX